BRIDGING THE GAP

Tampa youngsters gaze through a chain link fence, locked out of a segregated playground in the early 1950s. Photograph by Robert W. Saunders, Sr.

Bridging the Gap

CONTINUING THE FLORIDA NAACP LEGACY
OF HARRY T. MOORE

1952-1966

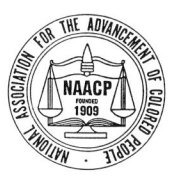

Robert W. Saunders, Sr.

UNIVERSITY OF TAMPA PRESS
TAMPA, FLORIDA • 2000

Copyright © 2000 by Robert W. Saunders, Sr.
All rights reserved

Manufactured in the United States of America
Printed on acid-free paper ∞

The University of Tampa Press
401 West Kennedy Boulevard
Tampa, Florida 33606

ISBN 1-879852-66-7

No part of this book may be reproduced or transmitted in any form or by any means, electronic or mechanical, including photocopying, recording, or by any information storage and retrieval system, without written permission from the publisher.

Unless otherwise indicated, all illustrations in this book are from the collections of Robert W. Saunders and the Robert W. Saunders Papers, Special Collections Library, University of South Florida, Tampa, or the NAACP.

Library of Congress Cataloging-in-Publication Data

Saunders, Robert W. (Robert William), 1921-
　Bridging the gap : continuing the Florida NAACP legacy of Harry T. Moore, 1952-1966 / Robert W. Saunders, Sr. — 1st ed.
　　p. cm.
Includes bibliographical references (p.　) and index.
　ISBN 1-879852-66-7 (alk. paper)
　1. Afro-Americans—Civil rights—Florida—History—20th century. 2. Afro-Americans—Legal status, laws, etc.—Florida—History—20th century. 3. National Association for the Advancement of Colored People—History—20th century. 4. National Association for the Advancement of Colored People—Biography. 5. Saunders, Robert W. (Robert William), 1921- 6. Moore, Harry T., d. 1951. 7. Afro-American civil rights workers—Florida—Biography. 8. Florida—Race relations. I. Title.
　E195.93.F5 S28 2000
　975.9004'96073—dc21

00-008604

Dedication

We enter life not knowing what tasks lie ahead, and as we age, we learn that certain goals and objectives become road maps. We at some time must decide which direction best helps us to serve humanity. At the end, our accomplishments will be measured by those who have benefitted because we wisely chose to help our brothers or unwisely forgot that some road maps are like stagnant pools of water.

I dedicate this book to my wife Helen, who gave me the benefit of her knowledge about Harry T. Moore and his family. I also dedicate this work to Robert, Jr., my son, who successfully tested Hillsborough County's segregated school system and the Tampa Boys Club. I must mention my grandmother, Marion Mathews Rogers—born in the Bahamas, raised in Key West—who was a pioneer in the early fight against Jim Crow practices in Tampa.

Finally, I would like to include Edward D. Davis for his guidance and support, Dr. Canter Brown, Jr., for his professional assistance, Mildred Roxborough of the NAACP Corporate Headquarters, Yvonne Shinhoster of the *Washington Post*, Daisy Young of Tallahassee, and all the other stalwarts who remain on the battlefront in the *"Fight for Freedom"*—the Florida State Conference of NAACP Branches.

Contents

Introduction	ix
Acknowledgments	xi

Part One: The NAACP in Florida, 1915-1966   1

    1. The Early Years   3
    2. My Life to 1940   27
    3. The Road to Walter White's Office   49
    4. Florida, the NAACP, and Me, 1952-1966   65

Part Two: A Time Line for Bridging the Gap   93

Part Three: Key People and Important Events   109

    5. Harry T. Moore:
        Profile of a Martyr for Civil Rights   111
    6. The Tampa Story   123
    7. LeRoy Collins: A Moderate Governor
        in the Deep South   147
    8. The Johns Committee: The NAACP
        Under Legislative Attack   159
    9. The Siege of Tallahassee   173
    10. Jacksonville: The Model Branch   185
    11. The NAACP at Home:
        Local Organizations and Activities   195
    12. The Challenge at St. Augustine   227
    13. Ruby Hurley, Youth, and the NAACP   243

Afterword   253

Appendices, Notes, Bibliography, and Index   255

    Appendix One   257
    Appendix Two   265
    Notes   272
    Bibliography   281
    Index   287

Introduction

Waiting for the truth, it seems to me, often is about the same as riding up and down on a historical seesaw. The perspectives of whoever controls political power, the economy, and the criminal justice system weigh heaviest upon those recording the past for us. Tragically for African Americans, this has resulted in the omission from history of many Black accomplishments, if not distortion or outright lies. In Florida, that sad fact has affected greatly the story of efforts to achieve freedom from racial bias by the state's Black population.

This situation becomes critical when our children, Black and White, grow up without any real sense of what it took to force the civil rights revolution upon the White South. Over the years, I have visited many schools where young people received or retained little information about the "Jim Crow" days or the fact that costs to change the system ran so high, even to the sacrifice of human lives. Perhaps the names of Dr. Martin Luther King, Jr., and a few others might merit recognition. Still, for Florida children—and most adults—great individuals such as Jonathan C. Gibbs, Joseph N. Clinton, Charles F. Dupont, James Weldon Johnson, A. Philip Randolph, Harry Tyson Moore, Marcellus D. Potter, Dr. J. A. White, Edward D. Davis, Theodore R. Gibson, Sr., Virgil Hawkins, and many others have escaped attention.

Let me acknowledge that, today, the truth of some of the past of African Americans gradually is unfolding. Students of Florida history are letting us know that Black Floridians were key participants in many of this state's successes. African Americans suffered, as well, as victims of avarice, subjugation, and political compromise. Because of the efforts of these students, we are aware of the high places of honor once held by many of our deceased Black leaders. We also now know how their accomplishments aided both Black and White citizens. Our young students are asking why crimes such as those that stained Jackson County, Rosewood, and Groveland went unpunished. Yet, the civil rights era remains shadowed, too distant in the past to be remembered by the young and still too recent to receive enough historical attention.

Which brings me to the reason why I wrote this book. From 1952 to 1966 I traveled the entire state of Florida as field secretary for the Florida state conference of the National Association for the Advancement of Colored People. I saw first hand the tremendous—though now mostly forgotten—role played by the NAACP in Florida's civil rights struggle, and I also witnessed the courage, sacrifice, and determination of countless individuals who led and participated in the NAACP's initiatives. Just writing these words I wish that I could name all of these heroes and heroines for the reader. They deserve to be remembered. Their work and the costs they paid for everyone's freedom should not be forgotten, nor should the previously unheralded role of the NAACP slip from our state's collective consciousness.

It would give me satisfaction greater than I can express if this book sparked renewed interest in Florida's African American heritage and the civil rights movement. I will be pleased if it records in a meaningful way for today's readers the fight led by the NAACP and its members against Jim Crow in Florida. At the very least, I hope that the facts of these events and personalities can now no longer be lost to the future.

Acknowledgments

I wish that I could name all of the many individuals interested in this work. Without doubt I will omit some persons inadvertently, but let me begin with those who energized me in one way or another to undertake this project. The first word should go to my wife Helen, whose early life involved friendship with Harry T. Moore and his family and who, in later life, offered me constant support and encouragement. After Helen, perhaps most persistent were and are NAACP leaders such as Charles Cherry of Daytona Beach; Mary Ann Pearson, wife of the late Rutledge Pearson, Jacksonville; Richard Powell, Miami; Robert L. Gilder, Ann Porter, and A. Leon Lowry of Tampa; jurists Leander J. Shaw and Joseph W. Hatchett; the young and dynamic NAACP leader Leon W. Russell of Clearwater; and Thomas H. Poole of Lake County.

The University of South Florida and its library provided well over a decade's assistance, first by offering a safe home for my personal papers and memorabilia and by making known to the general public the important information contained within them. The library's former director Sam Y. Fustukjian (now deceased), special collections heads J. B. Dobkin and Tom Kemp, and special collections expert Paul Camp afforded me numerous kindnesses and appreciated assistance. Also at USF, history professor Steven F. Lawson suggested the library as a home for my papers and arranged for the needed connections, always sharing an encouraging word.

As a sidelight to USF's role as repository for my papers, I must say that I have enjoyed assisting eager young researchers who have utilized them over the years. Students who are already opening new avenues in Florida's African American history include Erica Burroughs, a graduate of USF's Department of Anthropology, who worked with guidance from Dr. Susan Greenbaum; Caroline Emmons Poore at Florida State University; remarkable young Omar Rivers, son of Florida A&M University's distinguished history professor Dr. Larry E. Rivers; and Kissha King of Miami.

This book would not have found its way into print, at least at this point, without the generous support of the Tampa Bay History Center and its trustees and staff. With the leadership of President J. Thomas Touchton and Vice President George B. Howell III, the History Center made available to me over a period of almost two years the assistance of its historian in residence Dr. Canter Brown, Jr. An authority on Florida's history, Canter assisted me with research, editing, and final revisions of the text in a manner that was vital in telling my story. In doing so, he shared friendship and commitment of time and resources greatly beyond what I could have expected.

The process of finalizing the text required raising funds to pay a qualified researcher to pin down hard-to-find information. I am very appreciative of the efforts of Hillsborough County commissioner Ed Turanchik, who took it upon himself to find the money for me. Donors included the George Edgecomb Bar Association (T. Elaine Holmes and Thaxton Cooper facilitated this gift); Ellen H. Green; Patricia Bean, Paulette B. Brown; Patricia Tabone; Robin Rae Jones; Al Davis; Mary Padgett; Pauline Grant; and Connie Milito. Special thanks to Dr. David J. Coles of the Florida Archives for performing the needed research and to Hillsborough County commissioner Jan Platt, who has encouraged many others to become interested in the civil rights story.

Heartfelt thanks also go to all of those who helped with supplementary visual and factual contents, especially Marilyn Ibach of the Prints and Photographs Division and Mildred Hunter of the Photoduplication Service at the Library of Congress; Arsenio M. Sanchez; Richard Bernardy at USF Special Collections; Leland Hawes; Glenn Emery, curator of the Florida Collection at Jacksonville Public Library; Clarence Fort; Evangeline Moore; the family of Rev. Frank Pinkston; and the family of C. Kenzie Steele. I also extend sincere personal appreciation to the dedicated and creative staff of the University of Tampa Press—Dr. Richard Mathews, Ellen White, and Ana Montalvo—who actually brought this book into being. They understood its spirit and enhanced it in innumerable ways.

Finally, through fourteen and one-half years working as Florida's NAACP field secretary I met and worked with hundreds of dedicated persons of all races. While I cannot name each of them, my sincere gratitude and thanks spread across the wide range of Florida-land. Perhaps someday, perhaps soon, I will be able to give more of them credit for all that they did to help us come to the point where we are but from which we still have a long way to travel.

PART ONE

THE NAACP IN FLORIDA
1915-1966

Each year following the Civil War, Tampa's Black community celebrated Emancipation Day. It recognized President Abraham Lincoln's issuance of the Emancipation Proclamation on January 1, 1863. This group displayed the flag near the Scott Street Meat Market in the 1920s. Luther Alexander, Sr., a descendant of Florida's highly regarded Reconstruction-era political leader and A.M.E. minister Robert Meacham, is standing in a light suit, third from the right. (Photo courtesy of Luther Alexander, Jr.)

1
The Early Years

The National Association for the Advancement of Colored People beat me to Florida by about six years. I was born at Tampa in 1921, but the association had one branch and perhaps one local in place by the end of 1915. The story of how my poor and underpopulated state helped to lead in the expansion of this fundamentally important civil rights organization into the South is a fascinating one to me, both because of my professional ties to the NAACP and because of my own family's involvement in those early events.

First, a few words on Florida. At the twentieth century's beginning, the state contained only about 530,000 people. Some 44 percent of them were African Americans. Many lived in rural areas of North Florida, where large plantations had concentrated most of the state's slaves before the Civil War. Increasingly, though, the African Americans had begun to move into the larger towns and cities. Where most of central and southern Florida had been undeveloped or a frontier area previously, the construction of railroads and resorts in the 1880s and 1890s had brought tens of thousands of new settlers, tourists by the train and shipload, and nonagricultural jobs and business opportunities for Blacks.[1]

Through the first decade and one-half of the new century, these trends continued, except that many more White than Black newcomers boosted Florida's population. By 1915, 360,000 African Americans comprised only 39 percent of the total. The largest city then was Jacksonville, which held around 67,000 residents. Importantly, a majority of them were Black. Tampa came next with about 50,000, which was twice the number possessed by Pensacola. In fourth place Key West contained fewer than 20,000. Only a minority of these last three cities' inhabitants were African Americans: 42 percent, 25 percent, and 26 percent, respectively.[2]

The way that Florida developed created ironies and dilemmas for Black men and women. Early on its racial climate had been much better than it was going to become by the late nineteenth century. In the 1700s and early 1800s, the state had been a possession of Spain. That country's government had made the colony a refuge for runaway slaves. Places such as Fort Mose north of St. Augustine, the Negro Fort on the Apalachicola River, and free-Black settlements at present-day Bradenton on the Manatee River had given Florida's name a magical quality associated with freedom in the minds of southern slaves.[3]

Some of the Spanish traditions about race relations survived into the American era, which began in 1821. Following the Civil War, these traditions—coupled with other factors, including the fact that Blacks amounted to near a majority of Florida's population at the time of General Robert E. Lee's surrender at Appomattox—had assisted African American political leaders in playing roles in state affairs that perhaps were greater than in some of the other Confederate states. Black men remained in the legislature as late as 1889 and were still on city councils in places such as Jacksonville and Key West into the twentieth century. At the same time, the growth of urban areas benefitted Black tradesmen, artisans, professional men, and property holders. A Black middle class began to develop in the larger towns and cities, with schools, churches, fraternal and self-help organizations, and other institutions helping to provide a decent life for many one-time slaves.[4]

But, there was another side to the coin. The power of Black politicians in the 1870s and 1880s threatened conservative Whites. The state's frontier and rural traditions eased the way for many Whites to use bloody violence as a means of intimidation. By the 1890s, Florida had become one of the worst states for lynchings and other forms of racially motivated violence. Already, by 1889 White legislators had imposed a poll tax for voting, something that wiped out real Black political power, even in the cities. Then, in

1895 a terrible freeze destroyed the farms and livelihoods of thousands. It took years for the losses to be overcome.[5]

Bad times greeted most African Americans as the new century began, but by 1915 the middle class in the larger towns and cities had revived somewhat from the economic doldrums. At my home town of Tampa, for example, residents had created new institutions or revitalized old ones that were of tremendous benefit to the Black community. New church and civic structures provided focal points for association and actions for mutual benefit. One of them, St. Paul A.M.E. Church, would be of particular importance to my family and, eventually, to the NAACP. Other examples are easy to come by. The Afro-American Civic League labored for improvements in the public sphere, while the Paul Laurence Dunbar Literary Society did the same for the mental. Harlem Academy, under principal Christina Meacham, gave some children better access to schooling. Also, *The Tampa Bulletin*, under publisher Marcellus D. Potter, was on the way to becoming one of the best African American newspapers in the country. These kinds of advances were seen, as well, in the other major towns and cities.[6]

The improvements had focused mostly on economic and educational gain during the early 1910s, probably from the influence of the great African American educator Booker T. Washington. As the most famous race leader in the United States, he had accepted, for the time being, social segregation and the loss of political power so long as Whites assisted Blacks economically and educationally. One of his famous statements declared, "In all things that are purely social, we can be as separate as the fingers, yet one as the hand in all things essential to mutual progress." A 1912 tour saw him travel through most of Florida. An account in the *New York Age* summed up his reception. "Throughout the state, from Pensacola to the Southern points and up the east coast to Jacksonville," it stated, "Dr. Washington received one ovation, by white and colored people alike, as if the whole populace was responsive to his efforts to promote the progress of the Negro people in the South and to bring about more friendly relations between the races."[7]

Although Booker T. Washington's popularity extended far and wide in 1912, many refused to accept what they considered his philosophy of accommodation with racial prejudice. The intellectual leader of his opponents was W. E. B. Du Bois of Atlanta University. In 1904 he had publicly attacked Washington in a chapter of his book *The Souls of Black Folk*. It was entitled, "Of Mr. Booker T. Washington and Others." Du Bois asked, "If worse come to worst, can the moral fibre of this country survive the slow throttling and murder of nine millions of men?" He concluded, "By every civilized and peaceful method we must strive for the rights which the world accords to men, clinging unwaveringly to those great words which the sons of the Fathers would fain forget: 'We hold these truths to be self-evident: That all men are created equal; that they are endowed by their Creator with certain unalienable rights; that among these are life, liberty, and the pursuit of happiness.'"[8]

I cannot say for sure that particular Floridians read *The Souls of Black Folk* or any other of Du Bois's writings, but growing numbers agreed with him whether they knew it or not. One curious aspect of that fact, as later events were to illustrate, was that a number of the prominent individuals in Florida who rejected Washington's ideas in favor of Du Bois's had been public officials. Two examples come to my mind, whose actions I will refer to later in this chapter. Charles F. Dupont had been born a slave at Tampa in 1861, but at the age of twenty-seven he was elected sheriff of Monroe County. He served the full four years of his term with distinction. On one occasion he proved his courage and determination beyond doubt by holding off a Key West lynch mob. In the second case, Joseph N. Clinton, a graduate of Lincoln University, served both as a Gainesville city councilman and, in 1885, as a member of the Florida House of Representatives. By 1915, he was residing at Tampa, where I knew him when I was a little boy. He had served as deputy collector of internal revenue for the federal government before being fired in 1913 by the Wilson Administration.[9]

Dr. Du Bois's demands for the protection of the rights of African Americans resulted first in what historians have called the Niagara Movement, after a meeting held in Canada during July

1905. At that gathering, twenty-nine men agreed to a ringing "Declaration of Principles." It included this phrase:

> The Negro race in America [—] stolen, ravished and degraded, struggling up through difficulties and oppression [—] needs sympathy and receives criticism; needs help and is given hindrance, needs protection and is given mob-violence, needs justice and is given charity, needs leadership and is given cowardice and apology, needs bread and is given a stone. This nation will never stand justified before God until these things are changed.

The declaration boldly declared further that "We refuse to allow the impression to remain that the Negro American assents to inferiority."[10] Many of the document's phrases echoed through the decades to inspire civil rights activists. Who can forget, to give one example, ringing calls to aid the "lost, stolen, and forgotten." Yet, who today has heard of this call to arms?

Not surprisingly, Booker T. Washington opposed the declaration's call, but Du Bois and his adherents continued to insist on being heard, a fact that led within a few years to the creation of the NAACP. The tragic race riot that occurred at Springfield, Illinois, in 1908 gave Du Bois's arguments more weight, especially in the eyes of some liberal whites. Accordingly, the next year a National Negro Conference was held in New York City that led within two years to the incorporation of the National Association for the Advancement of Colored People as a bi-racial organization to advocate and protect the rights of all peoples of color. Oswald Garrison Villard, the White publisher of the New York *Evening Post*, became its first chairman of the board. Dr. Du Bois was made director of publicity and research, as well as editor of its publication, *The Crisis*.[11]

At first, the NAACP declined to make any serious attempts to organize branches in the South, which left Floridians on their own in protesting conditions and providing protection for themselves.

My grandmother, Marion E. Rogers, told me of an incident at Tampa in 1913, which brought the Black community together. It involved demands for a decent school to be located in the Odd Fellows Hall. She joined others in threats to sue the school district, just the type of action that the NAACP would have pursued.

In other cities similar actions were undertaken. At Jacksonville in December 1914, for instance, a "permanent organization" was "perfected for the purpose of perfecting the Negro's rights in this city." Three months later the Colored Board of Trade organized a legal defense fund to sue for a "more equitable" distribution of school funds. African American lawyers Isaac L. Purcell (a one-time Palatka city councilman) and Samuel D. McGill (a former law clerk to James Weldon Johnson) led the legal charge. The efforts paid off in August when Purcell won a court injunction against the board of education.[12]

In the absence of a statewide organization, the Knights of Pythias provided helpful leadership. In 1915 some rural White legislators attempted to push through a law prohibiting Blacks from practicing law and a "grandfather clause" amendment to the state constitution to further limit Black voting rights. Meeting at Tallahassee, the Knights selected a committee "thoroughly representative of Florida's leading colored citizens" to present objections to Governor Park Trammell and the legislature. Both measures eventually were defeated, although the constitutional amendment fell at a referendum only after the United States Supreme Court in June declared "grandfather clause" restrictions unconstitutional.[13]

It was just at this time that Floridians began to reach out to the NAACP, despite its reluctance to venture too deeply into the South. In April 1915 Charles S. Sturgis, a minister in West Tampa which then was a separate entity from Tampa, inquired of the national organization how he could convert the existing American Benevolent Association into an NAACP branch. H. E. Lester followed up the inquiry in June by contacting Dr. Du Bois. The response came from the national secretary, May Childs Nerney, who wrote, "As it is very difficult, however, to carry on this work in the South we think it would be better for you to consider organizing a local instead of a branch." Naming the local after Bishop Henry McNeal Turner, the Tampa activists finalized the organization.[14]

Soon, other events were to expand the NAACP network in Florida. Not without significance, in November 1915 Booker T. Washington died. This removed his monumental influence on the nature of race activism at a time when Dr. Du Bois's influence was growing through distribution of *The Crisis*. The next month Florida's first branch formally organized at Key West, with fifteen members. Former sheriff Charles F. Dupont was president and B. V. Gonzalez acted as secretary. Then, in February 1916 Du Bois came to Florida, spreading his gospel with speeches such as one he delivered at Tampa's Odd Fellows Hall.[15]

Du Bois's activist message fell on many receptive ears, for conditions in Florida were worsening with the opening of the year's political season. One gubernatorial candidate, Sidney J. Catts, in March denounced education for Black children. One month later authorities arrested several white Roman Catholic nuns at St. Augustine for teaching Black children in violation of state law. Catts drummed his anti-Black and anti-Roman Catholic message to ignorant White voters. Despite attempts at political maneuvering by some principals of the Democratic party, the bigot achieved election in November. They called him "the Cracker Messiah."[16]

Coincidence then occurred to offer some hope to African Americans in Florida. Just as Sidney Catts was elected in November 1916, national NAACP leaders had become convinced of the need for a full-time organizer. It chose a former Floridian, James Weldon Johnson, who took up his duties in December. "My first step as Field Secretary was an effort to organize in the South," Johnson later recalled. "It was my idea that the South could furnish numbers and resources to make the Association a power." He added, "This idea did not meet with the unqualified approval of all the members of the Board of Directors." At the time southern branches existed only at New Orleans, Shreveport, and Key West. In any event, Johnson immediately launched a tour of the southeast, which brought him to Florida in January and February 1917. At Jacksonville and Tampa he organized branches. Thirty-one individuals joined at the former city. At Tampa 107 persons signed their names to membership forms, making that Florida branch second in the South only to Atlanta. Joseph N. Clinton and my grandmother Marion E. Rogers figured prominently among them.[17]

Within weeks of Johnson's successful southern tour, the United States entered World War One with chilling results for the NAACP in Florida. Key activists were of age for military service and soon left the state. At Tampa, for instance, Daniel W. Perkins had become leader of NAACP activities, but the lawyer joined the Army after the declaration of war. Interim officers Dr. J. A. White and Christina Meacham attempted to carry on in Perkins's absence, but by mid-1918 the branch was languishing. James Weldon Johnson paid a special visit in June as a result of which fifty-six new members joined. Yet, the Tampa branch sorely missed Perkins's dynamism. After the war he relocated to Jacksonville, and, in his permanent absence, the branch lapsed by the early 1920s.[18]

Apparently only one Florida branch survived the war's end in good shape, likely the one at Jacksonville. It contained eighty-eight members. Unfortunately, the state's African American population needed leadership ever-more desperately. During the conflict thousands of Blacks left farms for better jobs in towns and cities, many of them in the North. With lynch law continuing to befoul the state, panicked planters and businessmen appealed to Governor Catts, who escalated a campaign to stem the tide of emigration. Eventually, law enforcement agencies rounded up those refusing to work and even detained hiring agents from northern employers. Responding to the governor's call, some towns demanded that Black men "work or fight"; that is, they had to seek employment in Florida in the war effort or else face immediate conscription.[19]

Following the peace in November 1918, conditions grew more violent throughout the country as African American aspirations for rewards for their contributions to the victory ran headlong into a White reaction. Dr. Du Bois had spoken of the aspirations when he wrote of returning Black veterans: "Negroes will come back feeling like men and not disposed to accept the treatment to which they have been subjected." Some southern newspapers saw a

The Early Years

H. E. Lester, completing work initiated by Rev. Charles S. Sturgis, was able to establish an NAACP local in Tampa in 1915.

Joseph N. Clinton was an active member of the Tampa branch. He was a neighbor and family friend.

Daniel Webster Perkins was an energetic young lawyer when he assumed leadership of Tampa's NAACP. After World War I he returned to Florida to practice law in Jacksonville.

W. E. B. Du Bois (left) was a charismatic personality and editor of the NAACP journal **The Crisis**. He and James Weldon Johnson travelled widely to speak on behalf of the national organization. Johnson, who was born and educated in Jacksonville, became the NAACP's initial Field Secretary in 1916 and began to organize the South. He visited Tampa first in 1917, when he recruited more than one hundred members. A return visit in June 1918 brought the chapter fifty-six more.

Du Bois photographed in the editorial offices of **The Crisis** c. 1915, probably a few months prior to his Florida trip. As editor of the journal, Du Bois enjoyed a tremendous national following, making his visit to Florida a catalyst to attract NAACP memberships.

11

"bloody fate" for those with the temerity to demand constitutional rights. The forecast proved accurate by the summer of 1919. Its twenty-five race riots earned the season the name, the Red Summer.[20]

The next year an additional element stirred racial animosities in Florida, as, for the first time, in 1920 women could cast votes in its local and national elections. A quirk in the poll tax law permitted African American women to register without penalty. Reportedly, 6,500 answered the call. With Black veterans persisting in their demand for political rights, the stage was set for confrontation. Tensions built as police arrested up to 500 of the women for minor violations of registration laws. Already in May a man had been lynched in Polk County near Tampa. In October, four more individuals—Ray Field, Ben Givens, Sam Duncan, and Milton Smith—succumbed to mob violence at Macclenny in northeast Florida. On the day before the elections, Mary McLeod Bethune, who was to play a very important role in my life and career, was compelled to face down angry Ku Klux Klansmen on the campus of her school at Daytona Beach. She had encouraged students and others to vote.[21]

Then, on election day, November 2, the eruption came. A number of African Americans led by veteran July Perry tried to cast ballots at the small town of Ocoee, which lies close to Orlando. Some Whites formed a "posse," dispersed the Black voters, and then attacked their neighborhood. Perry defended his family, killing two White men before he was lynched. Somewhere between ten and thirty others also died, as twenty buildings burned. In Florida, memories of the Ocoee Riot remained for years as a threat to the African American community.[22]

The events of 1919 and 1920 posed a threat to the NAACP as well, but, for a time, the local branches survived. The problem lay in the fact that many Floridians hesitated to put their lives or the lives of their family members on the line. Exceptions existed, of course. At Palatka, city councilmen Albert A. Browning and Joseph A. Nottage maintained a Black presence in public office until 1924. At Jacksonville in 1921, a ticket of five men attempted election to municipal office in that city, although a White backlash led by the *Florida Times-Union* defeated them. And, further to the good, when NAACP organizer William Perkins visited the state late the same year he stirred new or renewed interest at St. Augustine, Ocala, Tampa, and Jacksonville. This was the year that I born.[23]

The facts that I just mentioned were the high spots, and rough times lay ahead. The violence continued sporadically, then exploded anew. In early January 1923 Whites, believing that residents of the small community of Rosewood (near Cedar Key) were harboring an escaped prisoner who supposedly had attacked a white woman, started a melee. Blacks fought back, killing two attackers in a gunbattle. Three times as many African Americans died, as their town was consumed in flames. Survivors fled into the woods for safety, never to return to the site of their former lives.[24]

The blood that flowed at Rosewood bled the NAACP, although that outcome did not become evident for some time. Two months after the tragedy, national Field Secretary Addie W. Hunton visited Pensacola, Tallahassee, Jacksonville, St. Augustine, and Daytona Beach to stir enthusiasm. She reported mass meetings and impressive turnouts, especially at Tallahassee among students at Florida Agricultural & Mechanical College, where President Nathan B. Young "ofttimes spoke boldly for Negro freedom and Negro rights." Appearances deceived. By late 1924 the state contained only three honor branches (branches with paid up dues): Jacksonville, Key West, and a new branch at Blountstown. One year later only Key West maintained honor branch status. By 1926 none prospered sufficiently to earn the honor.[25]

Into the vacuum formed by the waning of the NAACP in the 1920s came bi-racial organizations that were more acceptable to Florida's White power structure, particularly the Urban League. That organization offered services of crucial day-to-day need in a state that entered the Great Depression in 1926, three years ahead of the rest of the country. As noted by historians of the Tampa NAACP, the League assisted "day-care nurseries for working mothers, alternative home placements for juvenile delinquents, family case work, the organization of clubs and recreation for black youth, and employment placement."[26]

Racial violence and legal discrimination remained areas of interest to the NAACP, and local incidents could provoke reorganization of a defunct chapter. This happened at Tampa in 1929 after Charley Durham was accused of raping a white woman. Led by Professor E. J. Wright, residents appealed for a new charter and welcomed national field worker C. S. Sutton to assist Durham. With Sutton's input, information was pieced together to prove Durham's innocence. The field worker also helped to clear up several other cases pending in local courts. The next year new executive secretary Walter White involved chapter members in the case of the Huggins family of Hernando County, members of which had been whipped because of a supposed theft. The national office, unfortunately, lacked the resources to send its own agent.[27]

Two great cases illustrate the NAACP's basic activities in Florida during the 1930s, as it attempted to stretch precious resources as far as possible. The first began with a robbery and murder and ended in a landmark United States Supreme Court decision. The facts in what become known as the case of *Chambers* v. *Florida* were summarized for readers of *The Crisis* as follows:

> On the night of May 13, 1933, an elderly White man was robbed and murdered in Pompano, Florida. Within the day some forty Negroes were arrested by dragnet methods, without warrant, and confined to jail. For almost a week, night and day, the prisoners were subjected to questioning and browbeating. They were not allowed to see counsel or relatives. Five days of persistent grilling elicited nothing but disclaimers of guilt. Walter Woodward, a young ignorant tenant farmer, then "broke." But his "confession" was considered unsatisfactory. The grilling continued. Finally Woodward, Isiah Chambers, Jack Williamson and Charlie Davis "broke" in a manner acceptable to the authorities and all gave "confessions." The four boys were thereafter indicted and arraigned. Williamson, Woodward and Davis pleaded guilty; Chambers pleaded not guilty.

At the Chambers trial, the four confessions were used and a jury returned a verdict of guilty. All the defendants were sentenced to death. Appeal was taken to the Florida supreme court, which affirmed. Application was then made to the Florida supreme court upon the suggestion that the confessions had been obtained by coercion and duress. That court granted leave to present a petition to the lower Florida court. The issue of the validity of the confessions was twice submitted to juries, which held against the prisoners; and the Florida supreme court ultimately affirmed, one judge dissenting.

The supreme court of the United States granted certiorari and reversed the judgment of the Florida supreme court. Despite the jury findings, it felt bound to reexamine the record to determine for itself whether the constitutional claim—that the convictions were secured through use by the State of confessions improperly compelled, a claim of right under the due process clause of the Fourteenth Amendment—was meritorious. And upon such reexamination the court found abundant evidence that the confessions were the manifest result of pressure dishonestly applied.[28]

The United States Supreme Court did not issue its final decision in the *Chambers* case until Lincoln's Birthday 1940. The protracted appeals process could not have been pursued without the assistance of the NAACP. First, local branches helped to raise funds to employ attorney S. D. McGill, who had been arguing civil rights cases since 1908. As *The Crisis* noted in praising him, "Due credit must go to S. D. McGill of Jacksonville, Fla., who carried the case five times to the Florida supreme court." The NAACP national organization afforded further assistance through the legal advice and talents of Thurgood Marshall and Howard University law faculty member Leon A. Ransom. McGill and Ransom successfully argued the case before the national court. In doing so they achieved one of the building blocks that ultimately helped to erect a wall of protection against a racist judicial system.[29]

The step forward won after such hard effort by the NAACP in the *Chambers* case is not so easily seen in a second 1930s Florida incident that resulted in more violence and yet another awful tragedy. In October 1934 at the Panhandle town of Greenwood, near Marianna, someone killed a young White girl named Lola Cassidy. Claude Neal was arrested, after which the local sheriff took him to Brewton, Alabama, where his safety, presumably, could be assured. Quickly, a mob formed, broke Neal out of jail, and returned him to the vicinity of Greenwood. The mob's leaders announced their intention to lynch Neal eight hours before the act. State and national NAACP officials pleaded for his rescue, but Governor David Sholtz declined to call out the National Guard and local law enforcement officials ignored the situation. At the appointed time, Neal was stabbed, mutilated, and shot repeatedly. His body then was dragged through the woods behind an automobile before it was hung from a tree limb.[30]

The fact that the NAACP pleas carried so little weight with governmental officials in the Neal case illustrated a problem that hampered the association's growth in Florida, because it was so easily ignored. It offered no statewide organization and precious few resources, including personnel. In the Neal case, one attempt to force change did result. It came from an idea of the young Roy Wilkins, who then was employed at the national headquarters. After reading a newspaper account of Neal's ordeal, Wilkins reacted strongly. "I put down *The New York Times* that day feeling sick," he recorded. Wilkins convinced Executive Secretary Walter White to let him and others picket a National Conference on Crime then planned for December 1934 at Constitution Hall in Washington, D.C. President Franklin D. Roosevelt was scheduled to speak, and Wilkins believed that the exposure might produce momentum for a federal anti-lynching law. Unfortunately, no federal law resulted, but Roy Wilkins did experience his first of many national-scale protests and endured the first of many arrests in the cause.[31]

Other than fraternal organizations such as the Knights of Pythias, only one African American organization possessed the kind of statewide network that might influence public policy during the

1930s. That was the Florida State Teacher's Association. While the organization lacked great financial resources, it did bring together many of the most capable Black leaders in Florida on a regular basis. Outstanding among them were individuals such as Noah Griffin of St. Petersburg, Edward D. Davis of Tampa and Ocala, and, from Brevard County, teachers Harry T. Moore and John Gilbert.[32]

With the support of hundreds of other African American teachers, they determined to improve the quality of education for Black children throughout the state. Especially after E. D. Davis assumed the organization's presidency in 1935, the FSTA launched itself into several initiatives, most importantly a legal assault to ensure equalization of teachers' salaries, without regard to race or color. The first suit was filed in 1937 by Noah Griffin in Pinellas County. The principal of Gibbs High School, his plea was rejected by local courts and the Supreme Court of Florida. For his trouble, Griffin was fired by the Pinellas County school board. The setback eventually worked to the benefit of the FSTA, which hired Griffin as its full-time executive secretary.[33]

At the time of Griffin's loss, the momentum for change could have been blunted had not a lucky series of inter-related events occurred. The chain began back with the NAACP's efforts in the *Chambers* case, which had impressed Brevard County teachers Harry T. Moore and John Gilbert. Particularly, it encouraged them to form a Brevard branch of the NAACP in 1934. Moore became president and Gilbert served as secretary, while also pursuing leadership roles in the FSTA. As the statewide organization committed itself to the equalization initiative, Moore and Gilbert utilized their NAACP contacts to seek funding to hire S. D. McGill as attorney for a Brevard County suit. The efforts succeeded, and on May 24, 1938, McGill filed the necessary paperwork on behalf of Gilbert, who then was principal of Cocoa Junior High School. As noted by *The Crisis*, "This case was the first in the Deep South [sponsored by the NAACP] and was watched keenly by other states."[34]

The Gilbert case resulted as unhappily as had Noah Griffin's suit, but the quest continued. Gilbert also was terminated as teacher and principal, and the Florida supreme court again declined to deal with the equalization issue in any positive manner. Success did not come for several years. Then, in January 1940 NAACP attorneys including S. D. McGill filed suit on behalf of Vernon McDaniel, principal of Washington High School of Escambia County. Faced with the possibility of an adverse decision, the local authorities offered a compromise leading to salary equalization. The dike had been breached, and other school districts were forced over the next decade to fall into line. Heroes and heroines of the fight included Jacksonville's J. L. Williams during his tenure as president of the FSTA, Charles Stebbins of West Palm Beach, Mary White Blocker of Duval County, Herbert C. Reynolds of Dade County, George H. Starke and Edward C. Davis of Marion County, and Hilda Turney of Hillsborough County, among others.[35]

The equalization initiative had proved several important things to the individuals involved. First, a statewide organization provided resources and contacts of immeasurable importance. Second, legal action could eventually force change through the courts in Florida, and the NAACP could offer crucial support to the success of legal cases. Lastly, if the leaders of the state's Black community did not act in concert, no one else was likely to stand up to demand change in a racist system.

At that point, the organization of a state conference of the NAACP seemed logical and inevitable, although no other state yet had taken such a step. Harry T. Moore and John Gilbert had proposed the idea as early as 1934, but action came in 1941, the year that Vernon McDaniel triumphed and that President Franklin D. Roosevelt signed the famous Executive Order 8802, barring discrimination in defense industries and in the government.[36]

At first, the Florida NAACP conference existed under an informal agreement of leaders of the nine branches, with Noah W. Griffin serving as president. That arrangement changed October 17-19, 1941, when the first annual conference met at Bethel Metropolitan Baptist Church in St. Petersburg. National Executive Secretary Walter White appeared to give his blessing to the innovation. "Before you lies two paths," he informed the delegates, "one is the path of indifference, laziness, cowardice . . . the downward path; the other will hold some imperfections and barriers, but in it there is courage, sacrifice and vision, which will help us reach our ultimate goal." Those in attendance selected Harry T. Moore as their first elected president.[37]

The war years that followed the creation of the state conference are not very well documented for Florida. Still, progress was made. Nationally, NAACP membership grew substantially and even-more-activist organizations such as the Congress of Racial Equality (CORE) were formed. Race leaders committed themselves to bringing real advancements out of the world conflict. Their symbol was the "Double-V," standing for victory over the enemy abroad and victory over racism at home. Back in Florida, Harry Moore worked the state. He built branches and enlisted new members, while aiding the fight against violence and against discrimination among civilians and at military bases such as Tampa's MacDill Field. By the end of 1944, the state conference contained 34 branches, with almost 3,000 members.[38]

What now appears to have been one of the crucial events of the World War Two era for Florida was the United States Supreme Court's 1944 decision in *Smith v. Allwright*. This decision struck down the Democratic White primary and opened up that party to African American voters. Harry Moore and other Florida NAACP leaders recognized its importance immediately and set about to take advantage of the ruling, with results that greatly affected Moore and the NAACP. Since the national organization stressed its nonpolitical nature, the Floridians quickly organized a separate entity called the Progressive Voters' League. Moore detailed its goals:

> To get the democratic primary open to Negro voters in every county in Florida; (2) to encourage the masses of our people to register and vote; (3) to make contact with the various candidates and to make recommendations to our voters on the basis of the candidate's recommendations and attitudes.[39]

League members had their work cut out for them. In 1944 only about 20,000 African Americans were registered to vote in

Florida, about 5.5 percent of the potential pool. To increase these numbers, Moore and his associates first depended on the NAACP organization. Under pressure from national officers, though, he began to rely more heavily upon the new organization, while continuing to utilize resources of the NAACP. By November 1945 he had issued a ringing call:

> Who are more directly responsible for the inequalities in educational opportunities, the lynchings, the police brutality, and other injustices suffered by Negroes, our state and county officials or the Administration in Washington? All of these evils can be traced directly to the prejudiced attitude of local officials. ... The fact is that practically every city, county, and state official in Florida is selected in the Democratic Primaries. In order to help select these officials, Negroes must vote in the Democratic Primaries.[40]

The results of the campaign soon evidenced themselves. In January 1946 the Florida Democratic party dropped its formal bar to Black participation. The next month two African Americans ran for the Dade County school board. In March, Moore's home branch in Brevard County sued for ballot access. And, so it went. By the Fall, Blacks voted in many urban counties and some rural ones. Three years later, the Tampa *Florida Sentinel* could proudly observe, "In 1947 the Negro participated freely, for the first time in years, in the municipal election of Tampa, and in 1949 in the State and County elections in most cities and towns of Florida." It continued, "There were a few places here and there which did not recognize the U. S. Supreme Court decision granting Negroes the right of suffrage in the Democratic primary, but they won't be many by next Spring, if any at all."[41]

These years were exciting ones, as progress seemed at last to be at hand. Let me give a few examples. In 1946 the NAACP filed a suit against the University of Texas, seeking to open state law schools to African Americans. The 1950 decision in *Sweatt* v. *Painter* then served as a precedent for arguments in public school desegregation cases that led to the 1954 decision in *Brown* v. *The Board of Education of Topeka, Kansas*. Also in 1946 President Harry S Truman announced the formation of a multi-racial civil rights commission. Its 1947 report, *To Secure These Rights,* called for an end to racial segregation and discrimination. Already that year, the President had addressed the national NAACP meeting, declaring that "Full civil rights and freedom must be guaranteed to all Americans."[42]

With excitement in the air and tangible results to be seen, Floridians joined the NAACP in record numbers and the organization grew more sophisticated. By late 1946, sixty-three branches covered the state, with youth councils organized and operating out of many of them. A little over one year later almost eighty branches reported to state officials, as Moore embarked upon a membership campaign with a goal of 25,000 members. Year's end saw the total at a modest 8,219, but the figure still represented a tremendous increase over the totals of just a few years before. Much of the credit for the growth must go to Moore. As a result of his Progressive Voters' League activities, he had been fired from his teaching job. So, in 1946 the state conference voted him full-time executive secretary. E. D. Davis assumed the responsibilities of president, with W. J. H. Black as first vice president, Frank Burts as second vice president, Emma Pickett as secretary, Mamie Mike as assistant secretary, and K. S. Johnson as treasurer.[43]

As events were to prove, things had begun to get out of hand for Moore and the Florida NAACP. The executive secretary stretched himself thin attempting to contribute to the NAACP, the FSTA, and the PVL. This came at a time when more and more of his attention was required in attending to the details of NAACP administration and fundraising. Moreover, national officials, including Walter White, were growing increasingly concerned about how Moore failed to carefully draw a line between his NAACP activities and those of the other organizations with which he was involved.[44]

Circumstances then took a turn for the worse. NAACP headquarters increased annual membership dues from $1 to $2. In 1949 national membership plummeted by 40 percent, with Florida suffering a similar decrease. Even the year before the state organization had been dealing with a budget deficit; now a crisis loomed. Moore attempted to take the initiative in 1949 by reorganizing the state into divisions based upon congressional districts. Each assumed some responsibility for the financial problems, and great hopes were manifested. By early 1950 the executive secretary also had begun traveling the state, gathering new members and rejuvenating branches. Unfortunately, by this time Moore's focus often was distracted to another—and important—cause.[45]

What became known as the Groveland case began in July 1949 in Lake County when a white woman alleged that she had been kidnapped and raped by several black men. The county possessed a reputation for vicious racism in its law enforcement circles, particularly on the part of Sheriff Willis McCall. So, when authorities arrested four men, fears for their safety immediately were felt. One mob attempted to grab the men at the Tavares jail, but, this time, McCall turned them away. Instead, the mob returned to Groveland where its members set fire to Black homes while firing into them with guns. Moderate governor Fuller Warren sent in the National Guard, after receiving NAACP pleas.[46]

I will write further about the Groveland case later in this book, but for now I would just mention that the NAACP's involvement grew. Lawyer Franklin Williams of the Legal Defense Fund gathered evidence that made the allegations highly suspect. The NAACP then associated with the defense White Florida lawyers Alex Akerman, Jr., and Joseph L. Price, Jr., as well as Black attorneys Horace Hill of Daytona Beach and Paul Perkins of Orlando. As the cases moved through the judicial system, the need for money to fuel the defense and keep the cause alive grew greater and greater. Harry Moore especially felt a responsibility to come to the defendants' aid, spending increasing amounts of his time and energy on the cause.[47]

Into 1950 Moore's problems were growing. National officers believed that he was not giving sufficient time to administration and was associating the NAACP too closely with political matters. Urban members chafed at his time spent organizing in rural areas. Budget deficits mounted to the extent that there was no money available to pay Moore's salary. All the while, he was becoming more vocal in direct attacks upon the White establishment. He attempted to block a federal appointment for former governor Millard Caldwell; he led the membership into a call for full integration of all public facilities; he demanded civil rights legislation from Florida's congressional delegation; and he charged "whitewash" in the Groveland investigations. These were but a few of his initiatives.[48]

The pace quickened for Moore as the 1951 state conference meeting neared, it being scheduled for Daytona Beach on Thanksgiving weekend. Some success had been achieved in the Groveland case. He began to organize "Groveland Sundays" as a technique to build defense funds, but mostly he turned his focus to membership recruitment and NAACP fundraising. It all changed in early November when Sheriff McCall gunned down two of the Groveland defendants in cold blood, killing one. From his home at Mims, Moore demanded McCall's suspension. "Human life is too precious to be gambled like this," he declared. His anger grew as state officials declined to act against the politically powerful McCall.[49]

When the Florida conference convened at Daytona, Moore's problems caught up with him. Representatives of the national headquarters attempted to remove him as executive secretary. The longtime leader fought back. Reported one official of the results: "Harry Moore was insistent upon continuing in that position and a compromise was reached whereby he is to work as state coordinator for a period, but is supposed to clear all of his activities through the president of the state conference." Moore recorded, "In some respects this meeting was about the worse we have had." He continued, "Really it was not a State meeting, because the National officers came in and took over."[50]

Tired and dejected, Harry Moore returned to Mims to celebrate the Christmas holidays with his family and his twenty-fifth wedding anniversary with his wife Harriett. That night members of the Ku Klux Klan, who perhaps did not even know that he was no longer executive secretary of the NAACP, placed three pounds of dynamite under his bedroom floor. At 10:15 p.m. the bomb exploded. Harry died on the way to the hospital, and Harriett survived him by only a few days. Although not too many people remember their names now, they were the first great martyrs of the Civil Rights Movement of the 1950s and 1960s.[51] Little could I have known, when I heard the news of his death far away in Detroit, Michigan, that within a matter of months I would become Harry Moore's successor.

Mr. and Mrs. Harry T. Moore were killed by the explosion that destroyed their home on December 25, 1951. Today they hold a place of honor in Florida's history as the first great martyrs of the Civil Rights Movement. (Evangeline Moore)

The Moore home as it appeared on the morning after the explosion that took their lives. (Florida State Archives)

The Early Years

Christina Meacham was an important Tampa NAACP leader during World War I.

Dr. J. A. White also took an active leadership role in Tampa after Daniel Perkins left for the war.

James Weldon Johnson was a continuing source of pride and inspiration for fellow Floridians.

The national leadership of the NAACP slowly was making progress by establishing legal precedents and by improving communications with influential political and public figures. In this photograph NAACP executive secretary Walter White and his future successor Roy Wilkins are standing with (seated) Dr. James J. McClendon, president of the Detroit NAACP branch, Eleanor Roosevelt, and Thurgood Marshall. Mrs. Roosevelt spoke at the national convention in Detroit in 1943, just a few years before I moved there and began to work with the energetic Detroit branch.

This 1921 Tampa view looks west across the Hillsborough River toward my childhood neighborhood of Roberts City. The J. W. Roberts & Sons Cigar Factory building is on the left, behind the burnt wreckage of the Bay Queen excursion boat. This area on the river's west bank between Cass Street on the south and the Garcia Avenue Bridge (now the North Boulevard Bridge) on the north, with North Boulevard as the western boundary, was called originally "El Barrio de Elinche" by the cigarmakers. (Arsenio M. Sanchez/Tampa-Hillsborough County Public Library)

Roberts City's diverse ethnic population arose from a thriving turn-of-the-century cigar manufacturing industry. The J. W. Roberts & Sons Cigar Factory at the corner of Green Street and Garcia Avenue was the first brick building in West Tampa. Built in 1893 as the Julius Ellinger & Co. Cigar Factory, a part of the Havana-American Company, the building was sold to the firm of J. W. Roberts on April 3, 1909. (Arsenio M. Sanchez)

2
My Life to 1940

While the NAACP was struggling to establish a toehold in Florida during the early decades of the century, I was growing up in Tampa. I was born there on June 9, 1921, in a section known as Roberts City. It got its name from J. W. Roberts, who owned a cigar factory situated at Garcia Avenue and Roberts Street. This was a neighborhood of four or five blocks just west of the Hillsborough River, a few blocks north of the Laurel Street bridge. To the south, not too distant, lay the famous Tampa Bay Hotel. Nearby to the west was West Tampa, a cigarmaking center that developed in the 1890s.[1]

My family's roots ran deep in Tampa and Roberts City. My mother, Christina Rogers Saunders, had grown up there. The Rogers side could trace their presence to about 1893. James W. and Marion E. Mathews Rogers were the parents of eight children, including my mother. They had come to town from Key West. Grandfather made cigars, and grandmother added to the family income by baking pastries and doing domestic work, mostly for Italian families. Doubtlessly, grandmother learned her cooking skills from her parents, who had operated a Tampa restaurant around the turn of the century. Relatively speaking, my grandparents' chances for a comfortable life were pretty good when mother came into the world on January 21, 1898.

Before going on, I should mention two points that come to mind when I think of mother's parents. First, just as was the case with J. W. and Marion Rogers, many influential Blacks in Key West and Tampa either were born in the Bahama Islands or descended from Bahamians. In my case, Harbour Island and its Dunmore Town especially were important. The same was true, to give another example, of Christina Johnson Meacham, the educator and activist after whom Tampa's Meacham Early Childhood Center is named.[2] Bahamiam traditions remained strong in these families and were passed down, even to a reverence for the king or queen of England. More importantly, though, race pride shone through, with an awareness and determination that the sorry conditions that had developed in the American South did not represent the only possibility for Black men and women.

The other point concerns grandmother Rogers. Given her background, her pride, her fierce determination, and her love, she probably influenced me as much or more than any other person. Until her death in 1951, she always demanded the best from me while giving me a foundation for pride and a living role model for activism. I can well remember her telling me stories of the famous "Buffalo soldiers," who came to Tampa during the Spanish-American War of 1898. Of course she mentioned their wartime exploits, but what I really recall is her story of how, after returning from Cuba, they broke their comrades out of jails at Tampa and Lakeland, where they had been incarcerated for resisting racist discrimination.[3]

Grandmother did much more than talk. When mother first attended school in Tampa, the entire facility amounted to one tumbled-down room. As mother told me, "there was nothing much to it." Grandmother simply refused to accept that for her own daughter or for other children. She helped organize local volunteers to demand action from white authorities, prodding male community leaders to action. "Men were kind of slow," mother remembered, "but she would always go." The school efforts succeeded to some extent but pointed out to grandmother the need for organizational resistance to racism. So, in 1915 she joined with others to found an NAACP local in West Tampa, once of the South's first. When membership waned in the 1920s, grandmother switched to organizing on behalf of Marcus Garvey's United Negro Improvement Association (UNIA). Later, she raised money to help defend the Scottsboro Boys. I know for a fact that, when white Tampa policemen attempted on one occasion to harass her, grandmother drove them off by threats to sue. As I mentioned, she was quite a role model.

My father's side of the family also had Bahamian roots. Willard Saunders traced their residence in the islands through his mother, Christine E. Hannibal, to escaped slave Shadrach Hannibal, who fled to Nassau from South Carolina. Grandfather John A. Saunders married Christine about 1889, and two years later they gave birth to my father, Willard. Before long the family relocated to Key West, where relatives and jobs awaited. Father matured there, learning the trades of bricklayer and master mason. He may have moved to Tampa by 1917, for he entered the army from the city for service in France during World War One. A corporal by the armistice, father took his discharge at Tampa. At the time the city was booming, and jobs were plentiful. He and mother met and courted in 1919. They married on December 25 of that year.

To say the least, the world into which my parents brought me in 1921 was a complicated one. To the good, Tampa was growing by leaps and bounds. During the decade, its population doubled to over 100,000, nearly making Tampa the largest of Florida's cities.[4] My childhood friend Rowena Ferrell Brady, who passed away not long ago, has published a beautiful book of photographs of Black Tampa during that period and afterward.[5] Looking through its pages I can recall many of the remarkable men and women who were able to forge a good life for themselves while contributing to the broader community and its needs. For some, the growth and prosperity that lasted at least until the Florida Bust of 1926 and 1927 brought opportunity for economic progress.

The other side of the picture is a tragic one. Tampa began in the late 1850s to develop a pattern of racial discrimination and violence that haunts it to the present day.[6] Brutal lynchings and vicious beatings occurred repeatedly. By the 1930s the American Civil Liberties Union had branded the city as one of the worst "centers of repression" in the United States.[7] The threat of one lynching in 1929 helped to revive the local NAACP branch, but that action did not forestall the castration of a young man in 1930 for "flirting" with a white nurse.[8] Four years later Robert Johnson was gunned down in cold blood for "suspicion" of assault on a white woman. The tragedy occurred even though police had discovered no evidence linking him to the crime. When a grand jury refused to indict anyone for the lynching of "this helpless and friendless negro," the *Tampa Tribune* admitted that the crime left "another black mark on the record of Tampa and Florida."[9]

The senseless violence did not choose its victims simply because of race, as Whites sometimes suffered too. In a celebrated 1930 case, suspected bomber John Hodaz was blasted with a shotgun as he was hung from the roof of an automobile.[10] At mid-decade socialist political activist Joseph Shoemaker endured a brutal flogging that killed him.[11] A personal experience came in late 1931 when our neighbor Fred Crawford was kidnapped, whipped, and tarred and feathered for his union and political activities. Police soon afterward raided his home, which was right across the street from ours, seized literature and political materials, and arrested Mr. Crawford. I was ten years old at the time.[12]

Even with the violence touching on my neighborhood, I have to say that I grew up in an immediate world that differed in very important ways from the larger world around me. Roberts City's atmosphere arose from a rich mixture. My family had neighbors from a variety of ethnic groups, including Cuban and Italian, as well as Black and Caucasian families. Local children played together, ate in each other's homes, fought each other, and protected each other. On the other hand, Florida's segregation laws and traditions did keep us from attending the same schools, eating in the same restaurants, and even drinking from the same water fountains. On Sunday mornings, my friends attended the Baptist church for Whites on North Boulevard and Green Street, while my family attended one of the traditional Black churches. Still and all, while I was denied many of the same opportunities as my White friends, I have fond memories of childhood in Tampa.

One other feature of the neighborhood deserves mention. In the 1920s there remained in Tampa and Roberts City a number of men who had served in public office in past years. I mentioned in Chapter One that former state representative Joseph N. Clinton was among them. He lived just down the street on the corner of Palm and Garcia Avenue. Memory of Mr. Clinton's legislative ser-

Willard Saunders and Christina Rogers Saunders in their wedding photograph, December 1919.

Christina Saunders stands on the sidewalk in front of our Roberts City home at 1608 Garcia Avenue. This photo was taken about 1956, four years after I began my NAACP work in Tampa.

vice was still alive. We knew that he had played a key role in important affairs, and local people respected him and what he represented. After his death late in the decade, his son Joe Clinton, Jr., moved in across the street from us on Garcia Avenue. Later, Mr. Clinton's grandson, Red Clinton, would become a popular musician. Joe Jr. and Red's presence in my life certainly kept Mr. Clinton alive to me. I knew that he did not go along with racial segregation. While he had been forced to accept it for the time being, he, nonetheless, was bitterly opposed to it.

Community institutions such as schools, churches, and civic groups also affected the way that I grew up. The first school that I attended was the old West Tampa Elementary School on Green Street and Fremont Avenue. I remember my first classroom, a corrugated tin structure that was behind a four-room wooden building which housed the upper grades. My first teacher was named Miss Higgins. The only toilet was in an outhouse behind my classroom. Then, in 1927 the new West Tampa School, now known as Dunbar Elementary School, was opened on Main Street and Rome Avenue. This new building was brick and contained eight classrooms. My teacher there was Mrs. Susie Lester, wife of Herbert E. Lester, one of the few Black postmen in Tampa and one of the founders of the Tampa NAACP branch.

St. Paul A.M.E. Church activities often took up my time when elementary school ended. My father belonged to the Episcopal church, but grandmother Rogers was a devout African Methodist. She had mother christened in the old St. Paul, which was replaced in the 1910s by the present sanctuary. Grandmother baked pies for the new structure's building fund. Besides the importance of religious commitment and the fervor it raised, St. Paul brought into my life many more important people and examples. I can vividly recall, for example, sitting in the balcony in January 1932 while Congressman Oscar DePriest spoke to a packed and excited audience.[13] What an impression it made on me as a youngster.

Probably even more important than guest speakers were regular members of the congregation. Many of them were leaders who would spearhead local civil rights initiatives in the years to come.

*Rev. Marcellus D. Potter was a community leader who, with his wife Mary, built the **Tampa Bulletin** into one of the leading Black-owned newspapers in the country.*

*Mrs. Mary E. Potter was assistant manager at the **Tampa Bulletin** and served as both editor and publisher.*

Rev. Andrew Jackson Ferrell was a stalwart at St. Paul A.M.E. Church and one of my positive role models in the community.

Dr. J. A. White started a Boy Scout troop at St. Paul A.M.E. Church, and we would often meet at the Lamar Avenue Urban League headquarters. Here the troop conducts a formal flag-raising ceremony there at some time in 1942. (Tampa-Hillsborough County Public Library)

I would imagine that the Tampa NAACP's early meetings were held in the church. My godfather, Chris Green, was a steward. Among the ministers were outstanding men, including Marcellus M. Potter and Andrew Jackson Ferrell, Sr. As a kid I was always sticking my nose in everywhere, and I saw these and other men at work doing something positive for their church and their community.

One prominent St. Paul member, Dr. J. A. White, inadvertently changed the direction of my thinking about the importance of institutions and organizations. Dr. White is remembered now mostly for his service as president of the Tampa NAACP branch. Less well known is the fact that, in 1931, he founded at St. Paul a Boy Scout troop for local boys. The program came from the influence of Cyrus T. Green, executive director of the Urban League, and meetings often were held at League headquarters. Favorite memories of mine include images of the jamboree I attended at Florida A&M College in Tallahassee in 1931. We camped there on the Commons. College all of a sudden seemed something more important and accessible to me. Some family members had been educated there, and grandmother Rogers already had made clear that she believed in education.

I have gotten a little off the point that I was trying to make about institutions and organizations. The incident occurred one day as I was coming home from a Boy Scout meeting, wearing my uniform or part of a uniform. I had just crossed the Fortune Street bridge over the Hillsborough River and was approaching Garcia Avenue. Suddenly, some Italian boys jumped me, and I knew that I was in for a beating. Then, one of the Italian boys stopped the rest, saying, "Don't bother him, he's a Boy Scout." My association with that organization provided protection from racial hostility, a lesson that I did not forget when I associated later with the NAACP.

By the time I joined the local Boy Scouts, I had lived elsewhere for two years and then returned to Tampa. My parents' marriage had begun to fall apart late in the 1920s. In 1928 they separated, later divorcing. I would not see or know much of my father after that, until I was an adult. From everything I have learned he was a fine man. He settled in Washington, D.C., and remarried. According to the rector of Saint George's Parish church, he was known as "a dedicated and faithful communicant, and hard worker."[14] He died in 1964 and is buried at Arlington National Cemetery.

After the separation mother also decided to move, in her case to New York City where she had relatives who could get her a job. In 1929 we traveled there by train. The trip was something that I will never forget. Coming from Roberts City where race relations were somewhat more amicable, I was shocked at the Jim Crow car in which we were required to ride. It was a "half car," so-called because it carried half baggage and half Black passengers. After leaving Tampa's train station with its segregated waiting rooms, we sat in this hot and smoky car for what seemed an unbearable period of time. As the car was coupled immediately behind the coal car, burning cinders flew through the air that we breathed.

Life in New York came as a revelation to me. The city had integrated schools, some of my teachers were White, and I was able to make friends easily. I attended Public Schools 103 and 48. It was also in New York that I first became a Boy Scout. We joined Emmanuel Temple A.M.E. Church. Our minister, D. Ward Nichols, was kind to us. Later, as Bishop Nichols he would be instrumental in Florida civil rights activities. My mother did not have as happy a time in New York as I did, however. She worked in a big downtown hotel but was dissatisfied. Also, she met a Mr. Jackson, about whom I remember very little. They married, but the relationship did not last. The best I can recall he passed away, although they may have simply gone their separate ways.

Mother's unhappiness prompted her in 1931 to transfer us back to Tampa, and once again the trip was a lesson in southern race relations. My aunt Marie Rogers (later Librand) had a brand-new 1931 Chevrolet and offered to come pick us up. We left New York very early in the morning. Thereafter, we drove day and night, without stopping. We were afraid to stop, for fear that we might find ourselves dangerously in the wrong place. Fortunately, we got to Tampa safely and without incident.

Back in Florida, the Great Depression already was in full swing. Actually, boom-time Florida had ended several years earlier, forcing conditions for many of the state's residents from bad to worse. Mother found work in a Work Projects Administration (WPA) sewing factory where women made clothing for needy children. It was a meager livelihood, made only marginally better by free food such as potatoes and yellow grits that were distributed to the poor. Thoughts of those hard times lay heavily on mother's mind for decades. In the 1980s she still would remember them with sadness and then declare, "I hope we don't ever have another Depression."

I went to work during the Depression years, too, but for me it was fun. Along with a few friends, I labored as a newsboy for our community's newspaper, the *Tampa Bulletin*. Several persons who later would figure very prominently in NAACP civil rights activities also were employed there. I would mention, to cite an example, Linnell DuPree, who then served the paper as a pressman. Considered one of the nation's best Black weeklies, the *Bulletin* was owned and operated by the Reverend Marcellus D. Potter and his wife, Mary E. Potter.

Mrs. Potter really ran the operation. Still, it was Reverend Potter's spirit that pervaded its newsroom. A tall, dark-skinned fellow, he exerted a large influence on a lot of us. His courage was renowned, as also was his kindness and generosity. Both the Potters treated the newsboys as their own kids. As an A.M.E. minister, Reverend Potter allied the *Bulletin* with the church. For that matter, we considered it the official organ of the A.M.E. church in Florida. The Potters also believed fervently in the NAACP. Their commitment was so strong that they willed one-third of the *Bulletin* to the NAACP, with the remainder going to their employees and to the Union League. Their example was not lost on us. Linnell, for instance, became one of Tampa's leading printers and publishers. He later aided me in NAACP work, often doing the printing when no money was available.

Working at the *Bulletin* was an education in itself, but that did not get me out of going to school. When mother returned us to Tampa in 1931, I started at Harlem Elementary School. Before long I moved on to Booker T. Washington High School, which accepted students beginning at the junior high school level, while offering vocational training for adults at night. The building was fairly new and was Tampa's first Black high school. Yet, it had no playground nor library. Those amenities were not available to us until the opening in 1935 of George S. Middleton High School, named for a respected postman who helped organize the Central Life Insurance Company. After Middleton opened its doors, Washington became a junior high school.

Ironically, many of my final high school days were spent at Washington. After I was in senior high, Middleton closed as a result of fire damage. During the time it was being rebuilt, high school classes were held at Washington. High school students attended in the mornings and junior high school students in the afternoon from 12:30 to 5:00. I remember that, one year, we went to school six days a week to make up for lost time. Clearly, some progress was being made during the 1930s toward better facilities for Black children, but what we had never approached those taken for granted by Whites.

Having said that, let me state that I had some fine teachers who made a lasting impact on me. They really instilled in me a desire to be something. Marian Anderson taught math at Washington and made us learn. The same went for seventh-grade teacher Elsie Turner. The discipline and high standards of Howard W. Blake, Washington's principal, left a very important mark. At Middleton, Dr. Frankie Berry instructed us in composition and rhetoric, insisting on perfection. She especially took a personal interest in me, living only three blocks down Garcia from us. Everett Rolfe, professor of trades, likewise gave much time to me, encouraging my interest in and tinkering with model airplanes. Our families were close, and we took pride in his brother's position as dean of the Meharry Medical College. There were many more, among them music teacher Frankie Thompson, James T. Hargrett, Anna Broughton, J. W. Lockhart, Helen Wilson, Olga Rolfe Blood, Garland V. Stewart, G. B. Brinson, Hilda Turney, and Chester Seaberry. These teachers did miraculous work in second-class conditions.

Music became an important part of my life during the high school years. Financially strapped Washington High had long since abandoned its student band when I entered the seventh grade, but in 1935 the WPA funded a program to teach some young people how to play musical instruments. Mrs. Faith McQueen Coleman's studio, on Green and Delaware, was the center for a chorus and for piano lessons taught by a "wizard" on the keyboards, Bill Anderson. I learned to play from him. Also, Captain W. Carey Thomas, a former bandmaster at Florida A&M College, instructed us. Rufus Spencer, a trumpet player, assisted him. I started out with them on the bass tuba and eventually learned all the brass instruments. The enjoyment of music seemed such a natural path to follow, since our home was filled with it. Mother and grandmother made sure that we were never without a piano and a gramophone.

Beyond the pure enjoyment of it, music broadened my horizons. I recall our pride at marching in the annual Strawberry Festival parade at nearby Plant City about 1935, nearly thirty years before a Black band was allowed to participate in Tampa's famous Gasparilla parade. Within our community, we became mainstays of public events, playing on occasions such as the dedication of Clara Frye Hospital. Out of the WPA band also evolved a dance orchestra called the Hard Rockers. Rufus Spencer organized it and played trumpet. I worked the piano. By 1938 we were playing proms and public dances, mostly in Tampa but sometimes elsewhere. In the process I came to know the area's big bands and musicians—Banjo Boy Hawkins, the Florida Collegians, and Red Clinton among them. At the time Ray Charles was living on Governor Street, just getting started.

I was earning a little money with music and having a wonderful time, but I had no thoughts of making a career out of it. I liked science and had some thoughts about training to be a lawyer. Grandmother Rogers meanwhile kept bringing up the possibility of my becoming a medical doctor. In any event, the influences most directly touching me—my mother, my grandmother, my teachers, and many community leaders—all pushed me toward college. And so, I delighted in music while accepting it only as a very enjoyable pastime.

It would not be correct, on the other hand, for me to imply that I had not seen some of life's temptations. I most certainly had. Beginning in junior high, I worked for Mr. O'Kelly, a shoe repairman on Central Avenue, the heart of Tampa's Black business district. By 1938-1939 the nearby Central Theater had employed me as a doorman. I worked from 4:30 to closing seven days a week for four dollars per week. Between the two jobs, I became acquainted with at least 75 percent of Tampa's Black population.

On the good side, the avenue thrived with our community's most prominent businesses and professional offices. There were restaurants, barber and beauty shops, ballrooms, fraternal organizations, and a hotel for visitors. One especially good restaurant was run by Moses White, and the Rogers Dining Room also deserves mention. Located in the immediate vicinity were the offices of Black doctors, dentists, and our one attorney, Z. D. Greene. I recall that "Colonel" Greene supplemented his income by teaching. Law enforcement came at the hands of Black policemen, although the officers could only patrol the Central Avenue area and could arrest only Black offenders.

Then there was the other side of Central Avenue life. Bars and clubs catered to virtually every clientele. Owned and managed by Black businessmen, they drew constant crowds. Among the popular bars—there were many more—were the Watts Sanderson Blue Room, Joyner's Lounge, Chick's Lounge, and the Red Lion. We used to call the Red Lion the "Bucket of Blood" because so many brutal fights occurred there. Gambling provided a major attraction for the avenue, as well, especially the game of bolita. Like every other kid, by age eleven I knew how it worked. Bolita was a numbers game in which anyone, regardless of age, could and, often, did play. The participant chose a number from one to one hundred. Every night at 9, each bolita house manager would choose the winner. One hundred numbered balls would be placed in a bag. The manager would shake the bag, then grasp a ball through the bag's cloth. He would tie a string around that ball before cutting the sack and revealing the number of the ball. The number so selected became the winner for that particular "throwing." The payoff was four dollars for every nickel bet, a tempting prize in those days, though it seems insignificant by today's Florida Lottery standards.

Tampa and Central Avenue contained any number of bolita houses, and they sometimes became the focal point for the worst kinds of violence. The houses usually were operated in connection with a bar. One owner, Charles Vanderhorst, who was better known as Charlie Moon, ran a game out of his Veterans' Rest, downstairs from the Apollo Ball Room, located at Central Avenue and Harrison Street. He may have been the only black man who actually owned his own game, the rest being controlled by Italians, Cubans, and a Cracker gangster named Charlie Wall. Without question, Charlie Moon and the other operators made thousands from poor Blacks trying to supplement their menial incomes. On the other hand, Moon was known to have provided soup kitchens for poor, hungry people who were victims of the Great Depression and to have engaged in other acts of charity. Accordingly, many residents held him in better regard than they might otherwise have.

As was the case with other bolita operators, Charlie Moon had to pay off crooked politicians and police officers, and his experience taught me lessons about crime and about abuse of power that I have never forgotten. As to crime, Charlie's violent demise well illustrated its rewards. When it came to abuse of power, I came to know the price paid when the rule of law was placed in the hands of a man like Pearl McAden.

As it happened, Charlie Moon was gunned to death early one morning in January 1944, at a time when he had begun to feel so secure about his power in the community that he had been spreading stories about the corruption of the white man's enforcer on Central Avenue. It occurred when I was serving in the military, but word got to me quickly just as it did to most Blacks with links to Tampa. Published reports stated that Charlie was gunned down outside his Little Savoy bar, but rumor had it that the killing occurred in the bar's back room, which Moon used as an office. Supposedly, the killer approached Charlie, declared "Moon, what's all this big talk you've been passing around about me?" then shot his victim three to five times. Charlie staggered out into street, before a friend drove him to the hospital where he died. Meanwhile, the night's gambling profits lay unsecured in Moon's office. Gamblers attacked the open safe in a rush that saw some of Charlie's closest friends getting as much cash as they could. Within a few months, several Black men opened businesses. Yet, no one questioned where they had obtained the investment funds. It was common knowledge that Charles Vanderhorst in death was the primary investor.[15]

Pearl McAden killed Charlie Moon. Most Black persons knew Pearl well and that he was a killer. As I mentioned, McAden was the white community's Black enforcer. For a while in the 1930s he was a police detective; later he served as a deputy sheriff. All the while he pleased his employers with the violence to which he so casually resorted. He seemed to enjoy roughing up "troublemakers," sometimes including Booker T. Washington High School students. As children we were deathly afraid of the mean McAden, whom we believed would have killed his own mother had a white man ordered him to do so.

I do not level the charges lightly. Besides the murder of Charlie Moon, for which he eventually was convicted, McAden was arrested as the leading suspect in his own wife's death in 1936. As a local newspaper reported, "She was shot at close range a few minutes after McAden had left her seated in his car on Buffalo avenue."[16] Pearl eluded justice in that matter, just as he had another murder a few months earlier. In that instance, McAden shot undertaker Stubb C. Pughsley from a moving car in front of the Pughsley home at 1510 Jefferson Street. The reason for the killing never was known, but the killer's name became public knowledge. Pughsley saw the gunman clearly and identified McAden to others before dying.[17] He was indicted, tried, and freed by an all-white jury after ten minutes deliberation.[18] Who knows how many others McAden killed with the tacit support of Tampa's white power structure.

Pearl McAden and what he stood for appalled me as a young man. I knew in my heart that his brand of violence was not the way that society should operate. In Roberts City I could see that non-Blacks were treated far better than this by the government. The fact that McAden was Black only made the problem worse. From the positive sides of my life, I had enough pride to know that something was fundamentally wrong. At home, at school, and at church voices that I respected told me that things would never change unless individuals stood up to make them change. In Pearl McAden's case, I particularly remember the courage of C. Blythe Andrews, Sr., in demanding McAden's punishment for the murders. He used his newspaper, the *Florida Sentinel*, to voice his protests. Finally McAden was convicted for Charlie Moon's death, with his sentence specifying exile from Tampa for a period after his prison term. In 1946, though, Pearl escaped from jail and, apparently, died without returning to the scene of his many crimes.[19]

The bitterness that I felt toward a system that protected and encouraged a Pearl McAden grew deeper as I saw and experienced more and more of the injustices of racial segregation. I already have said that friends and family provided me with a happy childhood at Tampa. Still, I could not avoid encountering indignities such as "Colored" and "White" water fountains. As a boy, I could not even sit on the benches placed out front of the S. H. Kress Department Store. I saw White officers violate Black people's civil rights as they entered homes unlawfully. I hated the Florida State Fair because Tuesday, the only day that I was permitted to attend, was "Colored Day." In the same vein, I detested the *Tampa Daily Times* for running a "Colored" page, edited by George Carr, a former Black educator, but distributed only to Black subscribers.

My growing anger at injustices such as these was shared by many of my friends at Middleton High School. Finally, although in only a small way, that anger boiled over. In 1938 I was a sophomore at Middleton. One morning, a number of Middleton students were riding the street car to school when White cops suddenly pulled a female student from the car. I cannot remember if it was Doris Williams or her sister Dorothy. This happened on the corner of Twenty-second Street and Seventh Avenue. The arbitrary act had no foundation other than intimidation, and it enraged us. At the time the White superintendent of Black schools was ignoring legitimate needs in order to pander to the White school board. I remember especially that athletic programs were funded at levels worse than paltry.

The combination of these circumstances compelled a few of us who were on the football team to action. First, we tore down the street car signs that read "White passengers will sit from front to rear; Colored passengers will sit from rear to front." When we got to school, we refused to enter the building. Instead, we built fires in the yard to keep warm while remaining out of doors. Some faculty and administrators quietly supported us, and the situation embarrassed the school superintendent enough to bring about some improvements. We were not punished. We also learned that collective action could bring positive results.

Football team members had joined in our protest, and football, in turn, played the key role in getting me to college. For three years I was proud to be one of the "Middleton Tigers." My position was tackle and guard, and, early on, I was promoted to first team. I was a good player, but we had some great ones to look up to. "Big Jim" Williams, to give an example, came two years behind me before going on to become a star player and coach for Florida A&M. Under Coach Chester Seabury we had a great year in 1939, losing only one game. In the process, the keen competition sharpened me, while traveling broadened my conception of the world outside Tampa. We contested games in locales such as Lakeland, Fort Myers, Gainesville, West Palm Beach, Clearwater, and St. Petersburg. We were treated well everywhere. I recall our car breaking down in Hobe Sound coming back from West Palm Beach on one occasion. We had to remain in that very beautiful community for several days. I was thrilled to see fellow Blacks faring well there.

My entree to college came about in an unexpected manner. First, since our team was attracting a good deal of publicity, we received a visit in late 1939 from Florida A&M's famous coach William "Big Bill" Bell, who had been an All American at Ohio State. He spoke with me, and I had hopes of a scholarship, which I needed to be able to attend any college. Unfortunately, no offer arrived from A&M. Then, perhaps from a good word kindly passed, I was contacted by Preston Peterson, coach at Daytona Beach's Bethune-

Cookman College. He not only arranged a small scholarship but also a National Youth Administration job on campus. I was to start in the Fall of 1940 after graduation from Middleton earlier that year.

During the months that separated my high school graduation from my departure for Daytona Beach, I did not give the future too much thought. Certainly, I understood that conditions around the world were worsening but I cannot say that I knew we soon would be fighting a world war. I had rejected any idea of a music or, for that matter, shady career in favor of a college education. Still, I looked forward to having fun while learning. Maybe, I'd then go on to become a lawyer. How little I understood what the future would bring; nor did I have any appreciation for the remarkable people and historic events that would change my life in ways that I did not dream of.

The corner of Garcia Avenue and Green Street (later Roberts Street) in 1915 included horse-drawn wagons loading up at E. Dominguez Wholesalers.
(Tampa Times)

Over the next decade, horseless carriages arrived and the corner near our home was bustling with business for the Roberts City Service Station. (Tampa-Hillsborough County Public Library System)

My Life to 1940

Most homes in Roberts City were convenient to work, like these just off Garcia Avenue, adjacent to the F. Garcia & Bros. cigar factory at the corner of Garcia Avenue and Arch Street. They were built close to one another, and many had open porches that were great spots to rest, talk, play, or just try to catch a cool breeze off the river. Maybe the fact that they were not shut up and air conditioned also helped us keep in touch with neighbors walking by or working outside in the yard or porch next door. (Arsenio M. Sanchez/Tampa-Hillsborough County Public Library)

The Roberts Cigar Factory (upper left corner of enlarged detail at right) also meant nearby work for residents. A careful look on the streets (at right and below) shows that automobiles were already starting to appear in the 1920s.

45

Another neighborhood landmark was the F. Garcia & Bros. cigar factory, just a few blocks from our home on Garcia Avenue. It was part of an economy that thrived in an atmosphere of ethnic and racial diversity. (Arsenio M. Sanchez/Tampa-Hillsborough County Public Library)

This view reveals part of Roberts City just a few years after I was born, in the early 1920s. There was still enough open land for farm animals to graze. (Arsenio M. Sanchez/Tampa-Hillsborough County Public Library)

Looking back, I am thankful that the community where I grew up afforded me at least a glimpse of life and work in a multi-ethnic, multi-racial atmosphere. The reality of racism was written unmistakably—and emphatically—in the larger, establishment community. Grandmother Rogers had even set an example by helping start a West Tampa local of the NAACP in 1915.

My mother Christina Saunders stands near our home looking south on Garcia Avenue in 1960. The back corner of the Roberts City Garage is visible in the right rear of this photo.

My training in the Army Air Corps led me from Tampa to Camp Blanding, Florida, then on to Spence Field in Georgia, and finally to Tuskegee Army Air Field, Alabama. There Captain Fred Minnis became a friend and mentor. It was partly his advice that led me eventually to work with the NAACP.

3
The Road to Walter White's Office

When I graduated from high school at the beginning of 1940, the world was changing around me, but, as I mentioned in the last chapter, my attention usually was directed away from such major events. At the time, the "phony war" persisted in Europe, while Japan seemed to be restraining its aggression in China. In the months that I waited for college to begin that fall, the situation exploded. Adolph Hitler's *Blitzkrieg* overwhelmed western Europe, and stories of the heroism of the Battle of Britain ran in every major newspaper. Then, Japan demanded military bases in Indo-China from the Vichy French government. In September, the Japanese government allied itself with the Axis powers of Germany and Italy.[1]

The reaction to these events in the United States proved complicated. Many conservative Whites opposed involvement in foreign affairs or else supported the Axis powers. Others simply feared the human and other costs of another world war. President Franklin D. Roosevelt attempted to assist Britain that summer, but it was an election year and he stepped very carefully. He did begin to build up the military, though, and in September achieved passage through the Congress of a selective service act. Meanwhile, African American leaders realized that Black men (and women) would be called upon to serve the war effort. Their allies pushed through an amendment to the draft law forbidding racial discrimination in the drafting and training of men. Led by Walter White of the NAACP and A. Philip Randolph, a former Floridian, they also insisted that the president commit the country to numerous civil rights advances. It was the beginning of the great civil rights movement to come.[2]

For the most part, I did not feel personally involved in these events. We were not yet at war, and my eyes were focused on college, upon which my mother and grandmother were insistent. I had been a little involved with the Tampa NAACP youth council. Yet, I was not a committed worker. What I looked forward to in college was preparing myself for some kind of professional program, probably law school. In the process, I intended to have the kinds of good times that college students everywhere look forward to having. As events proved out, my expectations in the short term happened as I thought they would. I could not have been more wrong about the long term.

My connection with the greater outside world began the day that I arrived on the campus of Bethune-Cookman College and met its president, Mary McLeod Bethune. That fall she was sixty-five years of age. She already had been teaching for forty-five years. Of course I had known about Mrs. Bethune long before I arrived in Daytona Beach. The fact that Eleanor Roosevelt, the president's wife, had visited Mrs. Bethune at the college had been hot news just before I got there. Her work with the National Youth Administration had introduced her into Mrs. Roosevelt's close circle of friends and, eventually, drawn her into the companionship of the president's "brain trust." The NAACP in 1935 had recognized her tremendous achievements by awarding her the Spingarn Prize.[3] Mrs. Bethune's relationships, in turn, had helped the college. Otherwise, my campus NYA job probably would not have been available.

Someone asked me not long ago what Mrs. Bethune had meant to my life. At first, all I could think to answer was "How often do you get to talk with great people?" The fact was that she played a key role in the lives of most—if not all—her students. At the small school she called us by our first names. We called her "Mame," which was a shortened version of "Madame," but only when she could not hear it. Almost always she was available to talk with us. In doing that, she inevitably insisted, in one way or another, that we prepare ourselves for important work. Her every action toward us laid a foundation for taking pride in ourselves. I will never forget the signs that she had posted in the chapel. Over

Mary McLeod Bethune began her educational odyssey as one of sixteen siblings on a five-acre farm in Mayesville, South Carolina. Her parents had been slaves. She first attended a mission school, followed by a scholarship to North Carolina's Scotia Seminary, and a scholarship to complete her studies at the Moody Bible Institute in Chicago. Later she worked near her home as a teacher to help send two younger sisters to school, eventually marrying and moving to teach at Palatka, Florida, in 1898. She continued missionary work devoted to the poor and imprisoned, coming to believe that their lives could be improved by education. That vision led her to establish what was originally called the Daytona Normal and Industrial Institute for Negro Girls in 1904, which merged with Jacksonville's Cookman Institute for boys in 1923 and at last became Bethune-Cookman College.

Mary McLeod Bethune speaking with students at Bethune-Cookman College in Daytona Beach in 1943. She started her school for girls in a rented cottage. (Florida State Archives)

the stage were emblazoned the words "Enter to Learn." Above the exit hung a sign that declared "Depart to Serve."

My own links with Mrs. Bethune came in ordinary ways. As part of my NYA job, I might be sent over to her house to do little chores. She would see me and strike up a conversation. We would talk with her in her office, too. I particularly remember her in another personal way. Mrs. Bethune insisted that we all work. I was often assigned to wash dishes, usually along with my Tampa friend Lutrell Bing (who later became a county commissioner back at home and was an instrumental figure in local school desegregation efforts). So, three times a day Lutrell and I could be found in the kitchen, and Mrs. Bethune occasionally would come by to cheer us on. Lutrell and I were there washing dishes listening to the radio on December 7, 1941, while most students were at Vesper services. Because of that, we were the first to learn of the Japanese attack on Pearl Harbor and we were the ones to carry the news to Mrs. Bethune.

My memories of those college days are warm, indeed, as are my thoughts of Mrs. Bethune. Unfortunately, the world imposed itself on those relatively tranquil days before I wanted them to be over. The end came in the late summer of 1942 when I was drafted into the army. With thirty-nine other young Black men, I was sent on a train from Tampa to Camp Blanding, Florida, for processing. After enjoying two weeks' leave, we returned to the camp and were given the wonderful news that we would be sent to "Boston." Cheerfully, we boarded another train car and off we went to the north. At the Georgia border, though, our car was unhooked from the train. Instead of continuing on to New England, we were attached to a second train headed west to Boston, Georgia, a rural community northeast of Thomasville. It seemed as if that train stopped every ten minutes to take on chickens and cows. We ended up at Spence Field in Moultrie, Georgia.

This disappointing journey eventually led me to service in the Army Air Corps. I was chosen for that assignment because of my interest in model airplanes, a hobby that my teacher Everett Rolfe had encouraged back at home. Training came at Spence Field, near Moultrie, Georgia. There, the personnel people immediately assigned me to work on the flight line. My job was to tie down AT-6 planes. As the weeks progressed, I learned to taxi them on the runways. One night, a first lieutenant took me for my first flight. For one hour we cruised alone above the Gulf of Mexico, a truly wonderful experience.

By the closing weeks of 1942, my army service took a major turn with reassignment to Tuskegee Army Air Field, Alabama. I really wanted to pilot airplanes, but poor eyesight forestalled that possibility. Instead, I was assigned to office duties because of my typing skills, I learned how to be an administrator. I worked in a maintenance squadron (Squadron A, 2143rd Army Air Force Base Unit). Within one month after my arrival, they made me a private first class. Corporal's stripes came late in 1943, with promotion to three stripes (buck sergeant) the next year. All the while, except as I will mention, I remained at Tuskegee. In February 1946, with the war long over, the army ordered me back to Camp Blanding where I was discharged. My uniform blouse then carried the Good Conduct Medal, the Atlantic Theater of Operations Medal, and the World War Two Victory Medal.

Just as had been the case with Bethune-Cookman College, my years at Tuskegee had passed happily. There I met many remarkable individuals. Benjamin O. Davis, Jr., had just made captain when I arrived, and Chappie James trained in the cadet corps—just to name two examples. One truly entertaining aspect of the experience came from meeting Alvin "Al" Downing, who was from the Tampa area. Al acted as the assistant band leader at Tuskegee. We found that we shared a love of music. As Al's presence indicates, Tuskegee Air Base was staffed with all kinds of talent. A group of us, with Al's help, pulled a musical show together, which we called "Roger." It was so well received that they sent us on a war bond tour. We traveled through Alabama, Georgia, Florida, Virginia, and the District of Columbia (playing there at the Watergate and at the Pentagon).

The friendship that Al and I launched at Tuskegee endured until his passing not long ago, but I cannot forget that service at Tuskegee also introduced me to another man who made a lasting impact on my life. As an administrator, I worked for Captain Fred Minnis. All along I had wanted to go back to school, and so I was taking several correspondence courses through the army. Minnis naturally approved of my determination, but he believed that I was setting my sights too low. "Don't waste your G.I. Bill," he told me repeatedly. "Go back to college because you've got too much on the ball." That was fine as far as it went, but Fred added something else: "Go to a northern school." He pointed out to me the many fine Black men at Tuskegee who, although their talents might be underutilized, possessed fine educations earned outside the South. I came to understand the importance of his advice and left the service intent upon finding a way to do something about it. I should mention that Fred Minnis later became one of the outstanding lawyers in the St. Petersburg, Florida, area, often lending his talents to the work of the NAACP.

It is ironic that racial discrimination drove me toward a type of employment after leaving the army that I came to really enjoy, but that is what happened. The G.I. Bill, as most everyone knows, provided educational benefits for veterans. Many today do not know that it also provided unemployment benefits. The program was called "52-20," because an unemployed veteran could receive $20 per week for up to fifty-two weeks. Since I could not immediately enter school and was unable to land work when I returned to Tampa, I went down to the local office to inquire. What I found there angered me mightily. White bureaucrats were directing Black veterans—many of them combat veterans—into only the most menial of jobs, even though they were qualified for far better work.

The more I thought about the injustice down at the job referral office, the more I was determined not to go back down there and submit myself to it. Instead, I followed up on a (slim) contact that I had made earlier. One of Tampa's two premier Black-owned newspapers was the *Florida Sentinel*, published by C. Blythe Andrews. I had written to him during the war in response to one of his editorials. Now, I went into the office and mentioned the letter to Mr. Andrews and that he had found it to be well written and insightful. I also reminded him of my work during the Thirties for the *Tampa*

Bulletin (Andrews had been writing a column for the *Bulletin* in those early days). Maybe just to get me off his back, Mr. Andrews offered me a job selling ads and doing general reporting. Soon he permitted me to pen a regular column. It delved into the personal side of life in the Central Avenue area, with which I was familiar thanks to other Thirties-era jobs. Called "Central Avenue Buckshot," the column debuted on April 13, 1946. Its first words posed a musical question: "Do you know that Mr. Eddie 'Clean Head' Vinson is one of America's greatest saxophonists?"[4]

The fun that I was having reporting for the *Sentinel* did not erase my determination for more and better education. The same month that my first column appeared I applied to Fisk University, where I hoped to study pre-law before enrolling in a northern law school. They accepted me, but then happenstance intervened. In August 1946 while in transit to Fisk, I stopped over in Cincinnati. Broke, as usual, I chanced to meet Jimmy Smith, the Cincinnati edition editor of the Cleveland *Call and Post*. After learning of my newspaper background and my financial condition, Jimmy offered me work as a circulation manager and reporter. At the time, it sounded like a good idea to me.

This Cincinnati sojourn, which lasted about one year, brought with it interesting experiences and profound lessons. I saw firsthand that the police could and would trick and frame Black men. Jimmy got me my first police pass, so I watched the actions of some Cincinnati cops up close. While doing so, we uncovered a major scandal. It involved a young Black veteran whom the police wrongly claimed had raped a white woman. White prosecutors, based on police testimony, convicted and imprisoned the man. This came despite the fact that the alleged criminal was being treated for venereal disease in a Kentucky veteran's hospital at the time of the crime. Our exposé of the travesty resulted in a retrial.

During that year I learned that corruption and racism were not limited to south of the Mason-Dixon line, while coming to believe that I needed to take a more personal role in changing this state of affairs. I can remember my thrill and pride at attending Jackie Robinson's first major league baseball game in Cincinnati. I can recall also my disgust that many white fans booed his presence while cheering his unsuccessful strikes at bat. To help make a difference, I began to work with the local NAACP to end discrimination in the use of public parks and facilities. Sadly, on one occasion—the night before a swimming pool on the East Side was to be desegregated—whites threw broken bottles into the pool. There was no question in my mind now about northern racial hatred.

By late 1947 I knew that it was time to move on from Cincinnati. My work for the *Call and Post* brought satisfaction but little money. I had married while there, to a Tampa girl whom I had known for some time, and she longed for the company of relatives in Detroit. I had no family ties in either Cincinnati or Detroit, but the latter city contained universities and law schools to which I could gain access through the G.I. Bill. The University of Cincinnati had provided me some evening credits in journalism and business English; yet, I needed academic degrees not random credits. For all these reasons, I left reporting behind for school further north.

Suffice it to say, nothing much worked out in Detroit as I had planned it. Wayne State University, where I first attempted to enroll, refused to accept my credits from Bethune-Cookman. For a time I attended there anyway as a non-matriculating student. In time I learned that the Detroit Institute of Technology would honor my earlier college work, plus their curriculum would allow me to study both sociology and journalism. So, I transferred there. The institute's faculty granted me a bachelor of arts degree in those subjects on January 26, 1951.

During the years that I was pursuing a college degree, other considerations were leading me into a new field, labor activism. The G.I. Bill only went so far, and, as a married man, I had assumed greater financial responsibilities. To meet them I sought work at the Ford Motor Company. Dressed out in a coat and tie, I applied only to be told "We're not hiring." Friends advised me to try again but to dress down. Attired in coveralls, I returned and was hired. They assigned me to the River Rouge plant in the machine shop.

It did not take very long at the River Rouge plant for me to learn the importance of the unions. Especially, I noticed how well

Ford Local 600, UAW/CIO was working. Many of the older guys around me related stories of the old days, the days of the "big strike." I read *The Legend of Henry Ford* about the goon squads and Ford's ruthlessness. The union had provided support and protection for workers when and where it could, an institutional shield that reminded me of how my Boy Scout uniform had protected me from the beating I almost got as a boy in Tampa.

In these circumstances, I actively pursued union affairs. Working in the frame and cold header unit (where metal was cut for frames), I served as a bargaining committeeman for the afternoon shift, dealing with management for about one year. This truly was an educational experience. My negotiating skills in the resolution of grievances received a fine honing. Additionally, I gained a great sensitivity for the impact of personality and other divisions within an institution such as a labor union. In my case, this manifested itself through union politics. All around me were factions within the union that represented extremes of opinion. Their members resented my refusal to join in their extreme positions and arranged for my transfer to the midnight shift. As a result, I was forced to resign as a committeeman.

My problems with some union members did not reflect my relationships with the local leaders. I spoke with them about my plans for law school. They, in turn, encouraged me to proceed, promising that a legal job with the union would await me upon graduation. They also urged me toward political involvement. While this aspect of my union work was cut short when I left the Ford job to pursue law school, I still ran for local Democratic party club office in 1951 as a union man.

My longtime dream of training to be a lawyer finally saw progress made in 1951. With a bachelor's degree in hand, I enrolled in the University of Detroit Law School. I attended throughout the year but found it increasingly difficult to carry the required fifteen-credit-hour load. Meeting my family responsibilities and unreimbursed school expenses required my working full-time. Plus, I was attempting to continue my NAACP volunteer work. Mostly, I was involved in voter registration, membership recruitment, and youth council activities. By January 1952 the load proved too much for me. My heart just about broken, I left law school behind forever.

That year of 1952, which began for me so sadly, ended with my life taking dramatic and unexpected turns. First, though, I tried to stay afloat financially while persisting with the NAACP efforts. The breakup of my marriage and subsequent divorce had been coming about for a long time, the strains resulting from the fact that each of us wanted a far different kind of life and relationship than did the other. In January I started employment at one of Detroit's major downtown department stores. Despite my college and law school training, they refused to hire me to work in either marketing or advertising. This, pure and simple, was racial discrimination. Instead, the managers put me to work on the loading dock. I finally had had enough of that by the spring and quit.

My main relief through these months came from the satisfaction and enjoyment that I gained from the NAACP work and the people whom I met through it. I could see that I was making a difference for the good and that meant everything to me. Although civil rights advances were coming slowly, the NAACP was achieving substantial wins, locally and nationally. For instance, the 1944 ruling in the case of *Smith* v. *Allwright*, which the association had backed, had seen the United States Supreme Court barring the exclusion of African Americans from Democratic party primaries, opening the way for Black political influence in the South. Six years later the court again heard the NAACP's calls and prohibited racial discrimination in public graduate and professional schools. As I was struggling in 1952, the momentum had grown, with the association appealing a series of public school desegregation cases, including *Brown* v. *The Board of Education of Topeka, Kansas*, to the highest court. Change resonated in the air.[5]

As to the people whom I met through Detroit NAACP work, I got to know many fine individuals but none finer than Gloster B. Current. A dark-skinned man of medium build, in 1952 Gloster was national director of branches. Previously, though, he had served as director of the Detroit branch. We had organized a youth council named for him, and I knew that he and I shared a great love of music. A brief conversation with him left you with the certainty that he was brilliant. In that regard and also because of his approachability, he reminded me of Mrs. Bethune. He possessed, as well, a wonderful sense of humor.

Given this measure of the man, you will understand that I was very pleased one afternoon in late summer 1952 to drop into the Detroit office to find that Gloster was visiting. I walked up to him and teasingly asked, "Are you folks hiring anyone in the NAACP?" We shared a little chuckle over that, and I thought little more of it. I should have. Before leaving Detroit, Gloster asked me if I was serious about working for the NAACP. One week later he telegraphed me to come to an interview in New York. Art Johnson, the Detroit executive secretary, had highly recommended me to him. Something had come up. Gloster and Walter White wanted to talk with me about it.

At the time I received Gloster's telegram, NAACP executive director Walter White faced a tremendous dilemma. As discussed in Chapter One, Florida's field secretary Harry T. Moore and his wife had been killed by the Ku Klux Klan the previous Christmas night. NAACP officials, including Walter, had demanded state action to find and punish the guilty. In reaction, Governor Fuller Warren had accused Walter and the NAACP agents looking into the deaths of being Harlem agitators trying to stir up problems for Floridians. In the meantime, the state NAACP organization remained rudderless, Black residents feared for their lives, and NAACP membership and activities declined significantly. Something had to be done—and soon.

The aftermath of Gloster's telegram to me came quickly. Two weeks later I presented myself at Freedom House, the NAACP's national headquarters at 20 West 40th Street in New York City. I was nervous, and I did not know what they wanted to speak with me about. Walter White probably was the best-known figure in the civil rights movement at that time. Certainly a leader of national importance, President Harry S Truman had appointed him to his civil rights commission. Walter's book, *A Man Called White*, enjoyed immense popularity in the Black community. Personally, I liked him from the first moment I met him. His attitude was straightforward and sociable. Beyond that, his dynamism impressed upon me that he was a man who was really determined to do away with racial discrimination and segregation.

The meeting's purpose became clear at the beginning. Also present were Florida NAACP leaders Ed Davis (then of Orlando) and attorney Paul Perkins, who had been working on the Groveland case. I chatted briefly with Ed about mutual acquaintances before Walter brought up Harry's death and the situation in Florida. He explained that he needed to send someone down who could not be accused by Governor Warren of being an outside agitator and who, in addition, possessed the organizational and leadership skills needed by the Florida NAACP. Before I knew what was happening, Thurgood Marshall walked in. If not before, I then knew that I was in big company.

Walter detailed the offer. The job paid $2,800 per year, plus five cents per mile. I would be working for the national office and would be paid from there. My task would be to implement national NAACP policy, with Florida becoming a testing ground for many initiatives. I cannot specifically remember saying yes, although I must have. I do recall Ed Davis warning me to "stay out of those little towns." And, like that, we reached the agreement that changed my life.

The news spread quickly. In mid-September 1952, the *Florida Sentinel* ran a national office news release, soon joined by the state's other Black journals. It began, "A Tampa son, Robert W. Saunders, has been appointed as the new secretary of the Florida NAACP." Its third sentence made clear my status: "Mr. Saunders is a native Floridian, having received his early training in Tampa public schools."[6] The *Sentinel*'s first October issue marked my hasty beginning in the job. "The NAACP opened state headquarters in Tampa last week at 1404 1/2 Central Avenue," the newspaper noted, "with Robert Saunders, assistant field secretary, in charge." It added in words that I would discover to be incredibly understated, "The new secretary will assist in revitalizing of old branches and in the formation of new ones."[7]

People often ask me why I took the job to succeed Harry Moore or else if I was afraid that the same end might await me. I must admit that, when I heard the news of his death, it did not strike me in Detroit as personally significant. I had met Mr. Moore once for about fifteen minutes in 1946, and I was saddened and angered by his murder. Still, I was not high up in the NAACP then. I was just a member. The job offer, on the other hand, was personally significant. To me, it was a once in a lifetime opportunity. As I have explained to others, "Don't too many people get those offers." I was honored, and I wanted to get to the job. Later, I would endure threats of violence, but at the time I took the position I did not think about danger at all. I just could not believe that these fine and courageous men had entrusted me with so precious a mission.

Before relating an overview of my years as Florida NAACP secretary, I would add an additional personal note. During the summer of 1953 a wonderful person entered my life, who has brought light and strength to me ever since. She has worked harder and shown more courage than just about anyone I have ever known, although she has shunned recognition for it. I would like to give her some here.

Helen was the daughter of Henry J. and Lucy A. Strickland of Mims, Florida. Her father labored in the citrus groves. Growing up, Helen was close to her family, but her motivation came from the neighbors, Harry T. and Harriett Moore. Mrs. Moore taught Helen in the local schools. Harry encouraged her to pursue his own loves of literature and Black poetry. Helen remembers when she and her friends memorized countless poems by authors such as Countee Cullen. The families spent time together, especially on Christmas Eve and Christmas day. Because of the Moores, Helen as a girl participated in the Mims NAACP youth council, before leaving for college.

The plans that Helen made for herself after high school did not work out any better than did mine. As I had a couple of years before, she attended Bethune-Cookman. There was little money in the large family to help her out, though. Then, in 1944 she learned that a temporary job was available at Tampa in the offices of the Central Life Insurance Company, with which Mrs. Bethune was closely associated. She had always heard that "When you come to Tampa, it's always hard to get away," and so she accepted.

She never got away. That's how come Helen was working at Central Life in 1953. I had met her once just after the war ended, in a restaurant. It was not love at first sight, on either part. In any event, seven years later I dropped by the Central offices to see Ed Davis, the state NAACP leader, who was the company's secretary. While I was talking with the receptionist, Helen and her friend Vicki Casellas returned from lunch. "Oh, Helen and Vicki, I'm so glad to see you two," I declared. "When I came in, I saw everybody else. And my heart sank."

My delivery did not impress Helen overmuch, but I persisted. A few days later I called her at her apartment, which she shared with Wilma Williams, the assistant treasurer at Central Life and a long-time associate of Mrs. Bethune. Helen was languishing there with a headache. In retrospect I am a little surprised that she agreed to my invitation to take a drive to deliver avocados to my uncle's store outside of town. With that beginning, though, our romance slowly blossomed. We were married at Tampa on January 21, 1954. It may have been the luckiest day of my life.

Helen and I receive an award for our work from Rev. S. M. Peck (left) at a 1959 banquet in Marti-Maceo Cuban Club. Seated at the table is Rev. LeRoy Watson, Tampa Branch program chairman, and Marguerite Belafonte, who was on tour to help raise money for the NAACP Freedom Fund in Florida. She also appeared at Tallahassee and West Palm Beach.

THE ROAD TO WALTER WHITE'S OFFICE

My military training, friendships, and experiences have remained important to me throughout my life. Here I am taking care of some paperwork and displaying my sergeant's stripes for the camera in the barracks at Tuskegee Army Air Field with a friend, Corporal Hollie Warthen.

The late Dr. Richard V. Moore, president of Bethune-Cookman College, introduces Dr. Mary McLeod Bethune and Mrs. Eleanor Roosevelt at a New York NAACP fundraiser.

Edward Davis was one of those present at that first meeting in Walter White's office. Ed was working then in Orlando and advised me to "stay out of those little towns." (Florida State Archives)

Dr. Bethune often entertained in her home, where I worked as a student. At this typical dinner, c. 1950, are (left to right) Arrabella Dennison, Marjorie Joyner, Ralph Bunche, Dr. Bethune, and other unidentified guests. (Florida State Archives)

63

Robert W. Saunders, c. 1952.

4
Florida, the NAACP, and Me: 1952-1966

In the third part of this book, I will go into detail about many of the important personalities and events of Florida's civil rights struggle during the years that I served as the state's NAACP field secretary. First, though, most readers likely will need an overview of that period of time in Florida, since it has been written about so little and so many people lack even a basic understanding of the NAACP's involvement in the parade of happenings. Much necessarily will be omitted. Still, the basic framework and chronology of events and the summary of NAACP policies, problems, and activities should prove helpful. Also, I have added Part Two as the next section of this book to provide a specific chronology of important events that should help clarifify these many complicated and sometimes confusing happenings as they relate to one another and to the historical context.

By the time state president Edward D. Davis joined me in opening up the new Tampa headquarters in late September 1952, I was beginning to realize the enormity of the task we faced. Our organization virtually was bankrupt, and many of our members—the totals had been dropping for several years—lived in fear in the aftermath of Harry and Harriett Moore's deaths. Ku Klux Klan intimidation and violence endured, tearing at the fabric of African American life in many parts of the state. To give just one example, the week after our opening a federal grand jury began hearings into the bombing of the Carver Village housing project in Miami.[1]

Somehow we had to regain the initiative and build momentum, confidence, and, eventually, optimism. To the good, I had national executive director Walter White's assurance of support, and Ed Davis likewise never wavered in his determination. So, we struck out boldly. At the headquarters dedication Ed proclaimed our goal to be "complete and immediate integration."[2] Within a day or two, southeastern regional director Ruby Hurley, for whom I came to have tremendous respect and affection, arrived in Tampa. Ruby, Ed, and I plotted strategy aimed at raising NAACP funds and visibility as we headed toward our annual meeting scheduled for Fort Lauderdale in late November. For public consumption, we announced a visit from New York Congressman Adam Clayton Powell, who would help us kick off a statewide membership drive.

The coming annual meeting offered us a vehicle for getting publicity. Walter agreed to deliver the keynote address, framed around the demand for complete and immediate integration. We pounded home those words in every way that our depleted resources permitted. Our sense of urgency mounted as the weeks passed, not only because of local conditions but also because the United States Supreme Court had scheduled hearings for early December on public school desegregation cases. As it happened, the meeting's turnout was good, although not everything we might have hoped. Still, in appearances there and throughout the Miami, Tampa, and Jacksonville areas, Walter, Ruby, and I argued for optimism. We met with some success but even more wariness. Walter raised about $2,000 for us, which helped but did not solve even our immediate financial problems. Clearly, the battle was going to be fought uphill.

All we could do was continue to plug away in every way that we could. Police abuses particularly gave us opportunities to call attention to serious problems while reaffirming the NAACP's legitimacy and role. In December 1952 case, Elmo Mims was shot in Fort Pierce while defending his home against a police invasion. Our state president William A. Fordham, who had replaced Ed Davis the previous month, alerted the press while dispatching NAACP attorney Francisco Rodriguez to defend Mims. I took to the public pulpit to insist on protection of civil rights. "We do not condone such actions from police who disregard the rights and privileges of citizens," I told audiences. "We shall continue to insist that elected officials use extreme integrity in selecting officers whether White or Negro to enforce the laws of this land."[3]

We appealed to government and the public in other ways. In January 1953 Governor Dan McCarty was inaugurated in Tallahassee. Many persons believed him to be a moderate reformer, and we decided to test him immediately. For the state conference, President Fordham and I appealed to the governor to "consider seriously the hiring of qualified Negroes to fill offices in all departments of the State Government." To his credit McCarty responded that "it will be my policy to give every consideration to qualified Negro personnel for appropriate positions during this administration."[4] Unfortunately, McCarty died of a heart attack on September 28. I do not know to what extent he would have fulfilled his pledge, but McCarty certainly would have traveled a different path than his successor. I will have a good deal more to say about that man, the reactionary and racist Charley E. Johns.

Through 1953 we endeavored to reach people in novel, as well as traditional, ways. For one thing, in January we started a radio broadcast over station WHBO in Tampa. Aired each Tuesday from 5:00 to 5:15 p.m., the program featured lawyer Francisco Rodriguez and others who assisted us in proclaiming the NAACP's cause and spreading word of its activities. The show reached at least some white listeners, a fact that added an important new dimension to our work. Beyond that, we tried everything we could. We held a statewide Miss NAACP pageant, Labor Day picnics, tag sales, musical programs, youth council rallies, and what have you. One publicity vehicle I declined to support, though, was the Jim Crow page of local newspapers, especially the *Tampa Daily Times*. These newspapers refused regular treatment of African American news, limiting coverage to a single page of items related mostly to the portion of the black community that editors believed acceptable. This policy, as I insisted in print at the time, was "detrimental to the progress of Negroes in Florida."[5]

And constantly we held membership and fundraising drives, trying to meet a statewide goal of just 10,000 members and to place our treasury on a reasonably stable footing. Mostly, we kept the goals and settled for less. What I had to say in seeking help from the National Colored Peoples Spiritualist Association convention in August 1953 echoed hundreds of other attempts. "The present need for funds to carry on the work of the NAACP is greater than ever before," I commented. "The cost of freedom is much greater than many of our people realize." My talk concluded with the earnest plea, "Each of us should give liberally to the fighting fund for freedom."[6] In retrospect I am amazed that racist and reactionary groups found us such a threat in the early and mid-1950s. If they had just known how precarious our situation remained, they might well not have overreacted as they did, giving us ammunition for fighting the civil rights war against them.

In the larger cities we made progress. I would spend weeks in Pensacola, Miami, or Jacksonville each year supervising membership drives. We received important help beginning in the summer of 1953 from the Black lodges of the Florida Elks, whose organization long had provided influential assistance to civil rights causes and had committed itself to "the uplifting of Negroes both economically and culturally."[7] Sad to say, opposition to our recruitment efforts sometimes came from within the African American community. I recall very well one Tampa minister who denounced fundraising memorial services held to honor Harry Moore as a "racket" and who went so far as to encourage membership in the Ku Klux Klan.[8] We experienced no shortage of opposition.

If cities gave us recruitment headaches, the rural areas posed almost impossible challenges. The Klan operated openly in many places, sometimes with a nod and a wink from local officials and sometimes with stronger and open support. Lake County's Sheriff Willis McCall is a case in point. Beyond the brutality and lawlessness that he encouraged, the man actually bragged openly about cross burnings, stirring racist mobs, and other anti-civil rights "victories."[9] But, more African Americans lived outside cities than in them and they could count on less protection.

So, it was to the countryside that Bill Fordham and I repeatedly pushed ourselves. Bill estimated that he covered over 6,000 miles in the first six months of 1953, and I'm sure that my tires

FLORIDA, THE NAACP, AND ME: 1952-1966

In 1952, several months after the killing of Harry T. and Harriett Moore, Walter White, Executive Secretary of the NAACP (seen at left), summoned me upon Gloster B. Current's recommendation to the NAACP New York national office for an interview. Present at the meeting were Edward D. Davis, Florida state NAACP president, and attorney Paul Perkins from Orlando.

Famous personalities supported our Florida efforts to raise funds and increase membership. Jazz great Lionel Hampton presented the winner of our statewide Miss NAACP pageant in Tampa in the early 1950s. Standing (back row left) is local activist Dewey Richardson, who led voter registration drives.

One of the first cases I worked on was a sentencing appeal in Ocala. Walter Lee Irvin (third from left) had been convicted of kidnapping and raping a Florida housewife. Our NAACP lawyers who successfully overturned the death penalty in favor of a life sentence were (from left) Paul C. Perkins, Jack Greenberg, and Thurgood Marshall.

When I came back to Florida in 1952, the South remained segregated, and civil rights were not a high priority on the national agenda. The national NAACP leadership, however, was playing a steadily increasing role in influencing the agenda. In January 1954 President Dwight D. Eisenhower met at the White House with Washington NAACP head Clarence Mitchell (center), national director Walter White, and other NAACP leaders for an open discussion of issues. In May the Supreme Court would justify NAACP legal efforts by ruling that "separate but equal" public education was unconstitutional.

Medgar Evers (left) and I (right) became good friends. We shared many ideals and ideas, and, as state field directors for Mississippi and Florida, we faced similar problems.

The steady, impressive accomplishments of our national organization gave credibility to our efforts in the South. Three important friends and advisers for my efforts in Florida were (left to right) Roy Wilkins, Walter White, and Thurgood Marshall, standing here in front of Freedom House, 20 West Fortieth Street, New York City.

suffered even more wear.[10] I will have more to say about my experiences in the rural areas later in this book, but I ought to note that the African Methodist Episcopal church assisted me greatly in reaching residents of small towns and isolated places. At one critical juncture, Bishop Cary Gibbs went so far as to name me director of social action for the A.M.E. churches in the Tampa region so that I could legitimately claim, if necessary for protection, that I was on church, rather than NAACP, business.

Through these years of 1952, 1953, and into early 1954, then, we labored to do some good while patching up the teetering NAACP organization in the aftermath of Harry Moore's tragic death. Fortunately, many good men and women bravely worked to assist us, but in those early years the numbers never approached the totals that truly were needed. All the while, we strove to prepare for the supreme court's decision on school desegregation. If the worst happened, we wanted to be ready to demand action in an effective way. We were not going to give up. To allow us a regional support system, Ruby Hurley began holding annual conferences of the southeastern region in 1953. At those meetings I cemented close personal and professional friendships with NAACP leaders from neighboring states. None would prove more dear to me than that with Mississippi's Medgar Evers, whose memory remains very much alive today in my heart and soul.

Plans devised at the southeastern conferences guided our state efforts. As one result, we headlined our state conference held at Orlando May 7-9, 1954, with the theme, "The Fight for Freedom," preparing our troops for the impending supreme court decisions.[11] Ten days later, the justices declared the doctrine of "separate but equal" to be unconstitutional insofar as public education was concerned. We have come to know the decision by the name of the first case listed, *Brown v. The Board of Education of Topeka, Kansas*. Of all places, I heard about it on the radio in a car while driving through Groveland.

Quickly, the Florida NAACP responded to the *Brown* decision with our own declaration. Our demands included immediate action aimed at "orderly implementation" of the decision and immediate admission of qualified applicants to junior colleges and public universities. We pledged support for protection of rights of black teachers and warned officials that we would file suit in every county in the state, if necessary. Since the latter warning carried potential financial costs greatly in excess of available funds, we urged "a program of immediate and voluntary desegregation on all levels [to] do away with the need of many test cases and [to] save the state useless expenditures of money to defend these suits." To add punch, we further announced "an accelerated program" of voter registration.[12]

For a time a kind of optimistic glow surrounded us after the first *Brown* opinion. The supreme court had not yet announced a timetable for implementation of its decision, but initially President Eisenhower seemed to express support and Florida Attorney General Richard Ervin created a committee to make recommendations. As late as March 1955 delegates to a "southwide" NAACP conference held at Atlanta agreed on a target date of September 1955 for school integration "throughout the South." When attendees raised the question of calls by some Whites for resistance by state governments, the gathering concluded, "We are not alarmed by those state governments . . . seeking to circumvent the Supreme Court's decision." The statement added, "These undemocratic and unconstitutional methods will fail."[13]

Unfortunately, our excitement clouded our vision. In Florida, newspapers soon were quoting Attorney General Ervin's opinion that the legislature should "seriously consider and probably abolish the public school system" as an alternative.[14] The gubernatorial election in 1954 came down to two Democratic candidates, Acting Governor Charley Johns and soon-to-be governor LeRoy Collins, both of whom supported continued racial segregation.[15] And, the building opposition already had begun to focus attacks on the NAACP, raising what, for the time, was the dreaded specter of communism. Already in August 1954 we had lost the services of Miami attorney Howard W. Dixon because of controversy around his legal defense of two accused communists. Dixon saw the furor as an attempt "to impugn the motives and character of the NAACP by placing on me a stigma of 'guilt by association.'"[16] It was only the beginning.

On a personal level, too, I was not as prepared as I wanted to be for the shock that was to come. My own world already had been shaken on March 21, 1955, when Walter White passed away. I was in Miami with Ruby Hurley. We had been working yet another membership drive, proudly reminding people of the NAACP's accomplishments of the past forty-six years. When I heard the news of Walter's death, it left me stricken, feeling more than empty and much more than sad. This great man had been responsible for many of those accomplishments that Ruby and I were proclaiming. Walter also had sent me to Florida and then had come down repeatedly to help me make a go of things. His sponsorship and his encouragement had meant more than I can find words to explain forty-five years later. I needed him to be alive. It could not be so, however. Eventually, I decided that all I could do for Walter and for myself was to work hard in the cause. That is what I did.

The optimism arising from the *Brown* decision burst on May 31, 1955, when the supreme court released its famous "all deliberate speed" decision, which segregationists read as giving them a license to delay desegregation compliance for years, if not forever. Our state superintendent of public instruction, Thomas D. Bailey, shirked responsibility, arguing that desegregation could only be handled on "the local level."[17] Many others were not so subtle. On our part, we insisted that the decision required a "prompt and reasonable start" toward full compliance. "Start," Bill Fordham explained, "does not necessarily mean we will have students in the White school, or vice versa, in September. But it means we expect them to offer some kind of concrete plan or blueprint."[18]

Crisis quickly built as event overwhelmed event. Before I describe the events, though, I want to note that some good soon came out of the crisis begun in 1955. Support for the NAACP increased substantially. First, many African American teachers and school principals who had held back from commitment now joined our ranks, sensing the divisions that were appearing on the horizon. Then, large numbers (for us at least) of young people began to turn to the organization as the vehicle for forcing change. To spur the movement we added to our youth council programs. To reach unaffiliated youth groups in churches and other organizations, we also commenced "Youth for Freedom Encampments," the first of which convened in August 1955 on the St. Augustine campus of the Florida Normal and Industrial College.[19]

Finally, we also began receiving signals that Governor LeRoy Collins was not the hardline segregationist that we feared. One early hint came in September 1955, when he appointed Henry H. Arrington as an assistant to Miami's state's attorney. It was a first in Florida history.[20] Incidentally, Henry's mother Ruby Arrington was a music instructor in Hillsborough County Black schools and organist at and a member of Tampa's St. Paul A.M.E. Church.

The bad news came more often and very quickly. Just as Governor Collins was opening the door slightly for African Americans to enter government, the board of control, which oversaw the state universities, refused to admit black applicant Virgil Hawkins to the University of Florida law school, at least until the state supreme court ordered desegregation. It did so in the face of objections voiced in the board's presence by Ed Davis, Bill Fordham, myself, Miami's Dr. G. W. Hawkins, and Jacksonville attorney Robert W. Gray. The NAACP pushed an appeal, one in a long series already undertaken over the years. Then, on October 19, the state justices refused to comply with the *Brown* decision by ordering Hawkins's admission, arguing that his presence on campus would "present grave and serious problems."[21]

Despite these and other setbacks, the NAACP's initiatives were gaining attention, so much so that right-wing elements intensified their attacks on us. They began accusing us of desiring desegregation in order to promote "the international Communist conspiracy to destroy the United States." They blasted the few moderate white officials as "hedging and pussy-footing" on the segregation issue. On behalf of the state conference, I countered the attacks by unmasking them, showing them as nothing more than a naked attempt to drive the growing numbers of Black voters out of the Democratic party and its primary elections. As to our patriotism, we of the NAACP refreshed the public mind about our history. "Negroes have fought, bled and died in every war this nation has fought," one of my speeches declared. "They have contributed richly to the welfare of the South and have done more to advance Dixie than many of the so-called members of the white race who enjoy far more of the benefits."[22]

The regional fever rose several degrees in December 1955 when Mrs. Rosa Parks refused to move to the back of a Jim Crow bus in Montgomery, Alabama, setting off the year-long Montgomery Bus Boycott and focusing national attention on the southern crisis. Early in the new year the federal supreme court ruled out delays in admitting qualified African Americans to public graduate schools, sending Florida officials, including Governor Collins, scurrying to defend the status quo. Collins even promised "to appear before the Supreme Court himself to plead the state's case."[23]

Meanwhile, demands on our resources multiplied as we backed desegregation actions in schools and public facilities, while maintaining our legal vigil for protection of other civil rights. The expense in time and personnel forced us to devote a tremendous effort to membership recruitment and fundraising. Gloster Current's generous allocation of his time and considerable talents made this much more pleasant for me, but it took us all away from concentrating as we should have on political developments. Democratic primary campaigns were on-going and passions were getting carried away. The situation became so absurd that one racist gubernatorial candidate called Governor Collins "the NAACP candidate." Showing modest political courage, Collins temporized. "If you want a governor who will get the white people to hate the Negroes and incite the Negroes to hate the white people then you don't want LeRoy Collins to be your governor," he declared.[24]

In the heat of this political battle national attention came to the Florida civil rights struggle in a dizzying series of occurrences. First, Tallahassee residents boycotted the capital city's bus system, with strong support from the local NAACP chapter and its leader Charles Kenzie Steele. (For Rev. Steele's account, as offered to the state conference of branches, see Appendix One.) At nearly the same time the NAACP filed suit to desegregate the Dade County school system, with future U.S. Supreme Court Justice Thurgood Marshall as lead counsel and Robert L. Carter assisting him. At our national meeting held in San Francisco, Thurgood specified Florida as a target state, one of those in which "we found not one instance on the part of the political leadership . . . to even consider the possibility of desegregating."[25] In addition, the Reverend Martin Luther King, Jr.—leader of the Montgomery bus boycott and soon to become founder of the Southern Christian Leadership Conference with Reverend Steele—backed our Jacksonville branch's spring membership drive, sending local racists into spasms of anger.[26]

Starting on July 1, 1956, the Florida situation heightened in intensity. On that day the Tallahassee bus company shut down its operations. Within a couple of weeks we had pressed the issue further by petitioning for desegregation of Tampa's transportation system. Governor Collins, by now the Democratic gubernatorial nominee and guaranteed victor in the November election, blasted the NAACP for "a miscarriage of ambition" and called a special legislative session to consider bills to preserve segregation.[27] The action, as I quickly insisted, was "unjust, retarding and a disgrace before man and God."[28] One popular initiative demanded by many lawmakers was to outlaw the NAACP, something that Mississippi and Alabama would accomplish during the year. Eventually, several pieces of restrictive legislation passed, including a measure setting up an investigative committee to examine the NAACP. The committee was the brain child of former Acting Governor Charley Johns who by then was back in the Florida Senate. Everyone called it the Johns Committee. The bill carried an appropriation of $50,000, and the governor permitted it to become law.[29]

The pace of events sped us along through the summer and into the fall. We held an extraordinary special session of our board with the presidents of local branches at Miami on August 11. Of the threat of the Johns Committee investigation we declared, "We have nothing to be fearful of, nor anything to hide."[30] A small step forward followed when Judge Charles Snowden, after urging from

NAACP attorney G. E. Graves, refused to hold Eleanor Fair on charges of breach of the peace after she refused to sit at the rear of a Miami bus. Then the Tallahassee boycott reheated when city authorities arrested carpoolers, requiring action on our part to provide legal aid.[31]

The police arrest scheme thereupon shifted to Tampa. In September attorney Francisco A. Rodriguez charged Hillsborough County officials with systematically excluding African Americans from juries. Likely in retaliation, police on October 1 detained our president William A. Fordham, an attorney, for doubleparking in front of NAACP headquarters, by then located at 705 East Harrison Street. When Bill asked to move the car instead of having it towed, the officers beat and kicked him. Thereupon, they charged him with resisting arrest. Authorities maintained the ridiculous charges against our protests. Later in the month the state conference met at Tampa. At the gathering Miami's A. Joseph Reddick, an A.M.E. minister, succeeded Bill Fordham as president. The next day Justice of the Peace J. Marion Hendry dismissed resisting arrest charges against Fordham and fined Bill $10 for double parking. What a disgraceful episode for my home town.[32]

Despite such travesties, we tried to avoid the trap of seeing all southern Whites as evil, something that many of our opponents failed to do as they smeared us with charges of being communists or communist dupes or what have you. We planned our efforts accordingly. When the U. S. Supreme Court threw out segregation on Montgomery's buses in November, I attempted to make the point clear. "The Montgomery bus situation is akin to the situation in Tallahassee and Miami," I explained. "All of these occurrences were brought about by a minority of whites in authority who forgot that human dignity was involved." I added, "If racial segregation in Montgomery is legally wrong then racial segregation in Tallahassee or Miami or any other Florida city is legally wrong."[33] I might add that the previous month we had been very pleased to honor a white state representative at our state convention. Dade County's John B. Orr, Jr., had been the lone voice heard in protest to many of the legislature's pro-segregation measures.[34]

Helen's energy is obvious as she mirrors the civil rights poster in the window of our state NAACP office in Tampa.

One of our most important activities continued to be voter registration. We knew the power of the ballot to shape political change and the sign this youngster carried through Tampa neighborhoods bore one of our favorite slogans. NAACP buses transported volunteers of all ages to the field, and potential voters to the registration office. (NAACP Collection, Library of Congress)

FLORIDA, THE NAACP, AND ME: 1952-1966

Attorney Francisco A. Rodriguez.

Benjamin Mays was executive secretary of the Tampa Urban League 1926-28. By the time I returned to Tampa he had become an important national leader. (Florida State Archives)

Father Theodore Gibson.

Leon Claxton of Royal American Shows presents a check to Daisy Bates to support NAACP life membership for the entire Claxton family. Bates was speaker at a 1957 mass meeting at St. Paul A.M.E. Church in Tampa.

Daisy Bates, an inspiring NAACP leader in the 1957 Little Rock, Arkansas, school desegregation crisis, visited Tampa later that same year to speak to our chapter. Gathered here at the head table are (front row, left to right) unidentified guest, Ellen Green, Daisy Bates, Helen Saunders, and Jesse Williams; (second row, left to right) attorney William Fordham, Leugenia Fordham, Evelyne Fordham, unidentified, Lucille Hammond, Mildred Douglas, Ozepher Harris, and Ray Williams.

Mrs. Althea Range, Miami business owner, introduces attorney Constance Baker Motley at a meeting in Miami's Greater Bethel A.M.E. Church, c. 1959. Motley was the NAACP Legal Defense Fund lawyer on Thurgood Marshall's staff who represented all school desgregation cases in Florida.

The Tampa Branch NAACP voter registration committee discusses its campaign plans with committee chairman M. P. Milner (center), who moved here from Virginia to help with the effort.

Rev. A. Leon Lowry, state president, commends some of the outstanding workers for their efforts in membership recruiting. Receiving certificates at this NAACP gathering at St. Paul A.M.E. Church are Helen Saunders, Tampa Branch secretary; Juanita Hall, representing Central Life Membership Committee; unidentified; and Melvin Stone.

Through the end of 1956 and into 1957 we combined our energies to face two continuing and tremendous challenges. We desperately needed more members and financial resources to cope with day-to-day demands, and we constantly faced the threat created by the legislature in the form of its investigative committee. It seems to me now that we rushed from fundraising drives and membership rallies to planning meetings and government hearings. Individuals such as A.M.E. Bishop D. Ward Nichols, C. K. Steele, and Joe Reddick drove themselves to aid us. From outside the state came Florida-born A. Philip Randolph, baseball great Jackie Robinson, Congressman James Roosevelt, and others. Still, it never was enough. Expenses mounted, and we prayed.

Sometimes we found ourselves praying to protect the lives of our friends, and sometimes we prayed that politicians hungry to cling onto offices by stirring race hate and prejudice would find some decency and humanity deep in their own souls. As to the former, a wave of shootings and related violence rattled Tallahassee in January 1957. Happily, no one in C. K. Steele's home was injured when an unknown gunman opened fire on it.[35] As to the politicians, how do you find forgiveness for someone such as Congressman A. S. Herlong, Jr.? He denounced civil rights supporters on the grounds that they "simply listen to what the Communist-inspired NAACP tells them are conditions in the South."[36] It was so important not to lose our tempers, not to appear as distant from reason as were many of our detractors. In October, for instance, U. S. Senator George Smathers charged that we were "as anxious to stir up controversy and discord as in accomplishing any real progress in behalf of [African American] people." What I wanted to tell him was a great deal more personal than what I did. "The NAACP seeks to have the laws of the nation implemented in a peaceful fashion," I commented. "It has always resorted to the courts and is ever willing to abide by their decisions."[37]

By the time I spoke those words in October 1957, I had passed a year that had swung from muddy depths to an inspiring high. I will discuss the NAACP's interaction with the Johns Committee further on, so for now I will say simply that, among many others, I appeared and refused to knuckle under to the bullying of its members and staff. They pressed us in every way that they could. Their interim report, issued in April, singled us out for repressive legislation, especially new laws aimed at curbing our ability to file lawsuits. In the end, questions of constitutionality short-circuited the plans, but the committee achieved a form of success by convincing the legislators to extend its life by two years.[38]

This one act of the Florida legislature imposed a tremendous burden upon us, as the Johns Committee embarked upon a witch hunt that would last for years. I have heard some persons insist that the committee drove the NAACP underground, but that is not really true. It did force us to change some tactics and the nature of our public visibility, however. Some employers—taking their cue from the headlines and, perhaps, a more organized effort—levied economic sanctions against activists, while baser elements of the population persisted in threats of physical violence. In the circumstances, we decided to keep secret the names of members, contributors, and many local officers to protect individuals from retaliation. In that climate, it could have meant the difference between life and death.

Many of our decisions were taken in May 1957, when the Florida NAACP leadership gathered at Tampa's Beulah Baptist Church (where A. Leon Lowry pastored) in the aftermath of the legislature's session. As I mentioned, the Johns Committee's bullying posture seemed to threaten individual NAACP leaders, as well as the organization. With Ruby Hurley's encouragement we nonetheless voted "to resist with non-violence every attempt to prevent compliance with the Supreme Court decision." More forcefully, Joe Reddick declared that "men would rather be dead than continue to have their civil rights trampled into the dust."[39] Our more well-known leaders now had to stand out even more forcefully, so that our work could progress while our membership could be protected.

To place these occurrences in context, the year 1957 witnessed the dramatic confrontation over racial integration at Central High School in Little Rock, Arkansas. That potential tragedy finally compelled a reluctant President Eisenhower to act in furtherance of the supreme court's order. The Congress also responded to public pressure by passing a moderate, but important, civil rights act, the first since the 1870s. These two events, taken together, gave us the high that I referred to earlier. In Florida, federal judge Emett C. Choate ordered an end to segregation on Miami buses, a key victory for us.

Given the climate surrounding the Florida legislative committee's investigations, though, the victories were few and far between and the frustrations great. Attorney General Ervin was only one of the men who stirred up segregationist fears of race violence, as most of our state and federal judges refused to enforce constitutional mandates. "The issue at hand is not one of tradition and morals but one of acceptance of law," I told reporters. "You cannot expect Negroes to go back to the days of their grandparents, who were forced to accept slavery."[40] Now it seems hard to believe that so basic a point needed to be drilled home to people forty years ago, but in Florida of 1957 it certainly did.

Through 1958 and 1959 we fought off attacks by the legislative investigative committee, while seeking to accomplish as much of our positive mission as we could. Governor Collins inched toward progress, but even he included the NAACP with the Ku Klux Klan when he ordered sheriffs in March 1958 to ban demonstrations calculated to incite riot or disorder. One day we would confront officials over segregated public facilities, the next we would assess the damages from hate bombings. We initiated legal actions whenever funds and personnel permitted, including one to test the legislature's attempt to allow school boards arbitrarily to assign pupils to schools (read segregated schools). We never backed away from demands for real change, setting as our state goal "complete racial desegregation in voting, schools, housing, government, and industry in Florida by 1963," the centennial anniversary of President Abraham Lincoln's Emancipation Proclamation. And, we committed ourselves to bringing up to 300,000 the total of registered African American voters in the state.[41]

Grand goals they were, but the legislative investigation took its toll as the months and years passed. At its every session the legislature considered segregationist legislation, passing any number of ridiculous and oppressive measures. One handful of bills enacted in 1959 compelled Leon Lowry, our then state president, and I to author a telegram to Governor Collins demanding that he "use the power of veto in keeping these heinous, reprehensible and undemocratic laws inoperative." The telegram, which said an awful lot about the state of affairs, continued, "It is most regrettable that men charged with the solemn responsibility of making laws in an enlightened age like this would bring shame on our state by enacting legislation designed solely to deny part of the citizens their democratic and equal rights."[42]

The very slow pace of progress speeded up in 1960, spurred by the actions of thousands of young people who took the civil rights fight into their own hands through the mechanism of sit-ins. Begun on February 1 at Greensboro, North Carolina, by students from that state's Agricultural and Technical College, the movement covered the South in what now seems like the wink of an eye.[43] I know that I was attending meetings about Tampa sit-ins by March, as the phenomenon spread over the state. Given that this was Florida, swim-ins aimed at integration of public beaches soon became a very popular cause.

Naturally, reactionary white judges attempted to mete out harsh punishments to the young people who embraced the sit-in movement, often denouncing them in the process. Judge John Rudd, for instance, lectured students from Tallahassee's Florida A&M University, denying their basic right to protest. I did not think that his action should go unchallenged. "Since when does a citizen of the United States have to restrict his criticism or protest against what he believes to be an abridgment of his constitutional rights, to his own locality?" I asked in an open letter. "Does this mean that Negroes in Tallahassee cannot express themselves freely when they are mistreated because they live in Tallahassee?" The letter continued: "Are you saying that a citizen of Tallahassee, who has been unlawfully arrested by police, cannot contest an abridgement of civil rights because the majority in Tallahassee are opposed to Negroes having equal rights? Does your pronouncement purport to make Tallahassee an non-democratic island where Americans moving in from other cities, cannot exercise historically established constitutional rights?" With more than a little cynicism, it concluded, "The unchristian and undemocratic nature of [your] statement leads us to believe that you have been misquoted by the press. We hope that you will forth rightly deny these statements or in the alternative, clarify your untenable position in this matter."[44]

As a personal aside, these and other comments about Rudd landed me in hot water with the judge. Attorney G. E. Graves and I were attending a hearing related to the sit-ins in Rudd's segregated courtroom, when he bellowed out, "Where's that Robert Saunders?" With Graves following, the judge took me to an adjacent room that was empty of any furnishings. There, he angrily demanded to know by what right I was criticizing him in the press. I remember so well his words: "Don't you know I could hold you in contempt of court?" Graves's advice saved the day. He kept repeating to me softly, "Keep quiet, keep quiet!"

While the sit-in movement endowed new energy in the civil rights struggle, Florida politics took a turn for the worse. The constitution barred Governor Collins from succeeding himself, and the eventual winner of the 1960 governor's race, Farris Bryant of Marion County, exulted in being a "firm" segregationist. Governor Collins said of Bryant that he was an apostle of "reaction, retreat and regret."[45] Beginning when he entered upon office in January 1961 and extending for the next four years, Bryant attempted to frustrate us at every turn. He went so far as to block federal programs designed to aid integration and would not even permit the state to join in a study of equal job opportunities. He fought the Civil Rights Act of 1964 and the Voting Rights Act of 1965.[46]

Still, we went at Governor Bryant and his administration with our own determination. The NAACP helped to force racial desegregation in the public school systems of twenty counties.[47] I am very proud to say that my son Bobby took the first step toward desegregation of Hillsborough County's schools when he entered MacFarlane Park Cuesta Elementary School in January 1962.[48] By March 1963 I could boast that "the move toward integration of

Florida's public schools leads the South."[49] Meanwhile, we attacked segregation and discrimination at service stations, cafeterias, and hotels, in the Florida National Guard, in housing and undergraduate programs at the University of Florida, in zoning decisions, and in just about every other segregated aspect of Florida society.

Through these years of the early 1960s we made measurable progress, partly thanks to assistance from other civil rights organizations. The Congress of Racial Equality (CORE) thrived in a couple of locations, especially on the campus of Florida A&M University. Beginning in 1957, the Southern Christian Leadership Conference (SCLC) attempted to inject needed dynamism into the cause throughout the region. Since many Florida NAACP leaders were ministers, our leadership overlapped somewhat with that of the SCLC. The name of Reverend C. K. Steele, an SCLC founder, comes quickly to mind. The sit-in movement added the Student Nonviolent Coordinating Committee to the roster of activist organizations, with chapters on the campuses of Florida's black colleges and university.

Let us not lose sight of the fact, though, that the NAACP laid the groundwork and provided essential support for civil rights initiatives in the state. We welcomed others to the fight. We did what we could to be good allies. Still, we were there before the others came, and we were there after some of them left. The nationally important demonstrations and related events at St. Augustine during 1963 and 1964 provide an example. As one historian noted, "At the beginning of 1963 NAACP officials developed plans for desegregating the community by exerting pressure at the local and national level."[50] Thereafter, our officers and members played crucial parts in focusing national attention on the situation in Florida and at St. Augustine. Although others received the lion's share of publicity, our organization proved its staying power. The St. Augustine demonstrations receive greater attention in Part Three. I would close here by saying thank the Lord for what other organizations did, but do not forget the NAACP.

All the while our fight continued to be fought uphill. Racist resistance taxed us tremendously, forcing us to come up with innovative ideas and new strategies, such as the idea of a "March on Tallahassee" and "selective buying" campaigns. All the while, we reached out to lend support to the struggle in other states and on the national level. We served as the organizing institution for Florida representation to 1963's March on Washington and endeavored to assist landmark integration initiatives such as James Meredith's 1962 attempt to enter the University of Mississippi.

We sometimes despaired at setbacks and personal defeats. One terrible time for me came in June 1963 when my friend Medgar Evers was gunned down in cold blood outside his home in Jackson, Mississippi. All of the southern state field secretaries lived day to day with the possibility of such racist violence. In 1962 Langston Hughes discussed our network. "Ruby Hurley . . . shows no fear when she gets off a plane at a southern airport to take a local bus to a remote hamlet New Yorkers never heard of," he wrote, "where mobs have just roamed the streets smashing the windshields and slashing the tires of all Negro-owned cars or stoning churches and homes." He continued, "Frequently enough, Gloster Current, director of branches; Herbert Wright, youth secretary; and field secretaries like DeQuincey Newman, Robert Saunders, W. C. Patton, and L. C. Bates find themselves in territories not unlike the Algerian villages of that you-never-know-what land on the Mediterranean." Hughes concluded: "The insurance premiums of these fighters must be high, their hearts stout, and their nerves like steel. Theirs is a labor of love."[51]

By 1964 our labors of love began to pay off. In January, the Twenty-fourth Amendment to the U. S. Constitution outlawed use of the poll tax. The Congress passed its landmark Civil Rights Act in July, providing protection against discrimination in education and the use of public facilities. It also created the Equal Employment Opportunity Commission and mandated an end to discrimination in federally assisted programs. A civil rights march from Selma to Montgomery, Alabama, helped set the stage the next year for enactment of the Voting Rights Act of 1965. Ironically, a key figure in the Montgomery march was Florida's former governor LeRoy Collins, by then President Johnson's director of the Community Relations Service. Also in 1965, President Johnson named Thurgood Marshall as solicitor general of the United States and two years afterward placed Thurgood on the U. S. Supreme Court.[52]

I wish that I could say that white Floridians had embraced the cause of civil rights as warmly as had LeRoy Collins and the Congress by 1964 and 1965. Unfortunately, it was not so. Hayden Burns, elected governor in 1964, blasted the Civil Rights Act of 1964 and denounced the NAACP. A moderate Democrat wrested the nomination from Burns in 1966, only to lose to Claude Kirk, a Republican who manipulated race hate with sophistication. All this notwithstanding, cracks appeared in the political barriers. To his credit, Burns told the legislature in his first address to the body that prejudice and bigotry had "no place in our government," and he appointed an African American, Clifton Dyson, to the state university system's board of regents. Kirk attempted to fill his political sails with wind from the anti-busing movement but went down to defeat, in turn, in 1970.[53]

By the time of Claude Kirk's administration, much of my time and energies were being spent elsewhere than Florida, although still in the service of the civil rights cause. I no longer represented the state's NAACP as its field secretary. Just as Thurgood Marshall had answered a call to a federal role, I also accepted employment with the United States government. In my case, the call came in 1966. The position was chief of the office of civil rights for the Office of Economic Opportunity, with headquarters in Atlanta. Through the job, I believed, I could utilize my experience for a greater good on a broader scale. Some good did come out of that work, but that is another story beyond the scope of this book.

Since I mentioned earlier my pride at seeing Jackie Robinson play baseball in Cincinnati in 1947, let me state here that he broke the news about my departure to Tampans. Gracious and generous man that he was, Jackie was speaking for us at a Tampa Freedom Fund dinner. I whispered to him that I was leaving. He asked me, "Who'll run the NAACP?" Before I could answer he was called to the podium. He began his remarks by passing on the word to his audience and, through them, to the community that had been my home and my headquarters. It was an honor to me that it mattered to him.

Leaving the state NAACP headquarters, I could look back on the years since 1952 with pride mixed with disappointment. We had accomplished so much and come so far, but the price had been very high. With better and more-representative leadership, the South could have avoided much of the agony that it suffered. The fight did not have to be to the death. Now, the passage of time has faded out memories of many racist leaders, and those who still live often are seen as kindly old figures out of a different world. I want young people to know that these men made our world worse for having lived in it. Trampling the constitution under foot, they clung to political office at the expense of lives, of real pain, and of destruction of trust that could have held our society together. They were defeated in the end, however, and I live with the satisfaction that I played a small part in bringing about their downfall.

Johnnie Brooks, NAACP national director for voting registration, helped get the racist politicians out of office by working tirelessly to bring new voters out for elections. Here he poses with a Gadsden County resident during a statewide Florida voter registration program inititated by the NAACP. The registration effort was successful because of the local branches, but support from Johnnie and others with national experience made quite a difference.

The NAACP Southeast Region staff met regularly to discuss problems and share ideas about how to fight racial discrimination. Southeast Regional Director Ruby Hurley is seated at the head of the table (lower left). Others attending this 1956 meeting are (left to right) Charles McClain, North Carolina Field Director; Medgar Evers, Mississippi Field Director; Rev. Holmes, Georgia Field Director; unknown; Robert W. Saunders, Florida Field Director; and W. C. Patton, NAACP Voter Education and Registration Director. (Sunland Tribune)

Flossie Currinton (seated third from left) joins Helen Saunders and Rev. A. Leon Lowry at the NAACP 50th Anniversary Dinner in New York in 1959. Mrs. Currinton served as the Florida State Conference secretary and secretary of the Daytona (Volusia County) Branch. She was one of many NAACP officials subpoenaed by the Johns Legislative Committee in 1957.

FLORIDA, THE NAACP, AND ME: 1952-1966

Every Black citizen in Florida owes a great debt of gratitude to the late Clarence Mitchell. Clarence was known as the 101st United States Senator. As the head of the NAACP Washington Bureau, he came to the rescue of many who were attacked by individuals such as Representative Bob Sikes of Crestview. He was able to bring pressure to bear in the highest government circles in the nation's capital. Clarence is credited with guiding the 1964 Civil Rights Act through Congress. He and his assistant J. Francis Pohlhaus wasted no time in following through on the many complaints registered by my office, most notably during the 1957-58 voting registration problems in Liberty County, Florida.

Many of my friends and co-workers are included in this staff photograph from the 1954 NAACP national convention in Dallas. Thurgood Marshall is seated at front left, and others are identified with their names or signatures on the photo. Roughly left to right, the others identified are Jack Greenberg, Clarence Mitchell, Constance Baker Motley, Ruby Hurley, Bob Carter, Frank Williams, Herbert Hill, Gloster Current, Cecelia Marshall, Mildred Roxborough, and Roy Wilkins. (Sunland Tribune)

PART TWO

A Time Line for Bridging the Gap

1916: James Weldon Johnson, born in Jacksonville, becomes NAACP national field secretary.

1938: Attorney S. D. McGill files an NAACP suit seeking equal pay for Black teachers, the first in the Deep South.

1940: Mary McLeod Bethune welcomes me as a student at Bethune-Cookman College.

1923: Flames engulf one of the cabins in what has become known as the Rosewood Massacre, January 4, 1923. (Florida State Archives)

A Time Line for Bridging the Gap
(1909-1966)

1909 **May-June** — The National Negro Conference held at New York City calls for a national organization to serve as a watchdog for the rights of blacks

1910 **May** — The new national organization has chosen the name National Association for the Advancement of Colored People (NAACP)

November — The first issue of the NAACP's *The Crisis* appears under the editorship of W. E. Burghardt Du Bois

1911 **June** — The NAACP is incorporated in the State of New York

1915 **September** — The Henry McNeal Turner Local coalesces at West Tampa after national NAACP officials discourage organization of a southern branch

December — An NAACP branch organizes at Key West, the first in Florida and one of the first in the South

1916 **December** — Floridian James Weldon Johnson becomes NAACP national field secretary

1917 **April** — The Tampa NAACP branch is formally chartered

1920 **November** — Florida's Ocoee Riot occurs

1921 **June** — I am born at Tampa

1923 **January** — Florida's Rosewood Massacre occurs

1933 **May** — Murders at Pompano, Florida, give rise to the case of *Chambers* v. *Florida*

1934 **October** — Claude Neal is brutally lynched at Greenwood, Florida

1938 **May** — Attorney S. D. McGill files a teacher salary equalization suit in Brevard County, the first such NAACP-sponsored action in the Deep South

1940 **February** — The United States Supreme Court renders a final decision reversing convictions in the *Chambers* case and, in the words of *The Crisis*, "enunciat[ing] in ringing terms the right of Negroes to justice free of oppression and coercion"

September — I begin studies at Bethune-Cookman College under the supervision of its president Mary McLeod Bethune

1941 **April** — A test case for equalization of teacher salaries is filed at Pensacola with S. D. McGill and Thurgood Marshall representing the NAACP

June — President Franklin D. Roosevelt issues Executive Order No. 8802, mandating nondiscrimination in national defense programs at the behest of the NAACP's Walter White and Florida-born union leader A. Philip Randolph

July — The United States District Court at Pensacola rules that teachers should benefit from equal pay irrespective of race or color

October — The Florida State Conference of Branches organizes as the first state conference in NAACP history, with Harry T. Moore as president

December — The United States enters World War II

1944 **April** — The United States Supreme Court rules the White primary unconstitutional in the case of *Smith* v. *Allwright*, prompting Harry T. Moore and others to found Florida's Progressive Voters' League, Inc.

1946 **January** — The Florida Democratic Party drops its formal bar to participation by African Americans in party elections

June — Harry T. Moore becomes full-time executive secretary of the Florida state conference of the NAACP

August — As a discharged World War II veteran, I begin a one-year stint with the Cincinnati edition of the Cleveland *Call and Post*

1947 **Fall** — I relocate to Detroit to pursue undergraduate and law studies

1949	**July**	— The alleged kidnapping and rape of a white woman in Lake County gives rise to the *Groveland* case
1951	**January**	— I receive the bachelor of arts degree from the Detroit Institute of Technology before entering the University of Detroit Law School
	November	— Lake County Sheriff Willis McCall guns down two *Groveland* case defendants
	November	— The Florida State Conference of Branches relieves Harry T. Moore of his duties as executive secretary
	December	— Ku Klux Klansmen assassinate Harry T. Moore and his wife Harriett Moore on Christmas night at their home in Mims
1952	**January**	— I suspend my law studies at the University of Detroit to pursue gainful employment and volunteer efforts for the NAACP
	August	— Walter White appoints me as field secretary for the Florida State Conference of Branches to replace Harry T. Moore
	September	— Having relocated Florida state conference headquarters to Tampa, I assume duties as field secretary
	September	— Ed Davis, president of the Florida state conference, announces "complete and immediate integration" as the NAACP's goal for Florida
	December	— Florida state conference officials help to protect Elmo Mims, who shot a Fort Pierce policeman while defending his home against police invasion
1953	**January**	— Florida state conference president William A. Fordham and I appeal to newly inaugurated governor Dan McCarty to eliminate discrimination in state employment
	January	— The Florida state conference commences regular radio broadcasts, beginning with Tampa station WHBO
1954	**January**	— I marry Helen Strickland at Tampa
	May	— The United States Supreme Court rules unconstitutional the doctrine of separate but equal as applied to

public education in the decision of *Brown* v. *Board of Education of Topeka, Kansas*

May — The Florida state conference demands immediate action toward "orderly implementation" of the *Brown* decision

1955 **January** — State Senator LeRoy Collins of Tallahassee, who had opposed the *Brown* decision, replaces racist Acting Governor Charley E. Johns as governor

March — Walter White passes away, to be succeeded by Roy Wilkins as national NAACP executive secretary

May — The United States Supreme Court encourages segregationists to stall implementation of the *Brown* decision by announcing its "all deliberate speed" doctrine

August — The Florida state conference inaugurates its "Youth for Freedom" encampments

September — Governor LeRoy Collins appoints a black lawyer, Henry H. Arrington, as an assistant state's attorney

October — The Supreme Court of Florida refuses to order the University of Florida Law School to admit Virgil Hawkins

December — Rosa Parks's courageous defiance sets off the one-year Montgomery, Alabama, bus boycott

1956 **January-February** — Klansmen disrupt voter registration efforts in Liberty County

March — The United State Supreme Court upholds Virgil Hawkins's right to attend the University of Florida Law School but the Supreme Court of Florida subsequently rules that Hawkins's right should be postponed

May — Florida A&M University students follow Rosa Parks's lead, taking action that resulted in the Tallahassee Bus Boycott

June — The NAACP sues to desegregate the Dade County public school system

A TIME LINE FOR BRIDGING THE GAP

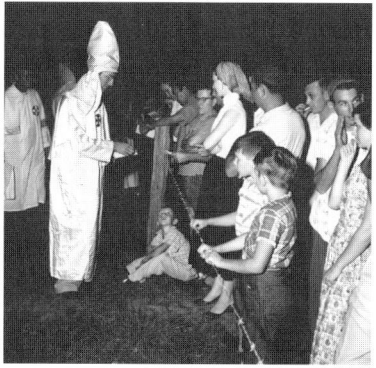

The 1954 Supreme Court ruling increased educational opportunity for Blacks in Florida's classrooms, but the Ku Klux Klan also increased its level of recruiting and demonstrating. In 1956, the year the photographs below were taken, the Klan disrupted NAACP voter registration in Liberty County and intimidated citizens throughout the state. (Florida State Archives)

NAACP attorneys (left to right) George E. C. Hayes, Thurgood Marshall, and James Nabrit, Jr., posed for the camera on the steps of the Supreme Court following the landmark 1954 ruling that the "separate but equal" approach in schools was unconstitutional. The case set new directions for our efforts throughout Florida and the South.

Helen Saunders (left) and NAACP office secretary Mazie Braxton stayed busy with many initiatives coordinated through our office at 705 Harrison Street, c. 1955.

Daisy Bates (right) was regarded as a civil rights hero when she came to Tampa in 1957 to help us launch our Florida activities. Her leadership in Little Rock, Arkansas, had been reported in all the media; her ability to reinforce abstract principles at the personal level helped make her visit here doubly rewarding. In this photo she is talking with Helen Saunders.

Father David Brooks, president of the Tallahassee branch, speaks with the NAACP's national director of voter registration Johnnie Brooks in Tallahassee in 1958. Our success at registering new voters throughout the state was one measure of our continuing progress. It was a team effort by each local branch with unflagging support from the national office.

Maxine Douglas, secretary to NAACP attorney Francisco A. Rodriguez, talks with James Johnson and a young secretary from our office in front of the Longshoreman building, where we also had our office, in Tampa in 1959. "Dean Johnson," as he was affectionately known, served as Tampa branch secretary from the 1940s until 1958.

August — The Florida legislature creates an investigative committee (that will become known as the Johns Committee) with the NAACP fixed as one of its prime targets

September — NAACP attorney Francisco A. Rodriguez charges Hillsborough County authorities with systematically excluding African Americans from jury duty

September — Tampa police detain Florida state conference president William A. Fordham

October — A. Joseph Reddick succeeds William A. Fordham as president of the Florida state conference

1957 **January** — Governor LeRoy Collins takes the oath of office for a four-year term as governor during which he will moderate many of his racial policies

January — Shootings and other violent acts occur at Tallahassee, including gunfire into the home of NAACP leader Charles K. Steele

January — The Southern Christian Leadership Conference is organized at Atlanta, Georgia

March — The Florida legislative investigative committee compels NAACP officials to testify at Tallahassee hearings

April — The Florida legislative investigative committee recommends repressive legislation aimed at the NAACP

May — The Florida state conference renews its commitment to civil rights advances despite legislative attacks

September — The United States Congress enacts the first Civil Rights Act since Reconstruction in the midst of the Little Rock, Arkansas, school crisis

October — A. Leon Lowry of Tampa succeeds A. Joseph Reddick as president of the Florida state conference

December — Florida NAACP leaders intercede to protect Lake County's Melvin Hawkins, Jr., after spurious rape charges are lodged against him

1958 **February** — Father Theodore Gibson defies the Florida legislative investigative committee at Miami hearings and is arrested

Wade-ins like this one in Ft. Lauderdale in 1960 helped bring integration to Florida's most popular recreational areas. (Florida State Archives)

In a wave of activity following the Greensboro sit-ins, Florida NAACP youth council members conducted their own sit-ins at lunch counters throughout the state. The reaction in this Tampa Woolworth's in 1960 was typical— when the young people sat down, the store closed its counter. (Tampa Tribune)

Segregated facilities were to be found all over the state. I made it a point to photograph examples, such as this waiting room at the train station in Wildwood, so that we could take steps to have the signs removed and the facilities integrated.

Klan members evoked fear in the symbol of the burning cross, as in the Tallahassee gathering (far left). The sign is typical of many planted by night in Florida during the late 1950s and early 1960s in the yards of those identified as advocates of desegregation. They were the work of the White Citizens Council or the Klan.

March — Governor LeRoy Collins includes the NAACP with the Ku Klux Klan in an order to sheriffs to ban demonstrations calculated to incite riot or disorder

November — Florida NAACP leaders intercede to prevent the lynching of Sumter County's Jesse Woods

November — The Florida state conference sets a state goal of complete racial desegregation in voting, schools, housing, government, and industry by 1963

1960 **February** — Students initiate the "sit-in" movement at Greensboro, North Carolina

February-March — sit-ins and "swim-ins" commence in Florida

August — Klansmen wielding baseball bats confront demonstrators at Jacksonville

November — Dr. Martin Luther King, Jr., speaks at Fort Homer Hesterly Armory at Tampa

1961 **January** — Hard-line segregationist governor Farris Bryant replaces moderate LeRoy Collins and acts through his four-year term to frustrate civil rights advances

May — "Freedom Riders" begin to test interstate travel conditions leading to a mob attack in Montgomery, Alabama

1962 **January** — Robert W. Saunders, Jr., integrates MacFarlane Park Elementary School, Tampa

November — Jacksonville's Rutledge Pearson succeeds A. Leon Lowry as Florida state conference president

1963 **February** — NAACP officials meet with St. Augustine members to plan efforts to pressure the city to end discrimination during its quadricentennial celebration

March — I proclaim that "the move toward integration of Florida's public schools leads the South"

March — The United States Supreme Court overturns the contempt citation issued by the Florida legislative investigative committee against Father Theodore Gibson

BRIDGING THE GAP

The Golden Anniversary national convention of the NAACP in New York City in 1959 was filled with promise. We were looking forward to building upon our past achievements and moving forward with new intiatives to implement change in the decade ahead.

A TIME LINE FOR BRIDGING THE GAP

In this panoramic photograph, I am standing with some close friends and associates beneath the banner on the back wall near the stage. In the enlarged inset you can see that on my right is Medgar Evers, and Ruby Hurley is standing at the end of the row on my left.

March — The March on Tallahassee

April — Dr. Martin Luther King, Jr., releases his "Letter from a Birmingham Jail"

May — Bombings and riots rock Birmingham, Alabama, prompting President John F. Kennedy to dispatch federal troops to keep order

June — Medgar Evers is assassinated at Jackson, Mississippi

June — Federal authorities compel Governor George C. Wallace to allow racial integration of the University of Alabama

Summer — Demonstrations continue at St. Augustine

August — The March on Washington

September — The Sixteenth Street Baptist Church is bombed at Birmingham, Alabama, killing four young girls

September — Klansmen assault Dr. Robert Hayling at St. Augustine

1964 **January** — Ratification of the Twenty-fourth Amendment to the United States Constitution, which outlawed the poll tax

February-March — Bombings, demonstrations, and riots shake Jacksonville

March — The Southern Christian Leadership Conference joins the escalating anti-discrimination battle at St. Augustine

July — The Civil Rights Act of 1964 becomes law

1965 **January** — Former Jacksonville mayor Hayden Burns takes office as Florida's governor to begin a two-year term during which he will blast the Civil Rights Act of 1964 and denounce the NAACP

March — The Selma to Montgomery (Alabama) march takes place

August — President Lyndon B. Johnson signs the Voting Rights Act of 1965

1966 **March** — I resign as Florida NAACP field secretary to become chief of the Civil Rights Division, Region IV, Office of Economic Opportunity, United States Community Services Administration, Atlanta

Roy Wilkins ponders a question at the lectern while I rest a little more comfortably in my seat at the front table knowing he is the one having to think on his feet during one of the workshops we conducted in Atlanta to educate staff from throughout the region regarding civil rights issues as they impacted initiatives of the Office of Economic Opportunity.

After I photographed these signs on US 441 near Lake Okeechobee and protested to Governor LeRoy Collins, the racist message was removed. However, Collins first stated that he had no authority because the "sign was posted on private property," c. 1959.

PART THREE

KEY PEOPLE AND IMPORTANT EVENTS

Harry T. Moore in about 1934 when he first became active in organizing an NAACP branch for Brevard county. (Evangeline Moore)

5
Harry T. Moore:
Profile of a Martyr for Civil Rights

I will always believe that the turning point in the struggle to end racial segregation and the Jim Crow mentality that existed in the South began after Harry T. Moore and his wife Harriett were brutally murdered.[1] Klansmen (call them Kowards) killed them with a bomb that destroyed the Moores' home at Mims, Florida, on their twenty-fifth wedding anniversary, Christmas night 1951. Both these crusaders for civil rights lay in bed at the time. I also believe that Moore lived his life knowing death lurked just around the corner because he so actively opposed racial discrimination in Florida. A prolific writer, Moore constantly challenged elected and appointed officials protesting lynchings, police brutality, prison abuse, unequal working conditions and salaries, and the deplorable conditions of the schools attended by Black students.

Both the Moores served their Brevard County community as educators and sources of inspiration. He pressed for salary equalization for Black teachers and professors, and he involved himself heavily in the original University of Florida desegregation suit filed in 1947. His and Harriett's students, among them my wife Helen, affectionately called him "Professor" Moore. Helen well remembers Professor Moore's great fondness for literature and Black poetry. To impress him, she and her friends would memorize poem after poem, especially those of Countee Cullen. The Moores often spent either Christmas Eve or a part of Christmas day with Helen's family. Helen had been at Mims that tragic Christmas Day of 1951, but had left to return to her job in Tampa by the time of the killings.

As time passed, Moore's experiences with discrimination against Black teachers and students incensed him all the more. In those days, all Black schools stood inferior in quality to those attended by White students. The facilities, furniture, and teaching materials all were unfit to provide a decent education for Black children. White schools boasted extracurricular activities and recreational programs as standard amenities. Black schools, barely funded by White school boards, found them an almost unattainable luxury.

The discrimination extended well beyond physical and program amenities to teacher training and compensation, issues that Moore pursued doggedly. To give an example, I would relate a story told to me by Edward D. Davis, our one-time state conference president. My recollection is that, in the late 1930s or early 1940s, the state had raised the annual salaries of the presidents of the University of Florida and the Florida State College for Women to $5,000. Black educators thereupon approached Governor Fred P. Cone about raising the compensation of the president of Florida A&M College. The governor, an avid segregationist, responded, "No nigger . . . in the state of Florida is worth $5,000 a year."

Harry Moore saw clearly that the courts could provide only so much relief for African Americans, whether the concern was school quality, teacher compensation, civil rights protection, or what have you. Accordingly, he devoted a great deal of his energy toward eliminating Florida's "Lily White Democratic Primaries" and pushing for increased voter registration for Black citizens. The initiative underlay his work from 1941 to 1946 as president of the state NAACP conference and later as its executive secretary. I have already mentioned that other NAACP stalwarts, including Edward Davis and Noah Griffin, labored alongside Moore in these causes.

Moore believed that the political best interests of the African Americans lay in the Democratic party, although that organization's local divisions in the South strove to maintain race prejudice and inequality. At the time, many of our leaders remained Republicans, the party of Abraham Lincoln and Emancipation. Moore outlined the reasons for his beliefs in a letter to the newly organized Progressive Voters' League on November 15, 1945. I find them both interesting and informative:

> In our attempt to clarify this situation [of which party to support], we should like to ask a few other questions. Are Negro citizens of Florida suffering more from discriminatory practices of local officials or of national officials? Who are more directly responsible for the inequalities in educational opportunities, the lynchings, the police brutality, and other injustices suffered by Negroes, our state and county officials or the Administration in Washington?

He continued:

> All of these evils can be traced directly to the prejudiced attitude of local officials. Negro teachers are paid less than white teachers with the same qualifications because the county superintendents and school boards have so arranged it. Jesse Payne was lynched on October 10, 1945, because the Madison County Sheriff permitted it. Who controls the election of these state and county officials, the Republicans or the Democrats? Regardless [of] our party beliefs, we must now face facts. And the fact is that practically every city, county, and state official in Florida is selected in the Democratic Primaries. In order to help select these officials, Negroes must vote in the Democratic Primaries. In order to vote in the Democratic Primaries, Negroes must register as Democrats. If we are to reap the full benefits of these opportunities, we must forget our old party affiliations and register to vote in the election that really counts—the Democratic Primary. Then when the general election comes, we can vote for the candidate of our choice.[2]

Moore made every effort to ensure that Black citizens would have the opportunity to exercise their privilege to vote. For instance, when he received letters from Black citizens in Taylor, Gadsden, and Suwannee Counties, all of whom were threatened when they tried to vote in the Democratic Primary of 1945, he immediately responded with a letter to Governor Millard F. Caldwell requesting protection for Black voters across the Florida Panhandle. Furthermore, after the Florida senate passed and sent to the house of representatives a proposed constitutional amendment that would require citizens to read a portion of the Florida and United States constitutions before they could qualify to vote, Moore protested.

In the case of the constitutional amendment, Moore's argument initially followed the reasoning that, if Florida was unwilling to support decent schools for Black children, it had no right to penalize them as adults for lack of a decent education. "It is obvious that this measure is designed to restrict the voting privilege of a certain group of citizens," he began in a letter to the house of representatives. "This measure, if passed is bound to cause unmerited hardships for prospective Negro voters." He continued:

> Florida Negro citizens have suffered many handicaps under our educational system. Our state has not made the same provisions for the education of its colored citizens as it has for the education of its white citizens. If you will just look back on our public school system as it was twenty years ago, you can easily see why a higher percentage of Negro citizens might have difficulty reading any section of the Constitution. Should Florida Negro citizens be penalized now for being victims of a system over which they had no control?[3]

Addressing points made by proponents of the proposed amendment, Moore rebutted with common sense arguments while reminding legislators that African American men had fought valiantly for their country during World War Two, a conflict just ended:

> A citizen does not have to read the Constitution to pay taxes. Many men who served in the armed forces would have difficulty

reading certain parts of the Constitution, yet they made their contributions to the defense of their country and democracy. Is it fair now to create new restrictions that might tend to deny these same men the fundamental right to vote?[4]

Moore's responsibilities and the scope of his work grew dramatically in 1946 when he became the executive secretary of the Florida State Conference. He organized numerous local branches across the state and provided leadership where voids existed and fear prevailed. The labors came with a high price. As a result of his civil rights agenda, Brevard County officials fired Moore from his teaching position in Mims. Likewise, they denied Harriett teaching opportunities in the county for three years, forcing her to look beyond the county's lines for work. The situation compelled the Moores to depend upon his salary from the state conference, but often it did not materialize. At the time of his death, the Florida NAACP's obligation to him amounted to some ten thousand dollars.

The demands placed upon Moore did not preclude his taking personal interest in individual instances involving miscarriage of justice. He especially took a strong stand against the travesties of justice surrounding the Groveland case.[5] Many believe that Moore's pointed criticism of the judicial system's handling of the case, coupled with his effective voter registration drives, directly led to his assassination.

I mentioned the Groveland case in Chapter One, but I did not go into detail about Moore's leadership in seeking justice. It will be recalled that, in 1949, three Black men and one youth were arrested and charged with raping a White woman in Groveland, a small town in Lake County. Then, a group of White mobsters burned the houses of Groveland's Black residents. Upwards of 400 men, women, and children fled their homes even as their dinner remained cooking on the stove. Many refused to return and eventually reestablished their lives elsewhere.[6]

Moore's reaction came quickly. On July 28 he demanded that state's attorney J. W. Hunter investigate the tragic affair and prosecute the mobsters. The task should not have posed a serious challenge, since county sheriff Willis McCall admitted that he knew many of the men involved. Obtaining no satisfaction with Hunter, Moore appealed to Governor Fuller Warren, demanding justice and carefully noting for the record Sheriff McCall's tolerance of mob violence. Met with silence, Moore committed himself to ensuring justice.[7]

The Groveland case took numerous twists and turns. The men eventually were sentenced to death by Florida courts. Increasingly preoccupied by the case, Moore campaigned on behalf of a "Groveland Defense Fund" and organized "Groveland Defense Sundays" while NAACP lawyers assisted appeals.[8] The United States Supreme Court overturned the convictions in 1951 and remanded the cases for retrial. It was then that McCall, while transporting two of the prisoners from jail to Lake County for retrial, shot and killed Samuel Shepherd and wounded Walter Irvin. McCall claimed the two men had attempted escape, although they were cuffed together, making escape difficult indeed. Further investigation by the NAACP, conducted at Moore's insistence, revealed that McCall had asked the men to get out of the patrol car on the remote clay road where they were shot.

The passion with which Moore pursued justice in the Groveland case matched his commitment in other areas, driving him to far greater public demands and highly visible attempts to pressure public officials to action. His success at getting an anti-lynching bill introduced into the legislature illustrated progress, but each step came at the cost of intensified opposition. The number of enemies grew, circulating among themselves word that something must be done about Harry T. Moore. Still, he demanded justice.

The final two months of his life played out as tragedy after tragedy. McCall shot the two Groveland defendants in early November. Moore urgently called for his suspension and insisted that the state conference follow his lead. Fellow NAACP leaders, in light of Moore's dogged pursuit of the Groveland case, chaffed at his neglect of state conference finances and members. Moore stayed his course. Within days the conference dismissed him as executive secretary, allowing him to retain for one year a position as state coordinator of branches.⁹

Broke, demoted, and exhausted, Moore nonetheless displayed a remarkable balance, dedication, and sense of decency. He did not abandon the cause of the Groveland defendants any more than he abandoned the NAACP. A letter that he wrote on December 2 to Governor Warren shows his steady thinking and unshaken determination. If not his last official letter, it was among them. It so well shows his patterns of thought that I will ask the reader's patience in quoting from it at length:

> Sane-minded Florida citizens of all classes, creeds, and colors must be shocked over the recent developments in the famous Groveland case. Despite the report of the coroner's jury that Sheriff McCall acted 'in the line of duty' when he shot Shephard and Irvin, those fateful shots fired near Weirsdale on the night of November 6th are still heard around the world.
>
> Thinking people naturally ask these questions: 1) in view of the mob action directed against these prisoners in 1949, was it safe to transport them to Lake County again with a guard of only two officers? 2) Did Sheriff McCall use sound judgment in attempting to drive his car and guard two prisoners at the same time? 3) Why did the officers follow a 'blind' clay road after leaving Weirsdale? 4) If the prisoners did try to escape (which is extremely doubtful), was it necessary to shoot them four times in order to stop them, especially when they were handcuffed together? 5) Since the three Groveland boys had complained of severe beatings and inhuman treatment by Lake County officers in 1949, why were they permitted to leave Raiford [the state prison] again in the custody of these same officers? 6) Is it true that in Florida the word of a Negro means nothing when weighed against that of a white person (as indicated by the three prisoners' complaints in 1949 and by Irvin's sworn statement last month? 7) In the face of such strong evidence of gross neglect or willful intent to murder the prisoners, why have those officers not been suspended?

> Yes, these questions are too important to be ignored. We need not try to 'whitewash' this case or bury our heads in the sand like an ostrich. Florida is on trial before the rest of the world. Only prompt and courageous action by you in removing these officers can save the good name of our fair state. We also repeat our request for ample and constant State guard for Irvin in future hearings on this case.

Moore closed the letter with a polite reminder to Governor Warren that Florida's Negro citizens had not forgotten that it was their votes that gave Warren the margin of victory needed to win the governorship in the 1948 election.[10]

That sane and reasoned voice, so clear to us today, was stilled twenty-three days later. On December 25 the Moores decided to postpone their Christmas celebration until the arrival of their youngest daughter Evangeline, who was due in from Washington, D.C. At approximately 10:30 that evening a bomb was placed beneath the bedroom of the Moore home. The explosion that ensued was so powerful that it ripped through the floor boards and blew the couple and their bed to the roof of the house. Harry died instantly, but Harriett hung on, only to die ten days later in a Sanford hospital.

What little investigation local authorities undertook revealed that the bomb was highly sophisticated. It was definitely constructed and placed by experts. Walter White, NAACP executive secretary, expressed to me the outrage felt among African Americans, labeling the killings as "one of the starkest tragedies that has befallen America in a long time."[11] When I was hired as Moore's successor, White confided to me that he believed some of the state's highly elected officials were involved in the murder plot.

The NAACP strove mightily, but unsuccessfully, to force public officials to do their jobs to bring the killer to justice. Walter demanded that Governor Warren take immediate action on behalf of the state, and he spoke at mass meetings in Jacksonville and Orlando in which he criticized the governor for his passiveness. Warren responded by issuing a statement in which he described the internationally respected White as a "ranting racialist" and a "hired Harlem hate-monger."[12] Although the case subsequently received national attention with rewards posted in excess of $20,000, no one has ever been arrested for the crime. In later years a disabled war veteran came forth with information and stated that he was involved in making and planting the bomb. However, the new information did not lead to any arrest.

Harry T. Moore spent his entire adult life fighting for the civil rights of Black Floridians. Speaking out against unequal educational opportunities, unequal salaries, the White Democratic primary, police brutality, and an unjust judicial system, Moore left no stone unturned. His words demanded attention and threatened the White power structure. Ironically, someone thought he had solved the civil rights "problem" by silencing Moore. In fact, the murderer made many Black citizens more determined than ever to fight for their rights. Admittedly, many were afraid to be associated with the NAACP immediately after the assassination, but with a little prompting Black citizens banded together in subsequent years. For decades after the deaths, Black Floridians remembered the ultimate sacrifices of Harry and Harriett Moore as they demanded the death of Jim Crow.

Harry and Harriett Moore

Peaches and Evangeline Moore

BRIDGING THE GAP

Harry T. Moore refused to let go of the Groveland case. Sheriff Willis McCall had emptied his revolver shooting two handcuffed defendants during an alleged escape attempt. The bodies of Walter Irvin and Samuel Shepherd were photographed on the ground next to McCall's car after the shooting on November 6, 1951. Moore called for an NAACP investigation that concluded McCall had asked the prisoners to get out of the car and then shot them. (Florida State Archives)

Two years earlier, jailer Reuben Hatcher (left) and Sheriff Willis McCall (right) stand with the three young men charged with rape in the Groveland case. They are (from left) Charlie Greenlee, 16, Samuel Shepherd, 22, and Walter Irvin, 22. Moore's tireless support helped them achieve a temporary victory when NAACP lawyers got their convictions overturned by the U.S. Supreme Court in 1951. (AP/Wide World Photos)

Today, Evangeline Moore is an influential author, speaker, and NAACP advocate. Her sister, Peachey, died of heart disease in the 1970s. (Evangeline Moore)

HARRY T. MOORE: PROFILE OF A MARTYR FOR CIVIL RIGHTS

An annual Memorial Service is held at the burial site of Harry T. and Harriett Moore in Mims, Florida. Standing in the center is Charles Cherry, 1976 NAACP state president.

Long-time NAACP supporters gathered at the memorial service in 1978 included (left to right) Richard Powell, Liberty City Branch (Miami); Earl Shinholster, Southeast Regional Director, Atlanta; Neal Adams, Liberty City; Robert W. Saunders; Dr. W. H. Gibson, national NAACP Board Chairman; and Albert Davis, Tampa Branch delegate.

When dozens of students from the NAACP youth council asked to be served at the lunch counter in Tampa's W. T. Grant department store, the manager refused service and posted a sign announcing that the counter was being "closed for cleaning purposes." (Tampa Tribune)

6
The Tampa Story

Racial discrimination always has been an issue in Tampa, although the situation usually has been complicated. As a child I lived in a West Tampa neighborhood with Cubans, Whites, and Italians. We played together, but we were not allowed to attend the same schools or churches. The implications of this situation were clearer to me than to other children in the area. Because I had lived in New York City for a brief time in my childhood, I had attended schools with all races and ethnic groups. At an early age, I had been able to see that differences existed.

In Florida, racial segregation was a way of life. I hated it. After being discharged from the Army Air Corps in 1946, I did return to Tampa for several months. The fact that White community leaders felt no obligation or responsibility for recognizing African American rights, even after our servicemen had offered the supreme sacrifice for their country, disgusted me. So, it was an easy matter for me to take Major Fred D. Minnis's advice and move North. While I lived and worked in Cincinnati and Detroit, I enjoyed the freedom to eat, shop, and ride buses without the stigma of segregation. Conditions in those cities were not perfect, but they made a real difference.

Being a newspaperman made things even better, giving me added confidence to demand decent treatment. I will always remember my first press pass issued by Cincinnati's Chief Weatherly in 1946. This pass opened many doors. I learned a great deal and gained experience needed for my future civil rights career, even though I did not dream at that time what the near future held for me. I came away from that experience certain that, as a Black man, I could make a difference in the face of White racism.

When I returned to Florida in 1952 as the NAACP's state field secretary, I was thrown back into the bitter Jim Crow system. I was not the same young man who had left the state, though, nor was I alone. I would enjoy the full support of the national NAACP to attack racism in every segment of life throughout the state. One of my first assignments, for example, was to take a lead in forcing elimination of "White" and "Colored" signs displayed in public facilities. Beyond that, we intended to attack discrimination in employment, housing, education, political activities, recreation, and transportation. The "Fight for Freedom," as the NAACP called it, knew no bounds. I vowed that I would work diligently to ensure that the NAACP program succeeded.

Because I located state NAACP headquarters in Tampa and because it was my home town, events that occurred there held special meaning to me and to my work.[1] I have mentioned earlier that the NAACP Tampa branch boasted a long history, stretching back to the mid-1910s. Even before that, my grandmother Marion E. Rogers and others had organized to demand better schools and living conditions. Reminders of those early efforts surrounded me as a child. My grandmother, of course, spoke of them to me. Every day, the delivery of the mail reinforced her stories. Herbert Lester, our postman, had stood forth courageously as one of the early leaders.

There were many others such as Mr. Lester who crowded into my early Tampa life. More than 110 men and women had put forward their names when the first Tampa NAACP organized back before World War One. Daniel W. Perkins presided. Soon, he entered the military and served with honor during the war. Afterward, as an attorney in Jacksonville, he pioneered legal initiatives on behalf of civil rights. Christina Meacham, a truly distinguished teacher and businesswoman, succeeded Perkins. Hundreds of my fellow students bore the stamp of her determination and character.

The names connected with the Tampa NAACP and with my life go on. From the 1920s and afterward they included Dr. Jacob A. White and attorney Z. D. Greene, who subsidized his law practice by teaching; E. E. Broughton, treasurer of the Central Life Insurance Company; C. Blythe Andrews, Sr., also of Central Life and later the editor of the *Florida Sentinel* and *Florida Sentinel-Bulletin*; Mrs. Jewel Archie, wife of Dr. E. O. Archie; Henry Hudson and Michael Lazarus, Sr., local union officials; Luther Maddox; Dewey Richardson, a relentless advocate of voter registration; James Johnson; Harold Reddick, a railroad porter; Matthew Gregory (Reddick and Gregory were close friends of Florida-born A. Philip Randolph and of E. D. Nixon, who organized the Montgomery, Alabama, protests); Willie Warren; Norman E. Lacey; Leonard Pressley; and Dan Malloy. Our courageous newspaper editor and A.M.E. clergyman Marcellus D. Potter of the *Tampa Bulletin* deserves mention all on his own.

While all of these individuals and others shared a desire to change conditions, they divided on how best to accomplish the goal. By the 1940s, two main factions existed within the Tampa branch. Broughton and Andrews, as leaders of the more-conservative group, advocated a "go slow" position. Reddick, Gregory, Warren, Lacey, Pressley, and Malloy were restless and more immediate activists. They protested police brutality and discrimination against Black people. They held strong positions on how to deal with Tampa's Jim Crow policies. Suffice it to say, the two factions found it difficult to agree on a unified program to eliminate segregation. The efforts made therefore suffered, since local power could not be focused to its full extent.

The NAACP attempted to resolve this situation in 1945. The national office dispatched Ella Baker, a field secretary, to mediate between the two groups. Baker had her hands full. Branch meetings sometimes became so heated that arguments ended with mild fisticuffs. Fortunately, the rancor calmed somewhat after Elder Straughn, the pastor of the Seventh Day Adventist Church, became president. The branch opened an office in Holsey Temple C.M.E. Church on Nebraska and Third Avenues. About that time Ella Baker returned for a second Tampa trip, providing crucial support for Straughn's conciliatory efforts.

Peace reigned to a sufficient extent by 1948 for the Tampa branch to join with the Urban League in support of a proposal for a "Negro Housing Project." The group's spokesman, C. Blythe

Andrews, pointed to the city's failure to provide adequate housing for its Black citizens. He contended that, for twenty-two years, most local Whites had met every effort to provide decent housing for Blacks with opposition. At the time, many Black families lived in virtual squalor in an area near downtown known as the "Scrub." Its boundaries were Central Avenue on the west, Nebraska on the east, Scott Street on the north, and Cass Street on the south. For many, the Scrub appeared synonymous with infectious disease, crime, and substandard housing. Truly a deplorable neighborhood, its houses contained no indoor plumbing nor electricity. Eventually, the united pressure from the African American community moved city leaders. They created in place of the notorious Scrub the Central Park Village Housing Development, which would experience its own problems as the years passed.

Although returned veterans from World War Two played increasingly active roles in NAACP activities in the post-war era, many early branch members remained involved in the protests that developed in the 1950s and 1960s. One such case comes quickly to mind. In that instance a White police officer killed a Black man named Sam Ingram. The NAACP's Matthew Gregory led a committee which demanded that the city take action to punish the three officers who were suspected of being jointly responsible for Ingram's death. The NAACP, at the urging of its senior leaders, also protested the brutal beating of a Black woman by Tampa police, who had entered her home forcibly. Similarly, they protested loudly when sheriff's deputies beat a seventy-nine-year-old Black man, Cole Newcross.

In that era of the late 1940s and early 1950s, these leaders achieved some progress, but the inherent conservatism of many sometimes resulted in unfortunate setbacks. To cite one example, in 1949 the Tampa branch missed a golden opportunity to end racial segregation in Hillsborough County's public schools. James A. Hargrett, Sr., a former Middleton Senior High School teacher and the owner of a grocery store, filed suit in federal court opposing separate but equal schooling. This effort stood a good chance of success, since the case came under consideration by the NAACP for inclusion in the group of suits that resulted in the 1954 *Brown* decision by the United States Supreme Court. Sadly, before a federal district judge could rule on Hargrett's case, Black leaders compromised with the Hillsborough County school board. All they received were promises to improve the county's segregated Black schools. Following this agreement, the national NAACP's attorneys dropped Hillsborough County as the fifth school district slated for inclusion as part of the broader legal attack on school segregation.[2]

In the decade that followed the debacle of the Hargrett suit, a new type of leadership, one that refused to accept compromise, emerged throughout Florida. Black World War Two veterans, educated under the GI Bill, returned as attorneys, physicians, and teachers. Many of them had earned graduate degrees. One such man who affected the subsequent course of events in Tampa was Francisco A. Rodriguez, the son of Afro-Cuban parents. A graduate of Howard University's School of Law, Rodriguez joined with William A. Fordham, an alumnus of the Lincoln University School of Law, to form Tampa's first Black law partnership. Rodriguez and Fordham both held offices in the NAACP. For a brief spell, the former served as Tampa branch president but resigned because of civil rights cases that he was handling as an attorney. With support from Edward D. Davis, Fordham would become state conference president in 1952. Harold Jackson and Delano A. Stewart, two additional lawyers, followed similar paths.

The schools offered great contributions to NAACP work. A. J. Ferrell, Jr., Richard Pride, Edwin Artest, Benjamin D. Griffin, Garland V. Stewart, Aurillio Fernandez, and Dora Reeder numbered among the active principals. Probably a majority of local members during the 1950s were teachers. I especially recall the work of Florene Jones in helping to promote the November 1960 appearance of Dr. Martin Luther King, Jr., at the Fort Homer Hesterly Armory. But, there were so many more.

The leadership corps that motivated the Tampa branch through the civil rights era furnished tremendous service to our cause. Their names and faces remain vivid to me. Let me mention Ellen P. Green. A Central Life Insurance home office employee, in

1960 she became the second woman to serve as Tampa branch president and the first to do so in the modern era. In addition to Ellen, Levy Turner, Charles Stanford, C. J. DaValt, Robert L. Gilder, and Elder Warren Banfield made up the roster of branch presidents up to the time of my departure as Florida field secretary in 1966. Buttressed by the *Brown* decision, the 1956 United States Supreme Court opinion dissolving racial segregation on intra-city public transportation, and the 1964 Civil Rights Act, these individuals instigated the University of Tampa desegregation suit and gave support to high school and college students organizing sit-in protests, among other actions.

The subject of sit-in protests compels me to mention Charles Stanford again. Before becoming Tampa branch president, Stanford served as the adult supervisor to the fledgling NAACP Youth Council. As advisor to the youth group, he worked with the state and national youth programs. He often led students in sit-in protests. This fine man once was arrested along with youth council members Gwendolyn Tim, Shafter Scott, and another youth whose surname was McMillan while leading a protest at Morrison's Cafeteria. This group also tested the discriminatory practices at the SuperTest Oil Company's midway on Columbus Drive and Dale Mabry Highway.

Although they did not actively participate in sit-ins and other civil rights demonstrations, several ministers lent their support. I already have mentioned Marcellus D. Potter, the distinguished A.M.E. minister who published the *Tampa Bulletin*. Following in his footsteps were G. J. Oates, an A.M.E. minister; John C. Robinson, pastor of First Baptist Church of College Hill; William M. Scott, also a Baptist minister; and J. C. Haisley and S. M. Peck, both pastors of Tampa's historic St. Paul A.M.E. Church.

Another local minister loomed large in NAACP and civil rights activities. The Reverend A. Leon Lowry accepted the pastorate of Beulah Baptist Church in 1955. While he never served as president of the Tampa branch, he labored on behalf of the cause. In 1957 I asked Lowry to consider running for president of the Florida State Conference. He agreed, and in October delegates from all over the

THE TAMPA STORY

Rev. A. Leon Lowry stands outside the White House entrance gate prior to a meeting of a select NAACP Convention Committee with President John F. Kennedy, June 1962. We had prepared a number of legislative proposals and reports on significant civil rights issues. There was a productive and open exchange of views and information which helped provide groundwork for the administration's initiatives on civil rights legislation.

Harold N. Reddick, Tampa Branch executive committee member, talks with W. C. Patton, NAACP director of voter registration for the Southeast.

This photograph of Rev. A. Leon Lowry in his study is a double exposure, but it seems to capture two sides of this active, versatile individual.

Harold Reddick welcomes one-time Floridian A. Philip Randolph to Tampa. Randolph was honored at the 1965 state convention in West Palm Beach. (The Harold Reddick family)

Our city's stubborn racism can be read in this graffiti that I photographed near Tampa's downtown public library in 1979.

Klan gatherings and cross-burnings were part of the rural landscape around Tampa.

Rev. Jackson E. Jones and I (fifth and fourth from right) stand with the newly elected officers of the Fort Walton NAACP Branch, c. 1962.

state elected him to succeed the Reverend A. Joseph Reddick. Lowry held the office until November 1962, when Rutledge Pearson, the young president of the Jacksonville branch, took over the responsibilities of the office. It should be mentioned that the Reverend Lowry's civil rights credentials stood among the best. His NAACP work earned him respect in cities and towns throughout the state.

When I returned to Tampa in August 1952, news of the Tampa branch activities cheered me, especially as I learned of the problems to be faced in other parts of the state. At that time the local claimed more members than any other Florida branch. True, the president, Matthew Gregory, was not a "degrees" man with college training, but he brought solid experience and connections with regional and national significance. The experience stemmed from his work with men such as Montgomery, Alabama's E. D. Nixon. Gregory and Nixon shared membership in the Brotherhood of Sleeping Car Porters, the labor organization led by Gregory's friend A. Philip Randolph. The Tampa branch, through Gregory, thus could reach in an instant into the highest circles of national Black life and activism.

Remember, though, that in 1952 many people feared open participation in the NAACP. Memory of Harry Moore's violent death whispered caution into every ear. The White power structure still controlled the everyday lives of Tampa's substantial Black population. Even those African Americans who belonged to labor unions felt vulnerable. A Republican Congress after World War Two had enacted the Taft-Hartley Labor Relations Act to undercut union strength. Florida politicians fought among themselves to express strongest anti-union sentiment. My friend Perry Harvey, Sr., a distinguished Tampa labor leader, exhausted himself in the struggle against the hostile climate. Beyond that, Tampa's police department, true to southern traditions, maintained and enforced racist policies that restricted Black citizens. The quality of public schools, despite the hard work of Black educators, sagged well below those for better supported White schools.

Young people today may not be aware, but in 1952 decent jobs were few and far between for African Americans. The few Black persons working at the county courthouse or city hall performed only menial tasks. Tampa's Black bellmen and waiters held the respected positions. Railroad employees likewise enjoyed great esteem. Importantly, insurance companies controlled by African Americans offered some good jobs. Those particularly worthy of mention included the Central Life Insurance Company of Florida, the Atlanta Life Insurance Company, and the Afro-American Life Insurance Company.

From this group of workers, the men who benefitted from the small pool of decent jobs, came a few of the independent individuals who were able to speak out without immediate fear of economic reprisals. Black businessmen supplemented their numbers. The names of Henry Joyner, Charlie "Moon" Vanderhorst, and Moses White should be remembered. All, though, lived subject to reprisal, a fact that permeated the atmosphere and forced unfair compromise time and again. Compromise often victimized Black leaders, and the compromises perpetuated a separate class of citizenry.

In light of these conditions, the fact of my appointment and presence in Tampa helped to strengthen the local NAACP leadership. As a nationally appointed NAACP staff person, I interpreted NAACP policy, provided direction, and implemented the local aspects of the entire national program. Importantly, I was not beholden to local sources for my paycheck, which was signed in New York City by Walter White and, after Walter's passing, by Roy Wilkins. I am convinced that this single small fact made a monumental difference in my ability to further NAACP goals in Florida.

The first six years of my tenure saw the Tampa branch active but mostly engaged in a rebuilding process; then, beginning in 1958, it entered a period lasting years that certainly proved tumultuous, perhaps the most tumultuous times since Harry Moore's death in 1951. If not before, the branch now involved itself in all arenas, including public facilities, public and private education, housing, employment, transportation, voter education and registration, and, of course, the brutal attacks on Blacks by White police officers. This also was the time of the sit-in demonstrations, race riots in several Florida cities, and the infamous attack on the NAACP by the Florida legislature.

While engaged in all of the fights that I have mentioned, the Tampa branch came face to face with what may well have been a much larger fight, one that would touch the community profoundly. It regarded the question of urban renewal. Tampa was just one of many cities that qualified for federal funding to improve living conditions and eradicate slum areas. At first, urban renewal sounded attractive. The federal government would grant certain cities funding to improve the slum neighborhoods that Black people had been forced to occupy for more than a century. Soon, though, it became apparent that unintended consequences lurked behind the promising facade. Rather than eliminate slum conditions, urban renewal plans would compel Black citizens to occupy new slum areas. Perhaps they would not be as run down as the old slums and perhaps they would appear slightly better, but they were not built to last. For this reason, we dubbed the Urban Renewal Program as "Urban Slum Removal."

The physical impact of urban renewal should not be underestimated. In Tampa, contractors cleared the whole of the Central Avenue segment, as well as parts of Ybor City from around 22nd Street to 14th Avenue and from 7th Avenue to about Ross Avenue. The entire area from Cass Street to slightly beyond 7th Avenue and from Tampa Street to the Hillsborough River were purged of long-time Black homeowners to make way for the Tampa police station, the library, a motel, and the Curtis Hixon Auditorium.

The NAACP did not sit idly by while the redevelopment occurred. In 1957 Madison E. Jones assumed the position of national NAACP housing director. When the Tampa branch learned that the city would be participating in the urban renewal program as well as the federal project for constructing the new interstate highway system, it also discovered that the projects would adversely affect 60 percent of Tampa's Black population. Yet, the city had attempted little or no consultation with the Black population, including the NAACP. Accordingly, local branch officers asked Jones to visit Tampa to study plans for implementation of the new programs and to advise the NAACP of its role. Subsequently, Jones met with Mayor Nick Nuccio and city planners. He then advised the local branch to activate its steering committee on housing immediately. Jones also met with several Black realtors to let them known what was happening. The Reverend William H. Gordon took a leadership role as chairman of the housing committee.

The main thrust of Jones's advice came in a letter to Gordon that was mailed from New York City shortly after the official's return to national headquarters. "Of first importance is the problem presented by the proposal to build a courthouse and police station in the area of Scott, Estelle, and Fortune Streets," Jones wrote. He noted the residential character of that neighborhood and its high percentage of Black population. "The Mayor must be made aware of the fact that unless these people can be rehoused, and according to our policy dispersed throughout the city, we should oppose the program," he declared. "Therefore unless the city can come up with a rehousing program acceptable to us, we cannot go along with the present proposal." Finally, Jones advised Gordon to meet with the city planner as soon as possible to discuss the city's ultimate plans for those affected by urban renewal.[3]

Unfortunately, the suggested and critically important meeting never took place. I learned the facts after Jones asked me to inquire as to why his suggestions were not followed. Gordon, after reminding me that he operated one of the city's oldest Black funeral homes, replied that the committee could not delve into the city's affairs because, among other things, his funeral home received indigent bodies. I gathered from the statement that Gordon was not going to sacrifice his business with the city in order to fight for fair housing for Black residents.

On a happier note, the situation soon began to improve as new leadership took over the Tampa branch. Thereafter, the branch and its officers eagerly supported efforts to end housing discrimination by protesting Tampa's failure to comply with urban renewal requirements, including a fully representative citizens committee designated to consult with the urban renewal committee. One key statement that we issued in 1961 expressed the new consensus. "The overall practice of planning *for* and not planning *with* minority groups in the development of an Urban Renewal program for the entire community," the statement began, "has a tendency to relegate the affected minorities into positions of having others plan for the housing needs irrespective of the rights guaranteed as citizens of the state and nation." It continued, "It is essential that minority groups be represented in this planning and by persons who will defend their rights against encroachment while realizing that the program of Urban Renewal benefits the entire community when administered fairly."[4]

The NAACP realized, of course, that it would have to follow the city of Tampa's every move to ensure that Black citizens affected by urban renewal would have a fair chance to argue their positions, a circumstance that found echoes in most Florida cities. The Black communities throughout the state indeed were divided over the complicated issue. As such, Tampans fared little different than residents of other Florida cities. On the one hand, Black people anxiously desired to live in better housing, and some people did not mind that urban renewal plans would perpetuate racial segregation by forcing them to move to all-Black neighborhoods away from the city. On the other hand, a majority resented moving away from the neighborhoods in which they had lived and worked all of their lives. And, added to the equation, were those who hated the fact that the city masked its plans to ensure segregated housing by appearing to promote better housing for those affected by urban renewal.

Federal regulations offered us a foothold from which to launch our attack on Tampa's plans. Particularly, requirements of the federal urban renewal programs called for all those affected by urban renewal to have the opportunity to present their opinions. I knew that our 1961 statement, from which I quoted a few paragraphs ago, would not be enough to persuade the city to comply with federal regulations. So, I enlisted national office support from Jack E. Wood, Jr., who had succeeded Madison E. Jones. Wood assured me that, in his opinion, Tampa leaders would obey the federal requirements rather than risk losing federal funding. Then, as we agreed, Wood denounced a mayoral proposal to satisfy consultation requirements for one project, known as the Maryland Avenue Project. That particular scheme afforded a special panel of Black citizens only two weeks to review the plans and their impact.[5]

We then utilized Wood's protest to the Tampa mayor as a pretext for the Tampa branch's own response. Branch president Ellen P. Green received authority to file a complaint against the city with the office of Dr. Robert C. Weaver, Director of the Federal Housing Administration. She telegraphed Weaver vehemently opposing the city's defiance of federal requirements for representative citizens advisory committees. As she noted, the mayor's special committee constituted no more than a mockery of the Urban Renewal Administration's mandate. The Tampa branch suggested that the federal government consider removing Tampa from the urban renewal program.

Meanwhile, we strove to identify specific concerns about Tampa's approach. By June 15, 1961, I was able to list five important problems that the local branch had identified. In order to afford a feel for how far-ranging these concerns were, I think it appropriate to list them here:

> 1) The urban renewal commissions included seven people, all of whom were White. No Blacks had ever served on any of these committees.
>
> 2) Blighted areas already were being cleared and Blacks already were being removed. Not once did the commission establish a representative citizens advisory council.
>
> 3) All relocations efforts were following the same segregated housing patterns as before; Blacks were not being informed of certain regulations of fairness with regard to purchasing homes; and Blacks were being directed into buying housing in areas labeled "Negro communities."
>
> 4) Mayor Julian Lane's special committee for the Maryland Avenue Project, although 50 percent of its members were Black, was not fully representative. The Black people who served on the committee all shared the mayor's opinions.
>
> 5) As Blacks relocated into integrated areas, non-Blacks moved

out of the neighborhoods which, as a result, quickly were becoming all Black. Soon these homes would no longer have the market value at which Blacks had purchased them, because the area would have become racially segregated.[6]

There followed one year during which we endeavored to enforce change but city leaders dragged their feet. On June 23, 1962, the local branch again appealed to the city, pointing out its failure to comply with the federal regulations. Months passed. Five months later I directly requested that Mayor Lane appoint Black citizens to the urban renewal board. The response came when, late one night not long thereafter, Lane called my home and pleaded with me to withdraw the NAACP's complaint. He promised that the city would comply with the mandated regulation from then on. Accepting this as a good faith offer, the NAACP withdrew its petition, and Lane established a biracial committee and a city planning committee. Even then, the biracial committee failed to represent all viewpoints.

Attempts to further this little bit of progress, so hard won, stalled, partly due to persistent divisions within the Black community. For the time being the city ignored most of the NAACP's complaints. This came, in good part, because some Black leaders who stood to profit from urban renewal chose to support the city. Black Tampans paid the price. The destruction of the Maryland Avenue neighborhood compelled many residents to move to Progress Village, a housing development whose residents were and are all Black. Similarly, the core of the Black business district along Central Avenue faced the bulldozers and wrecking balls. Some businessmen transferred to West Tampa; others never reestablished their concerns.

And, the NAACP's battle over housing in its various forms had only begun. To cite an example, Leon Lowry in 1962 addressed the issue of hotel and motel segregation as it affected Black troops. Managers denied Black airmen from MacDill Air Force Base rental space in several trailer parks. This time, the federal government could resolve the problem without recourse to local officialdom. Responding to our initiatives, federal authorities barred all military personnel from renting housing in trailer parks that had discriminated against Black service personnel. Given some fits and starts, the action effectively addressed this legitimate concern.

The Tampa branch's housing efforts finally took a major step forward following passage of the 1964 Civil Rights Act, although the posture of some Whites still left us shaking our heads. In that year Robert Gilder served as branch president. He and I met with officials of the Tampa Housing Authority and asked them if they knew what the passage of the act would mean for fair housing. They told us no. At that time the authority had yet to implement any anti-discrimination safeguards in its housing programs. Now, though, the law read clear. With assistance from Federal Housing Administration officials, we worked out an agreement with the Tampa authority to assign housing on a racially non-discriminatory basis. All eligible applicants' names would be listed on a first-come, first-served basis. Applicants would be assigned accordingly. Soon, other branches followed the Tampa branch's lead and were able to entertain the Fair Housing Program with the aid of Jack E. Wood and the state conference.

The challenge of ending racial discrimination in public accommodations posed serious difficulties, just as did ending public housing discrimination. Here, though, the sit-in protests gained significant victories in Tampa. In achieving them, we were fortunate to benefit from the experiences of Edna Branch. Edna had participated in youth activities at Savannah, Georgia, but she spent summers visiting relatives in Tampa. In Savannah, she had gained a great deal of insight into how protests were carried out.

Edna Branch's knowledge informed members of Tampa's 1960 NAACP Youth Council, a group that consisted of high school and college students who were eager to contribute in any way they could to the civil rights struggle. My office served as the main meeting place for these students. Before the sit-ins they already had proved a ready asset to us. They designed posters, helped prepare mailings, and performed other tasks. The group also worked on voter registration projects. Still, these activities were not enough to exhaust their energies. Edna worked diligently with me to help direct those energies in peaceful, nonviolent protests. With a total membership that rarely, if ever, exceeded 110, the Youth Council soon led the attack against discrimination at restaurants and lunch counters. They protested, as well, by picketing local movie theaters. So that their contributions can be remembered, let me especially mention Youth Council members Clarence Fort, Arthenia Joyner, Lorenzo Brown, Gwendolyn Tim, Terasea Van, Henry Carley, Shafter Scott, James Hargrett, Jr., and Cheryle Pride.

Whether directly or indirectly, adults naturally assisted the young people, including some surprising ones who were White. The Reverend J. C. Haisley, pastor of St. Paul A.M.E. Church, offered his sanctuary as the starting point for marches to businesses that continued to discriminate, including Grants and Woolworth. Leon Lowry, NAACP state conference president and pastor of Beulah Baptist Institutional Church, sometimes joined the marchers. I am very pleased to say that all of those who courageously demanded their rights received better treatment in Tampa that in some other places. At Jacksonville, for instance, the Ku Klux Klan, armed with baseball bats, met youth protestors. At Tampa, though, Mayor Julian Lane instructed the local police to protect demonstrators and to arrest anyone who threatened them. Indeed, the law enforcement officers arrested several White men, some of whom were carrying baseball bats.

One community mechanism helped to encourage the cooperative attitude illustrated by Mayor Lane's action. In 1959 the mayor had appointed a biracial committee called the Community Relations Board. Black members of the board included Leon Lowry, Perry Harvey, Sr., C. Blythe Andrews, Sr., Raynell Sloan, Elder Warren Banfield, the Reverend W. H. Calhoun, and Clarence Wilson. A number of White community leaders joined them, among whom were attorney Cody Fowler, Sandy Moffett, "Bob" Thomas, A. R. Ragsdale, Father Wilson Dodd, and Byron Bushwell. This group had supported modest changes, although the White community opposed their implementation.

When the sit-ins began in 1960, they had the effect of compelling less activist Blacks and Whites to move forward, however reluctantly. Members of the Community Relations Board met with the youth leaders and NAACP officials. Interestingly, in the face of insistence by their elders for accommodation, youth council members refused to compromise. Terasea Van at one meeting pursued her argument so insistently that, when one Black member of the board mentioned that other adult members should not support the protests, she started banging on the table with her shoe. The sit-ins continued, and peaceful change resulted with the acquiescence of important segments of the White leadership.

Another youth activist group helped to bring about the progress that was made at Tampa. James Hammond organized the Young Adults for Progressive Action. I did not always agree with him on ideas and tactics, and I felt that there was no need for another organization while the NAACP was playing such an important role. Yet, Hammond and his organization gave support to the "fight for freedom" by making substantive contributions. I respected Hammond because he was a fighter. He responded to my attempts to press for one organization by noting that many young adults were reluctant to be identified with the NAACP. Some were teachers, and others held jobs with White establishments. They feared economic reprisals and the recent legislative attack against the NAACP.

An illustration of Hammond's determination to fight racial inequality relates to an event that involved his command as an Army Reserve officer. As a captain, Hammond once led an interracial company of soldiers traveling by Greyhound bus to Fort Benning, Georgia, for summer training. Arrangements had been made for the group to dine at the Greyhound terminal in Tallahassee. As was typical for the time, Black travelers were forced to eat in a dingy, often crowded and dirty area reserved for "Colored." Hammond knew that bus company officials would demand that he segregate the soldiers by race. White soldiers, regardless of their rank, would be allowed to dine in the "White" dining room. Black troops, with Hammond among them, would be subjected to the indignity of being ordered to use a separate part of the restaurant.

Looking ahead to this potential problem, Hammond made plans before his departure from Tampa. First, he and I met to discuss the situation. He insisted that he would not disgrace his position as the commanding officer by allowing his company to be racially segregated. He told me that he would insist upon his entire group eating in the "White" dining area. We agreed that, in order to allow some alternative, I would contact Dr. George Gore, president of Florida A&M University; explain to Dr. Gore what we expected would occur; and ask him to accommodate the group if Hammond's attempt failed. Dr. Gore in fact agreed to have the university's dining room prepare to accommodate all of the soldiers if the Black men were refused service in the White dining area. I also contacted Clarence Mitchell, director of the NAACP Washington Bureau, as well as Tampa attorney Francisco Rodriguez and officials at the United States Department of Defense.

Hammond thereupon carried through with his determination, at what became a great threat to his military career. As expected, the cafeteria manager refused to serve the Black and White soldiers together. He demanded to know who had the nerve to bring Black soldiers into the White restaurant. Though Hammond responded that he was the commanding officer and that they were traveling under orders that required the men to eat together, the manager refused any reconsideration. Rather than segregate the command, Hammond ordered the troops to reboard the bus. They went to Florida A&M University, where the staff received the men with warm hospitality. Without Dr. Gore's help—though little appreciated by some, he stood tall against pressures from segregationist legislatures and the Florida Board of Regents—Hammond would have been forced to segregate his troop.

The matter did not end there. United States Representative Bob Sykes, whose district ran through the Florida Panhandle, fumed at Hammond's action. A rabid segregationist from Crestview, Sykes accused Hammond of embarrassing the White soldiers and called for the captain to be decommissioned. Hammond stood firm in the face of this bullying, and the army agreed with him. He retained his commission. We all took pride in Hammond and in what he had done.

Tampa's racial problems were too numerous to include all of them in this chapter. Suffice it to say that the NAACP, with limited resources, was faced with a tremendous task as it sought to bring about institutional change. In Florida, we often began those efforts with initiatives at Tampa, my home and the NAACP's state headquarters. Even then, without financial assistance from the national NAACP office and the NAACP Legal Defense Fund, challenges to illegal discrimination in the courts and on the streets often would have been impossible. I should mention that Tampa's Francisco Rodriguez and other Black lawyers gave their talents to this fight, often without remuneration. Black people owe a tremendous debt to this group of professionals and to the many men, women, and children who put their own lives and lifestyles on the line for civil rights progress.

I wished constantly with all of my heart that it was not so, but truthfully our efforts at Tampa—this was true elsewhere, as well—barely scratched the surface. Change came at an excruciatingly slow pace and at great cost. For many, the changes appeared imperceptible. How often did I and other civil rights advocates explain to the man in the street that the annual two-dollar membership in the NAACP was not an insurance policy? To the man in the street it was often difficult to explain the benefits of the NAACP's work, however strongly my heart compelled me to want to do so.

NAACP Youth Councils often led sit-ins at local lunch counters. Rev. A. Leon Lowry was state president when he joined the young people at Woolworth's in Tampa on the second day of demonstrations there, March 2, 1960. (Clarence Fort)

Clarence Fort was the 21-year-old president of the Tampa NAACP Youth Council in 1960 (photo at left). He is also in the photograph above, seated second from the right at the Woolworth lunch counter on the first day of demonstrations, February 29, 1960. As he sat at the counter, he read from the Bible. The protest ended when he and others were served peacefully. A few years later we successfully integrated the Hillsborough County schools when my son Bobby (below, second from left) became a sixth grade student at MacFarlane Elementary School. (Top two photos courtesy of Clarence Fort)

Florida enjoyed top-notch representation at NAACP national meetings. Mrs. Vernell Albury, treasurer of the Miami Branch, and Mrs. Eula Johnson, Ft. Lauderdale chapter president, prepare to board a convention train from the 1962 Philadelphia meeting. The entire convention adjourned for Washington, D.C., to lobby for civil rights legislation. Both of these women were called to testify before the Florida legislature's witch-hunting Johns Committee.

This is me trying to look as official as I can, seated at my state headquarters desk in 1958.

Here I was talking with Rutledge H. Pearson and Lloyd Pearson in 1962, shortly after Rutledge achieved election as state conference president. He spoke at St. Paul A.M.E. Church in Tampa. (Florida Sentinel-Bulletin)

The Tampa Story

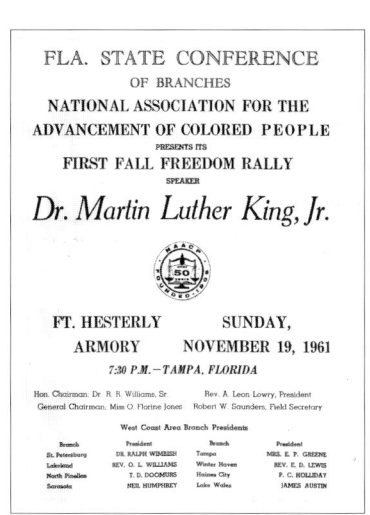

When Dr. King spoke at our November 1961 "First Fall Freedom Rally," racists phoned in a bomb threat and forced evacuation of Tampa's Fort Homer Hesterly Armory. The threat failed to stop Dr. King or our freedom rally.

A committee of sixty persons representing the NAACP met in the White House Oval Office in 1962 to call for far-reaching civil rights legislation. Our suggestions formed the context for the 1964 Civil Rights Act. Following the meeting, President John F. Kennedy offered us a tour of his office. Aaron Henry and I are to the left of the President; Patricia Harris and Theodore Berry are standing at far right.

Florida's Governor LeRoy Collins, a one-time segregationist who, with prodding from the NAACP, eventually offered Florida positive leadership for change, speaks at a 1984 banquet in Tallahassee sponsored by the Florida conference of NAACP branches in honor of the 75th anniversary of the founding of the NAACP. State Conference President Charles W. Cherry is in the background. (Florida Department of Commerce Division of Tourism)

7
LeRoy Collins:
A Moderate Governor in the Deep South

Perhaps no Florida governor in the twentieth century has received the critical praise that has been bestowed upon LeRoy Collins, who served in the executive office from January 4, 1955, to January 3, 1961. The fact of his personal integrity and honesty remains unquestioned, but we really remember him for his reputed liberalism on racial issues. As two University of Florida scholars noted in an analysis of Florida's chief executives during this century, "While he personally opposed the [*Brown*] decision [ruling racial segregation in public schools unconstitutional], he blocked repeated efforts by the legislature to close schools to prevent integration." They continued, "In his last two years as governor, he led an educational effort to persuade white Floridians that integration was inevitable and that they should begin preparing for it."[1]

I would not challenge Collins's ranking when judged next to most of Florida's other twentieth-century governors, but he was a politician and, as such, my working experience with him was mixed. His political courage concerning racial matters never led him too far out front of the White voting public, and his actions often required prompting by the NAACP and other civil rights groups. Collins lived as a decent human being, not a saint. He deserves to be remembered that way.

Collins's past little suggested his emergence as even a reluctant ally of the civil rights movement, growing up in mostly rural Leon County, where Old South ways remained alive. Still, there were signs. Edward D. Davis, who served as president of our state conference at the time I was employed as field secretary, knew the future governor when he served in the Florida legislature as a state senator. I remember Davis remarking, "Collins was born in the heart of the Jim Crow South, but even during his legislative career, he could see beyond the horizons of racial prejudice and support the Constitution of the United States."

During his early political years Collins proclaimed his adherence to the doctrines of racial segregation, a fact that made his later denunciation of that pernicious creed so surprising to Black Floridians, the NAACP, and the Florida legislature. Naturally, the NAACP at first remained skeptical of Collins's change of heart, but as national attention focused on his decisions to resolve discrimination in schools, restaurants, and other public facilities, we became pleasantly assured of the governor's personal commitment to ridding Florida of its Jim Crow heritage. For instance, to our delight Collins supported the NAACP when, in Jacksonville, peaceful demonstrators from the local NAACP Youth Council were confronted by the Ku Klux Klan, whose members threatened and attacked the young people with baseball bats. Following the incident, Collins sent a staff member to work with the community to resolve the racial problems in Jacksonville.

Decisions such as those Collins made in the Jacksonville crisis gave Black Floridians a new sense of hope in the state's White leadership, but the change away from his segregationist past came only slowly. As I will discuss in the pages that follow, his evolution in thinking and policy resulted partly from NAACP pressure and partly from his reaction to a zealous segregationist opponent in his 1956 re-election campaign.

During the early days of Collins's tenure as governor, he made comments that left the NAACP wondering just what his position on civil rights really was. In one of his speeches, for example, he declared that "the heavy hand of coercion whether by judicial or bayonets or otherwise should be taken off the South and allow Southerners to resolve our sins of racial discrimination, such as it may be, in our own time."[2] This statement left me confused. After all, Collins had to realize that, without judicial mandates, the South would never change. I agreed with Ruth Perry, the White secretary of the Miami NAACP branch who also authored a weekly column in the liberal *Miami Times*. "Parts of his last speech would be considered very liberal by diehard segregationists," she wrote. "But I am wondering if Collins is speaking as a politician or with sincere belief." Perry continued: "I must confess that every time anyone mentions letting the South resolve its own problems, by its own efforts, in its own time, I take a very dim view of the whole thing."[3] In fact, most Black Floridians took a very dim view of Collins's comments. How could we, faced with threats of economic reprisals or—worse—violence against us and our families, agree with the governor?

Collins further disappointed the NAACP during his first term in office when he refused to take a firm stand against segregationists in the case of Black voters in Liberty County, located in the Florida Panhandle's most rural region. I became personally involved with this situation after I became acquainted with the Reverend Dee Hawkins in 1956. A native of Liberty County, he struck me as a truly fine man, especially after I saw how deeply devoted he was to the care of his mother of more than ninety years. In any event, Hawkins had emerged as the county's leading Black activist with a strong commitment to the civil rights struggle. To further his goals, the minister attempted to establish an NAACP branch, but he received little support from the county's intimidated Black residents. In order for the NAACP to maintain a presence in Liberty County, we helped Hawkins organize an authorized committee, which required only seven members.

The next step for Hawkins came with his determination to register Blacks to vote in local elections, a tremendous challenge in a county where African Americans had not cast ballots since the nineteenth century. Early on he requested that I meet with him and his committee on several occasions at nearby Blountstown. Ater the last such session, he urgently insisted that I come to his house in the woods outside Bristol. Ku Klux Klan members, who prowled the county at will, had threatened to burn his home. With rumors swirling of potential racial violence, my wife Helen expressed her concerns for my safety and insisted that she accompany me to this remote area. Accordingly, she and I traveled by automobile one Sunday morning from Tallahassee to Bristol. When we arrived, quiet marked the little town. Few people, particularly Black people, were walking the streets.

The meeting occurred at Hawkins's home. He lived in a roughly honed, unpainted wooden frame house. I remember that the grass surrounding it had been freshly cut to a line of pine trees. Hawkins told us that he owned all of the land, including several acres of the pines. "Each week I have to threaten some Whites to stop them from cutting my timber," he declared. "Black folks up here continue to face danger in protecting our own property." He continued, "We can't vote, and we have to send our children into another county to go to school." I felt his keen anguish and frustration as Hawkins talked. He possessed a fierce determination to register Blacks to vote, for he believed that voting provided the only means by which Blacks effectively could make a difference in their lives.

After listening to Hawkins that day, I promised him that the NAACP would do everything possible to protect his voters. Then I cautioned him against retaliating against White provocations with violence. I also gave him Clarence Mitchell's telephone number as NAACP Washington bureau director and instructed Hawkins to call me and Mitchell should an emergency arise. As Helen and I drove back to Tampa that evening, we worried about Hawkins and his elderly mother residing in such an isolated, wooded area.

Events in Liberty County thereafter evolved in terrible ways. Through Hawkins's persistent efforts, he managed to get twelve Black citizens, including himself, registered to vote. White segregationists, as expected, began intimidating these individuals. Hawkins called me with an urgent plea for help. "All Hell has broken loose up here," he declared. "Since we went down and put our names on the rolls, the KKK has threatened me and the rest of us." Hawkins added: "We been told that if we take our names off the books, nothing will happen to us. I'm trying to tell others to don't give up." His voice filled with emotion and desperation as he told me what occurred on his property each night. "They hide in the brush behind the trees, and they keep telling me to come out and talk with them," he explained. "But I ain't going to do it." Hawkins continued: "They threw some kerosene rags and talked about burning me out of the house. I tell them that the first one that shows his face will get shot cause I got my gun fully loaded. I ain't gonna let them harm me or my mother."

It was at this point that my hopes for Governor Collins plummeted. I wrote the governor on February 10, 1956, to report the incident to him. I requested that he take measures to protect the registered voters to ensure that their voting privileges were not threatened.[4] Collins responded by promising to investigate the incident. Then all of us, including Collins, learned from the media that ten of the twelve newly registered Liberty County voters had withdrawn their names from the books, supposedly on a voluntary basis. I wired the governor, demanding that he provide protection. He refused to send assistance, an act that insulted me and those courageous Liberty Countians. He insisted that, since the voters withdrew their names on their own accord, his hands were tied. How could he actually have believed that the voters gave up their constitutional rights and voluntarily withdrew their names? Hawkins, a true hero, never gave up. He later relocated to Tallahassee. I learned that he had lost most of that rich timber that had graced his land when White segregationists burned his property.

Collins's refusal to intercede in the Liberty County crisis came during the year in which he sought re-election as governor, but, after he achieved a primary victory later in 1956 (the win assured a general election triumph), we noticed a definite change in his position. He had been forced to run against an arch-segregationist from Tampa, and I think that the experience disgusted Collins. In the aftermath, he began to support the NAACP's efforts more consistently. To cite one example, when the Democratic Party Site Committee chose Miami as the party's 1960 convention site, the Reverend A. Leon Lowry, NAACP state conference president, attorney Francisco Rodriguez, and I asked that the Democratic Party require the state to end racial segregation. We knew that, otherwise, hundreds of black delegates would be forced to endure untold discrimination as hotels, restaurants, train and bus stations, gas stations, and other public facilities remained strictly segregated. Unfortunately, rather than confront the state legislators, the site committee chose Los Angeles in place of Florida's largest city. Rather than criticize us for our actions, Governor Collins agreed with the NAACP and declared that the state, itself, was to blame for losing lucrative business opportunities.

Another incident that reflected Collins's more aggressive support for civil rights related to the kidnapping of a Sumter County man, Jesse Woods. The story began in November 1958 when Woods was arrested at Wildwood. The charge stemmed from a complaint that he had whistled at a White woman inside the local A&P food store. The police incarcerated Woods in the Wildwood jail. During the night, a mob of White men broke into the jail and took Woods away with them. On the same night, the Florida State Conference of the NAACP was in session at Tampa. Delegates from across the state were attending the annual Freedom Fund Dinner. No one, including me, had heard of the Woods incident.

As fate would have it, Roy Wilkins, national NAACP executive director, was scheduled to speak the following day at a mass meeting at St. Paul A.M.E. Church in Tampa. Roy was traveling by train, which happened to stop at Wildwood where it was broken into sections. One section continued to travel to Tampa while the other went east and south to Miami. Roy heard about the kidnapping during the layover. I met him at Tampa's Union Station, whereupon he immediately asked me, "What about the suspected lynching of a Black prisoner last night?" His words caught me by surprise. Here was my boss telling me about an incident that had occurred less than 100 miles away from a convocation of almost every NAACP leader in the state.

As I prepared to leave for Wildwood early the next day, I stopped by my office at 705 East Harrison Street, the same building in which the International Longshoreman Association also kept their headquarters. When I arrived that Monday morning, I chanced to see Perry Harvey, Sr., the union's local president. He and other members advised me against traveling alone to Wildwood. One union member (he still lives in Clearwater but, unfortunately, I cannot recall his name) volunteered to go with me. I was grateful for the assistance for, during my six-year tenure with the NAACP, I had never investigated a lynching.

The scene that we encountered at Wildwood proved chilling. The streets lay deserted. Though I had been through the town many times, never had I seen the streets so empty, particularly for a Monday morning. We noticed an elderly Black man who was standing beside the road and asked him to direct us to a restaurant. He got into the car, promising to take us to a small place owned by a Black woman. Our new-found friend and guide began asking us questions. He wanted to know if we had come from Tampa. "Are you from the NAACP?" he asked as if he had been expecting us. I assured him that I was the state field secretary, and I gave him one of my cards. "Good," he responded, "we've been expecting you."

The guide took us elsewhere than the promised restaurant, and his diversion inadvertently brought us into contact with Governor Collins's staff and suspicions that lingered about him. At the man's directions, we drove east on Highway 48 for several miles until we came to a dirt road. There we came upon a tiny settlement of small, wooden frame houses. He asked us to stop at the house with all the reporters in front. He pointed to one heavy-set man seated on the steps talking to a Black woman. "The fat man you see talking to my sister said he's from Governor Collins's office," our guide told me. "But we ain't talking to him or no one else." He added: "Keep driving further down the road until you come to another house. We'll talk there." The second house also belonged to relatives of Woods. Here our friend introduced us as the NAACP men from Tampa. Only then did the real story of what happened to Jesse Woods begin to surface.

One of Woods's relatives told us what happened after the arrest. They put Woods in jail and left it unguarded. Late that night, some White men broke into the jail and took Woods out into a wooded area. There, they beat him and left him for dead. They drove off unaware that Woods was still alive and able to crawl to the edge of the dirt road. His uncle, who was leaving for Fort Walton Beach where he worked on a road construction project, found him there early on Sunday morning. The uncle took Jesse, who was bloody and sore, back to the settlement and gave him first aid. Woods's uncle and others then rolled him into a rug and placed him in the back seat of a car. They did not know for sure where Woods was taken, but they believed that he had made it to a section of Miami called Liberty City. They wanted me to find him quickly before his abductors realized that he was still alive.

On behalf of the state conference, I agreed to undertake the search. My union friend and I drove back to Tampa from where I called Father Theodore Gibson, president of the Miami branch, and Richard Powell, a Liberty City branch officer. I asked them to go to the address given to me by Woods's relatives to see if Woods was there. I cautioned them not to reveal to anyone what they were doing. Late that night Father Gibson called to say that their mission had proved fruitless. This meant that I would have to return to Wildwood for additional information.

On the return trip I enjoyed the company of a new companion. Bettye Murphy, a member of the family that owned Baltimore's African American newspaper, was a friend of Francisco Rodriguez and was visiting in Tampa in order to cover the Wildwood incident. They asked if she could go with me on Tuesday. I agreed, and we set off for Woods's uncle's home at Wildwood. As it turned out, the uncle did not know where Wood was but said that he would show us where we could get more information. We drove to a fishing camp. There we borrowed a rowboat from the owner and proceeded down the Withlacoochee River. Approximately one mile downstream, we encountered six people fishing with cane poles. Woods's uncle began talking to an elderly Black woman. He told her that I was with the NAACP and could be trusted. The woman hesitated briefly before telling us to go to her house and lift up the rug where a loose floor board could be found. Underneath we would find a letter with a Fort Walton Beach address. Woods, she revealed, was located at that address.

The search now had led us just about from one end of Florida to the other. Back in Tampa, I discussed my next move with attorney Rodriguez. Meanwhile, members of the media began to show up at NAACP headquarters. Apparently, they suspected that I knew something about Woods's whereabouts. But I was not talking. Rather, I was preparing for more travel. Bettye Murphy eagerly desired to leave for Fort Walton Beach and agreed to pay for my round-trip airfare if I would let her accompany me again. I agreed. Traveling as Mr. and Mrs. Smith to avoid the media, we flew to Panama City where we then set out for Fort Walton Beach by car.

Disappointment again greeted us when we reached our destination, but events soon led me into closer contact with the governor. First, we found no one at home at the Fort Walton Beach address. Murphy insisted on entering the house anyway. As the door was unlocked, we gave in to temptation and stepped inside. In the back room we discovered blood-soaked bandages and a blood-soaked rug. We also found a bottle of medication. Yes, Woods had been there and we were on the right track. When the occupants returned home, I introduced myself and Murphy and showed them the letter that had been given to us with their address on it. They told me that, only one hour previously, Woods had been moved to Dothan, Alabama, where a local minister had taken the injured man into his care. The news tempted me to go to Alabama, but I resisted because I knew that the NAACP had been enjoined from operating there. We returned to Tampa by way of Tallahassee, where we stayed at the home of Dr. Nick Williams, a dentist and supporter. Bettye, while making a telephone call to Baltimore, was overheard by an operator telling of our discovery. The word soon leaked.

Federal authorities and Governor Collins thereupon assumed active roles in the drama. Having returned to Tampa, I was greeted by two Federal Bureau of Investigation agents who came to my home. They wanted to know Woods's location. I agreed to give the information only after they agreed to guarantee that Woods would be protected once he was apprehended. The two agents contacted Collins, who assured them that the state would protect Woods. Only after learning of the governor's promise did I reveal Woods's refuge. Several hours later the agents called me to confirm that they had found Woods and that he was in protective custody. The governor issued a strong statement condemning the acts of the cowards who abducted Woods. Florida NAACP officials praised his leadership; yet, to this day, I do not believe that the NAACP ever has been credited with finding Woods.

Before closing this chapter, let me add an additional instance of LeRoy Collins's positive leadership, one that found him supporting the NAACP in a case that involved Lake County's notorious racist sheriff, Willis McCall. My involvement started on Christmas Eve 1957 when Melvin Hawkins, Sr., brother of Virgil Hawkins (the plaintiff in the University of Florida desegregation suit), met with me and attorney Rodriguez at my home. Hawkins appeared visibly upset that his son Melvin Hawkins, Jr., had been arrested and charged in Lake County with the crime of raping of a White woman. Someone had told him that they overhead Sheriff McCall telling one of his deputies to arrest "young nigger Hawkins" because he was the nephew of "that nigger who was trying to get into the University of Florida."

Clearly we needed to move fast, and only the governor possessed enough power in the state to restrain McCall. It was near 11:00 p.m. when I called the governor's mansion in Tallahassee. Mrs. Collins answered the telephone. I asked to speak with the governor. When she replied that he was asleep, I explained that this was an urgent matter. I spoke with the governor, who then talked with Hawkins for about one hour. He gave Hawkins his word that his son would be located and protected. The next day young Hawkins was released from McCall's custody. He remained in Lake County, a law-abiding citizen, until his death in 1994.[5] After Hawkins's release, authorities arrested someone else for the rape. It turned out that the culprit was a teenaged White youth said to be suffering from a mental illness.

Governor Collins continued to support desegregation efforts and, in doing so, won the favor of the NAACP. As his decisions drew national attention, the President of the United States even favored him. President Lyndon B. Johnson invited Collins to serve as the director of his Community Relations Service. NAACP leaders in Florida believed that we had helped to prepare him for the outstanding job that he did as the agency's director. He proved to us that, in the end, he was a good man who had outgrown his past and deserved to be remembered for the good that he accomplished.

Father Theodore Gibson, president of the Miami Branch NAACP (left), and Richard Powell, one of the officers of the Liberty City Branch, stop for a photo in front of the Miami Branch office. Both of them were activists during the Collins years. When I began the search for Jesse Woods, one lead reported he might have been taken to an address in Liberty City, near Miami. I asked Gibson and Powell to check on it, and Gibson phoned me late that same night to report they could not locate Woods. By travelling throughout the state, I had the opportunity to build teamwork and establish friendships with some exceptionally dedicated and talented individuals.

Rev. King S. DuPont, Dr. Gilbert L. Porter, and Rev. Metz Rollin stand outside the Florida State Capitol during Johns Committee hearings in 1958.

The Johns Committee held hearings throughout the state, but many of them took place in Tallahassee. Questioning me (in the shadows at the far right of this photograph) is the Johns Committee's lead counsel Mark Hawes, seated next to an unidentified member of the committee. This hearing was held in the Old Capitol building. (NAACP Papers, Library of Congress)

8
The Johns Committee:
The NAACP Under Legislative Attack

The Florida legislature's infamous Johns Committee already has received some attention in the first part of this book, but its blatantly unconstitutional attempts to abridge civil rights in the state and the NAACP's response to them deserve additional attention. To recount what already has been mentioned, Florida's "pork chop" legislature originally formed the committee in 1956 as an attempt to preserve racial segregation and Jim Crow discrimination in the aftermath of the United States Supreme Court's decisions in the *Brown* public school desegregation cases. History has remembered the panel by the name of a state senator, Charley E. Johns, who urged the funding of, and eventually chaired, the witch hunt. A resident of rural Bradford County, Johns state senate president had occupied the governor's office for a time during 1953-1955 subsequent to Governor Dan McCarty's death. LeRoy Collins, McCarty's friend and ally, ousted Johns from the governor's mansion in a campaign that featured Johns's opposition to a law to unmask the Ku Klux Klan.[1]

The legislature initially charged the committee with investigating organizations and institutions accused of being communistic or which did not endorse the state's Jim Crow practices. The panel, in turn, employed a staff to press its inquiries. Its initial target was the NAACP. To head up the probe, the committee employed as its counsel a native Tampan named Mark Hawes. A tall, heavy-set man, close shaven and red faced, Hawes also served as counsel for the racist Florida Association for Constitutional Government. The NAACP took priority as his first target.

Eager to establish a political base for himself, Hawes labored tirelessly to oblige committee members and their hate-driven allies. With an initial $50,000 appropriation from the legislature, the counsel employed a former Federal Bureau of Investigation agent to travel the South and to report on how other states were managing to by-pass the *Brown* decisions. He discovered that Louisiana, Texas, Mississippi, and Alabama lawmakers were aiming to outlaw the NAACP from operating in their jurisdictions. Hawes impressed upon his committee that Florida could do the same. If not before, the NAACP thereby emerged in the eyes of white supremacists as public enemy number one.

Disingenuously, the committee asserted in public that its purpose was to look into the activities of organizations whose missions were not in the best interest of Florida. When it came to the NAACP, then-chairman Henry Land, a state representative, directed a letter in February 1957 to Roy Wilkins, Thurgood Marshall, and Robert L. Carter. Re-reading this letter today, knowing what I know of the committee's subsequent actions, makes me shake my head in wonder about how low supposedly God-fearing public officials could stoop. "Contrary to what has been reported at various times by the press," Land declared, "this committee was not set up solely to investigate the NAACP or any other organization." He continued:

> The Act reads as follows: "It shall be the duty of the committee to make as complete an investigation as time permits of all organizations whose principles or activities include a course of conduct on the part of any person or group which would constitute violence, or a violation of the laws of the state, or would be inimical to the well being and orderly pursuit of their personal and business activities by the majority of the citizens of this state. Such investigations shall be conducted with the purpose of reporting to this legislature of the activities of such organizations to the end that corrective legislation may be adopted if found necessary to correct any abuses against the peace and dignity of the state."[2]

Land's letter notwithstanding, the NAACP understood that the committee intended to destroy it through supposedly legal means. Patterns soon evidenced themselves. First, the panel began targeting principal NAACP leaders, key branch members, NAACP attorneys, and allied organizations that supported the NAACP's work. On March 9, 1957, subpoenas issued forth. Mine directed me to appear before the committee in Tallahassee on March 11, 1957, at 9:00 a.m. It also ordered me to bring all books, records, correspondence, and other memoranda of the NAACP or the NAACP Legal Defense and Educational Funds, Inc.

Other key NAACP officials received demands to appear, as well. They included Leon Lowry, state conference president; attorney William Fordham; one-time state conference president Edward D. Davis; Father Theodore Gibson, the Miami branch president; Vernell Albury, treasurer of the Miami branch; Ruth Perry, Miami branch and state conference secretary; Richard Powell, a Liberty City branch officer; participants in the University of Florida desegregation suit; attorney Horace Hill of Daytona; several Florida A&M University faculty members; and former officers of the Florida State Teacher's Association, an organization comprised of Black teachers. Being an eyewitness and participant in the subsequent hearings, I made it my practice to leave immediately following each hearing and either telephone the national NAACP office or, if a typewriter was available, prepare a report to be submitted to New York while the proceedings were still fresh in my mind. To give the flavor of the proceedings, I am including several excerpts of testimony from these reports.

The committee planned its hearings to highlight at the beginning the University of Florida desegregation suit and to attack its plaintiff Virgil Hawkins. When called to testify, Hawkins asked for counsel, and attorney Horace Hill responded to this request. The questions and answers that followed quickly targeted the NAACP. Among them were these:

> Hawes: When did you first file to enter the University [of Florida]?

> Hawkins: 1949
> Hawes: Did you talk with anyone concerning your filing?
> Hawkins: Yes. I talked with many people including Edward D. Davis.
> Hawes: Did you pay attorney's fees to Alex Akerman?

Hill objected at this point, stating that such testimony was privileged, but the objection was overruled.

> Hawkins: No.
> Hawes: Did the steering committee represent any organization?
> Hawkins: No. The steering committee did not represent any organization.
> Hawes: Did the NAACP agree to pay attorneys in this case? Did they agree to pay Horace Hill any money?
> Hawkins: NAACP has never agreed to pay any money.
> Hawes: Has the Progressive Voters' League paid any money?
> Hawkins: I don't think so.
> Hawes: Did the steering committee ever discuss with you the process for raising money?
> Hawkins: We talked about it.[3]

Hawkins's testimony lasted approximately two hours before the committee moved on to NAACP officials. Hawes continued to question the witness about the source of funding for the desegregation case. He wanted to know if Hawkins had received funds from the NAACP Legal Defense Fund. When Hawkins was allowed to step down, the committee council called Ed Davis. Similar questions to those asked of Hawkins ensued:

> Hawes: Did you receive any money from the NAACP during the early days of the University of Florida case?
> Davis: A few dollars from Harry T. Moore.
> Hawes: What was his office?
> Davis: Executive Secretary, Florida State Conference of

Branches.

Hawes: Did you receive any money from the NAACP Legal Defense Fund?

Davis: No. Mr. Akerman said that he would solicit aid and counsel from Mr. [Thurgood] Marshall.[4]

This testimony went on for some time, all bordering on the source of money for the University of Florida desegregation case. Davis also told of his tenure in office and how long he had been an NAACP member. In fact, he confided to me after the hearing that he thought the whole thing was a waste of his time and was truly boring.

Attorneys William A. Fordham and Horace Hill followed Davis to the stand. Fordham's testimony began with inquiries about fundraising. He was asked to disclose how plaintiffs were solicited. He replied that it was not NAACP policy to solicit plaintiffs. Then, calling Hill to testimony, the committee's counsel sprung a surprise. Hawes had obtained several of Hill's memoranda and letters written to and from the national NAACP office, as well as bills for attorney's fees, photocopies of canceled checks, and other material related to the University of Florida desegregation case. Hawes clearly intended to prove that the NAACP was paying Hill for his services in the suit. When Hawes asked, "Didn't these letters come from your files—weren't they in your office?" Hill found himself caught off guard. He had not expected his private records to be brought into evidence. Nevertheless, he answered coolly that he did not know the source of the letters and other materials. He had not given anyone permission to search his files. Therefore, he could not testify as to the authenticity of the photocopies.

Extending their ultimately unsuccessful attempt to prove that the NAACP paid plaintiffs to serve in their suits, the committee members scored a small victory when they uncovered an NAACP check written to Virgil Hawkins. Actually, the check had been drawn from contributions made to support the University of Florida suit and constituted a loan made to Hawkins because he had suffered economic reprisals as a result of his involvement in the litigation.

Still, the committee pressed the matter. It recalled Hawkins and continued to interrogate him the next day. The questions delved into his private finances, including his salary, bank account history, and other sources of income. Even his wife's salary and the names of their debtors came under scrutiny. Hawkins used the opportunity to make the point that his debtors had begun to pressure him after the suit had become well publicized in 1956. "I wish I knew why they did it," he told the committee. "But they even wanted my automobile."[5]

The committee thereupon turned its attention to the Florida State Teacher's Association, with which the NAACP had enjoyed a long history of cooperation. The legislators intended to show that the FSTA financially supported the NAACP's litigation efforts. They called Shirley Wayne Curtis, principal of Pinellas County High School in Clearwater, to the witness stand. Curtis also served as the FSTA's executive secretary. After inquiring into the organization's structure and the duties of its officers, Hawes asked Curtis if the FSTA had ever contributed money to the NAACP. He said that he did not know. Hawes pressed further:

>Hawes: Was the question of financing the University [of Florida] case ever brought before the Board of Directors?
>
>Curtis: No. The question was never brought before the Board of Directors.
>
>Hawes: Has the Association ever given money to the NAACP?
>
>Curtis: As I recall, they have given an annual contribution of about $25.00 per year to the National office and nothing to the state.
>
>Hawes: Did the steering committee make an appeal for funds for the Hawkins case?
>
>Curtis: They made an appeal, but there was not an agreement about supporting this case.
>
>Hawes: As far as you know, the FSTA has not put any money into the University of Florida case?
>
>Curtis: As far as I know, no.[6]

Frustrated by his failure to nail the NAACP or the FSTA, Hawes summoned Dr. Garrett T. Wiggins to testify. The president of Pensacola's Washington Junior College, Wiggins had held office during 1952-1953 as FSTA president. With the distinguished educator Hawes continued the same line of questioning that he had pursued with Mr. Curtis. I could see that he ached to elicit an admission that the FSTA had supported the NAACP's University of Florida desegregation suit. However, Dr. Wiggins insisted that he knew nothing about the FSTA financing of the plaintiff's case.

The frustration of the committee and its counsel grew as its hearings produced little of use to its purposes. This failure came in good part because the panel proved unable to gather in most of our state conference records. Fortunately for us, we had had enough time before the hearings began to export many of our files to the national office, where they could be protected. The paucity of records that were produced offered a focus for many of the questions that were put to me:

> Hawes: Now, you had a subpoena duces tecum, calling for all of the records in your possession of the NAACP, and you brought us this box of stuff here. Has anybody gone through those records and taken anything out of them, stripped them in any way?
>
> Saunders: Not as I know of.
>
> Hawes: That box of records is very general press releases of the national office of the NAACP, in large?
>
> Saunders: I don't understand the nature of your question.
>
> Hawes: Are you familiar with these records here? Are you familiar with these records?
>
> Saunders: I am.
>
> Hawes: About three-fourths of the material in there consists of news releases, doesn't it, such matters as this?

Here Hawes showed some of the materials that I had submitted.

Saunders: I believe so, yes, with the exception of my personal communication.

Hawes: There are very few of your personal communications in that box, aren't there?

Saunders: I don't understand what you mean, sir. Do you mean that . . .

Hawes: Are all your communications that you wrote and received in the last year in that box?

Saunders: Generally speaking, I'd say that they are.

Hawes: Don't you know that they're not?

Saunders: I don't know that. I'd say that everything—that practically everything that I have received, with the exception of what has been—was moved when we invested the other office, in April or May, is there.

Hawes: As a matter of fact, what you've brought me in that box is the most infinitesimal amount of your correspondence imaginable, isn't it?

Saunders: May I ask the Counsel a question, if it pleases?

Hawes: I'm asking you. Isn't that true?

Saunders: I'd say no, that it isn't.

Hawes: That's not true.[7]

The committee's 1957 report substantiated our conclusion that the panel's primary purpose was to attack civil rights groups in general and the NAACP in particular. Beginning with what was generally known about the NAACP, its purposes and objectives, the report laid the foundation for an outright attempt to establish legal grounds to drive the NAACP from the state and punish officers and attorneys who had represented the organization and who were filing school desegregation suits. Here are excerpts:

> The NAACP is directly responsible for securing the decisions of the United States Supreme Court holding separate but equal facilities in education, both elementary and at the higher levels, to be in violation of the United States Constitution. Having secured these decisions, the NAACP has set itself up as a sort of

executive arm of the federal courts to execute the integration decrees of federal courts which, standing alone, are not self-executing under the law.

In order to accomplish its aim of complete integration, the NAACP has promulgated a very concrete and highly effective set of plans. A national legal department is maintained in the New York offices of the Legal Defense and Educational Fund, Inc. A legal staff is likewise maintained at the regional, state conference, and branch levels. It is the primary duty of the various legal staffs to accomplish the aims of the NAACP by carrying on integration litigation in the cases furnished by the various local branches of the NAACP. . . . A carefully planned program of attack, legally, legislatively, and publicity-wise, is being executed.[8]

To furnish ammunition for punitive legislation, the report sought to establish that the NAACP used names of plaintiffs without their knowledge in filing school desegregation suits. I know of only one situation that remotely resembled the charge. In that instance, a Tampa mother had filed a petition with the school board. Under pressure and questioning by a committee representative and Hawes, she stated that she had not known what she was signing. She was also alleged to have said that, if she had known the petition was to desegregate schools, she never would have signed it. At no time was the NAACP aware that people were being asked to sign petitions without fully understanding the petition's purpose. The report went on to claim that our national office had complete control over the lawsuits and plaintiffs involved. It declared that plaintiffs had no control over their cases, could not disagree with the attorneys, and essentially were at the mercy of the NAACP once they agreed to serve as plaintiffs. The report concluded:

> The great bulk of the NAACP's activities, above described, are in the opinion of [the committee's] counsel contrary to the spirit and letter of the canons of ethics and general laws governing the conduct and practice of law; and amount to an abuse of

the judicial processes of the courts in which these cases are carried on.⁹

The report ended on an alarming note. "Evidence now available to the staff strongly indicates that the Communist Party has sought to, and to some degree may have actually, infiltrated the NAACP and sought to use it," the text read. "Unfortunately, it is impossible to conduct the type of investigation and to hold the necessary hearings to determine the true nature and extent of this situation within the lifetime of this committee."¹⁰

The investigative committee succeeded in 1957 only in saving itself. The panel, its members, and supporters in the legislature pushed a number of bills aimed at curbing the effectiveness of NAACP legal initiatives and forcing disclosure of our finances and membership rolls. Supposedly the laws would have applied more broadly, but reports bubbling out of the Capitol specified the NAACP as the "top trouble maker of the state's growing race tensions." In the end, only a measure extending the committee's life for two years achieved final approval after legislative leaders realized the broad impact on all citizens' rights of many of the punitive proposals.¹¹

With its new lease on life, the committee pursued its inquisition in a way that could not fail to dampen enthusiasm for public support of civil rights. I especially remember a committee meeting on February 26, 1958, at Miami's City Hall. Members of the Seaboard White Citizens Council and other hate groups active in the Dade County area occupied most of the several front rows. The fact that Father Gibson and Ruth Perry, the White secretary of the Miami branch, were scheduled to testify had been publicized widely. Rumors had it that this meeting would witness the showdown between Mark Hawes and the NAACP.

Those present particularly awaited Ruth Perry's testimony. Clearly, the committee had targeted her because she was a White civil rights activist who despised racial segregation. Despite tremendous stress, she endeavored to stand fast. However, the pressure touched Mrs. Perry too heavily when Dade County state representative Cliff Herrell, angrily pacing the floor, yelled out that "any person who fails to cooperate with this committee is not fit to be a citizen of the state of Florida."[12] I saw this dramatic outburst as simply another play for publicity, considering the audience present. However, Ruth Perry, having been browbeaten already by the committee, burst into tears in the wake of Herrell's insult.

Subsequent to Herrell's theatrics, the committee recessed for lunch. Miami attorney G. E. Graves, one of the NAACP counsels, told me to ask Father Gibson to join us for lunch in his office. Frank D. Reeves, dean of the Howard University Law School and an NAACP attorney who had participated in the *Brown* cases, joined Father Gibson, Graves, and me in our rental car.

Never before have I revealed the content of that very important conversation, but, during the course of the lunch recess, the four of us carefully calculated how we could effectively end the committee's tirade against the NAACP. Reeves asked Gibson if he was ready to break up the hearing. The priest, angry with the committee's abuse of Ruth Perry, quickly responded, "Hell yes." We advised him of the consequences that he could face, the likelihood that he would be held in contempt of the committee. Gibson answered that he did not care. Our preparations continued in Graves's office. The two attorneys prepared a statement for Father Gibson to read. They rehearsed him on the questions that he would have to answer and suggested the appropriate time for him to read the statement.

Events then took their course. After we had returned to the hearing room, Hawes sought out the Reverend Edward T. Graham as his next witness. Graham had not yet arrived, and Graves persuaded Hawes to call Father Gibson. Our friend took the stand and answered the opening inquiries. When Hawes began to inquire about his office with the NAACP, Gibson interrupted him. In his polite but pointed manner, Gibson declared: "Just a minute sir. I have a statement that I would like to read to this committee." As he stood up from the witness chair, I could see that there was no stopping Gibson now. He scolded the committee, I thought, in a priestly manner, refused to turn over NAACP records, and stalked out of the room. I heard Hawes's thunderous voice, "Are you refusing to cooperate with this committee?" Proudly, Father Gibson turned his head and looked directly at the committee. "I am doing just that sir," he slowly articulated.[13]

Father Gibson's courageous act instantly propelled him to the center of attention as newspaper reporters and photographers swarmed around. The lights from the cameras followed him out of the hearing room, leaving the committee members and spectators in stunned silence. As expected, the committee moved to cite him for contempt. The case was heard first by the state courts. Utlimately, it landed in the United States Supreme Court which ruled, although not unanimously, in favor of the NAACP. Meanwhile, with the litigation pending the Johns Committee turned its attention to investigating Tampa's University of South Florida for allegedly promoting homosexuality and communism.[14]

The Johns Committee's witch hunts brought shame to the state of Florida and, in the process, forced the NAACP for years to conduct its operations in a manner far more secretive than formerly had been the case. Many individuals, fearful of reprisals at the hands of committee supporters, backed away from civil rights activism. Donors to NAACP causes knew that racist investigators might someday be hauling them into legislative hearing rooms. I cannot help but ask, where were Florida's supposedly progressive White leaders when this disgraceful chapter in our state's history was written?

Attorney Francisco A. Rodriguez smiles for friends as he walks from a car in Tallahassee where he helped represent Florida NAACP chapters during the Johns Committee hearings.

THE JOHNS COMMITTEE: THE NAACP UNDER LEGISLATIVE ATTACK

Charley Johns holds forth on the floor of the state senate chamber in Tallahassee. Johns indulged in tirades aimed against various minority groups and interests. His bullying tactics brought him statewide attention and grabbed temporary notoriety for the Johns Committee. Ultimately, however, his name has retained negative associations in the state, similar to those McCarthyism has in national politics. A reference to "Johns Committee" tactics connotes abuse or misuse of governmental investigative powers. (Florida State Archives)

Miami attorney G. E. Graves was a key member of the NAACP legal team who sympathized with Rev. Gibson's anger over the committee's unkind and disrespectful handling of witnesses. He supported Gibson's decision to walk out of the hearing. (The G. E. Graves Family)

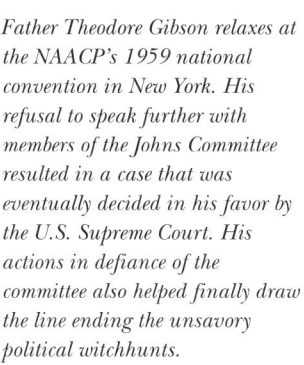

Father Theodore Gibson relaxes at the NAACP's 1959 national convention in New York. His refusal to speak further with members of the Johns Committee resulted in a case that was eventually decided in his favor by the U.S. Supreme Court. His actions in defiance of the committee also helped finally draw the line ending the unsavory political witchhunts.

Students from Florida A&M University marched in the state's capital in 1956 to support two coeds arrested for refusing to move to the back of a public bus.

9
The Seige of Tallahassee

Numerous protests during the Civil Rights era focused on Florida's capital city, Tallahassee. Earlier in this book I mentioned, for example, the 1956 Tallahassee bus boycott and the NAACP's role in that early and bitter struggle. The fact that Tallahassee constituted the state's center of government naturally contributed to its importance for civil rights demonstrations, as also did the presence of students from Florida A&M University, located a short walk south of the Capitol. It will not come as too much of a surprise, then, that the most significant demonstration of NAACP-sponsored strength occurred in that city with what we termed the "March on Tallahassee." The story of its conception, implementation, and success provides an illustration of the commitment of individuals, as well as of the organization, to the "Fight for Freedom."

NAACP leaders first conceived the idea of the March on Tallahassee during the annual meeting of our state conference held at Sarasota during October 1962. Our purpose was to promote the enactment of a federal civil rights law through highlighting continuing racial problems and widespread public demand for change. After years of struggling with the intimidating activities of the legislature's Johns Committee, we sensed that the time was right for a major and public push. We had achieved some substantial advances that year as protests covered the state from Pensacola to Key West. To cite one victory, in September the University of Florida had desegregated its undergraduate programs and campus housing.

Still, change came slowly in Florida while the regional and national pictures seemed less than promising. Riots recently had erupted on the campus of the University of Mississippi when that state's governor refused to obey United States Supreme Court orders to admit James Meredith to the undergraduate program. He remained only with the armed assistance of United States marshals. Dr. Martin Luther King, Jr., and his Southern Christian Leadership Conference allies meanwhile faced continuing frustration with their protests at Albany, Georgia. Clearly, stronger federal laws were needed, but congressional committees labored under the domination of southern segregationists who stymied attempts to enact legislation. Public pressure needed to be brought to bear.

Details of the anticipated march began coming together at an NAACP Church Committee meeting called for February 1963 in Orlando. At that session, the assembled ministers accepted my proposal that the march be held at Tallahassee at a time in late March when the Congress was debating civil rights and, not insignificantly, only eight days remained during which Floridians could register to vote before the books closed.

In addition to the other reasons I have mentioned, the capital city provided an ideal forum for the march because it would place special pressure on our new governor Farris Bryant. A known and avowed racist, Bryant presented himself as a polar opposite to his predecessor LeRoy Collins. During the last several years of his six years in office, Collins had taken increasingly strong stands against racist agitation. I recall one of his radio addresses from those days when he remarked, "As far as I'm concerned, I don't mind saying that if a man has a department store and he invites the public generally to come in his store, and trade, I think then it is unfair and morally wrong for him to single out one department . . . , and say he does not want or will not allow Negroes to patronize that one department."[1] On the other hand, Bryant believed in racial segregation and had done nothing to improve race relations in his home county of Marion or, as will be discussed in a later chapter, the troubled city of St. Augustine. Accordingly, the NAACP wanted the march to stand as a vivid protest to the new governor's segregationist agenda.

The organization and personnel for the march quickly took shape. As the planning proceeded, the Reverend C. K. Steele presided over Tallahassee's NAACP local branch. As such, Steele chaired the march committee by appointment of the church committee head, the Reverend J. H. McKissick of St. Augustine. We also invited other civil rights, civic, and fraternal organizations to participate. Several members of the Congress of Racial Equality also joined us. They included Patricia Stevens, a Florida A&M coed and Florida's CORE field secretary. In addition, Father Theodore R. Gibson, whose contempt conviction at the instigation of the Johns Committee would be overturned by the United States Supreme Court that March, and Edward T. Graham, both of the Miami branch, served on the march committee with Steele.

Before further commenting on the details of march planning and execution, I would like to sidetrack slightly to cast some positive light on a man who has been criticized, I think unfairly, as failing to promote civil rights from his influential position. I am speaking of Dr. George Gore, president of Florida A&M University. My digression is linked to this Tallahassee protest story because Chairman Steele invited Dr. Gore to serve as a march sponsor, something that the distinguished educator understandably hesitated to do.

The circumstances that prompted Dr. Gore's caution were years in the making. Florida A&M students had engaged in protests since the Tallahassee Bus Boycott days and had accelerated their activities with sit-ins during the early 1960s at popular white-owned Tallahassee businesses. All the while, as a state-supported institution of higher learning, the university risked the wrath of racist legislators. Particularly, Representative Thomas Beasley of Walton County, who twice had presided as speaker of the legislature's lower house, threatened to dismiss faculty members who advised students in protests. The threats especially found targets in Dr. James Hudson, a faculty member, and Daisy Young, the adult advisor for the college NAACP chapter and a university employee. Greater threats against the university loomed in the background. The Johns Committee, for instance, insisted that Dr. Gore appear before its members, who then menacingly hinted to him of reprisals if he did not force students and faculty into line.

My concerns for FAM's position were longstanding by the time I reported on them to Roy Wilkins, NAACP national executive director, as early as March 1960. My report for that month noted:

> Suggestions are being made by the legislative members because of the intense student activity to:
>
> 1) close Florida A&M University or move it to another part of the state if Negro students continue their demonstrations,
>
> 2) expel all students who took part in sit-down demonstrations,
>
> 3) prevent enrollment of northern students at both universities [in Tallahassee; that is, FAM and Florida State University].[2]

Over the years I had developed respect for and a friendly relationship with Dr. Gore. He had admitted to me the burden of pressure that he felt as a result of protest activities. Yet, his personal commitment to racial justice persisted. He appreciated, as well, the NAACP's contributions, especially the fact that, when fifty FAM students had been arrested for violating a court order against picketing, the state conference had saved the day for him by paying the fines. Subsequent to that incident, Dr. Gore had promised that I could use the university's facilities at any time.

These facts will help to explain why I understood when Reverend Steele told me of his lack of success in soliciting Dr. Gore's support and why I suggested to Steele that I have a personal conversation with the university president. The next morning I flew from Tampa to Tallahassee. My meeting with Dr. Gore resulted very productively. I spoke with him about what we needed. In response, the president asked a professor to supervise preparation of signs, with frames, for the march. He give us, as well, use of a large field on campus for a staging area for participants. He indicated that he could not excuse from classes the students who wanted to take part in the march, but he assured me that the administration would not object to the participation of those who did not have class conflicts. With this support, I knew that the march would succeed.

Then, as the day of the march drew near, controversy developed between CORE members and the NAACP. It seemed that CORE was not pleased with the march route that Reverend Steele and his assistants had designed. The chairman had designated a line of march that proceeded north from FAM along Monroe Street, which soon would lead marchers to the east and in front of the Capitol toward a baseball park directly across from the governor's office. He furnished copies of the plan to the state conference, Tallahassee city officials, and the governor's office. Steele reported to me that Governor Bryant had agreed to the route. CORE insisted, to the contrary, that marchers proceed north of the Capitol into the downtown area.

Serious complications followed. CORE asked Reverend Steele to request a change in the march route, something to which city officials would not agree. CORE refused to give up. On March 26, on the eve of the march, CORE members came to the Tookes Hotel where Ruby Hurley, the NAACP regional director for the southeast, and I were staying. They demanded to see us and then insisted that we attend a meeting at the Episcopal parish hall that evening to listen to their demands. I told Ruby that I would attend the session and that there was no reason for her to leave the hotel. The meeting lasted until after midnight. I let the CORE representatives know that the NAACP intended for the demonstration to follow the original route. The CORE members decided that they would not participate and predicted that the march would fail without their presence. We hoped they were wrong.

Excitement filled the air as everything was readied on the morning of March 27, 1963. Buses began to roll in from Tampa, Fort Myers, Ocala, St. Augustine, and other locales. The arrival of five or six buses from Jacksonville capped the affair. I was proud. We had pulled it together without much money. Some critics have said that the number of marchers totaled fewer than one thousand, although other observers insisted that the figure ran as high as three thousand. My estimate, as of the time we starting marching, was that about two thousand marchers set out.

The elation that I felt on that occasion has dimmed my memory of the some of the details, but I remember clearly passing the Capitol directly under the governor's office and spotting a small group of CORE members standing on the street corner as we walked by. The Reverend Eugene Tillman of Daytona joined with me and Reverend McKissick in issuing a statement that declared, "We did not come to Tallahassee for a confrontation with the Governor, but to deliver a demand that Black Floridians were ready to push harder for complete freedom from racial segregation." Later I learned that Reverend Steele had wanted to invite Dr. King to speak, but state conference president Rutledge Pearson had demurred. As he told me, "This is all Florida and all NAACP." He added, "We respect Dr. King, but we have the strength and know-how here in our state."

The Tallahassee march succeeded. I do not believe that, as of that point, any other state conference in the southeastern region had conducted a similar project. It served notice on the entire state that African Americans would stand up for their rights together, that the murderers of Harry T. Moore and their sympathizers were no longer considered threats to Black people in Florida. It set a precedent, as well, that had national reverberations. It was, after all, the following August that witnessed the renowned March on Washington. Our march additionally succeeded by furthering the leadership reputation of Reverend Steele. He received serious consideration for appointment to the NAACP's national board and served as the SCLC's first vice president. The NAACP appreciated his leadership as president of the Tallahassee branch and gratefully acknowledged that the march would have failed without his precise planning.

Just as it lauded Reverend Steele's leadership, the NAACP also recognized the great contributions of FAM students to the civil rights movement in Florida. I can recall in the aftermath of the Tallahassee march watching Roy Wilkins as he stood at the lectern of the campus's new auditorium to praise Black Tallahasseans generally, while singling out FAM students. Some of their accomplishments I mentioned briefly earlier in this chapter, but I did not go into detail. Perhaps a few words would be in order now.

The sit-in movement, commencing in early 1960, showcased the determination of FAM students and the university's chapter of the NAACP. I remember one protest in March that caused quite a stir in Tallahassee. A group of FAM students "sat-in" and picketed several downtown stores. "The Mayor and the ex-mayor led police and commissioners to the various stores," I reported at the time to Roy Wilkins of the events that ensued. "Arrests were made at the order of the Mayor-Commissioner of Tallahassee." The report continued: "Students were told they would have three minutes to get out of the store. While in the process of leaving, the order to arrest was given."

The White Tallahassee authorities proved themselves devoid of any sense of southern hospitality, and policemen did not disguise the fact that they were allied with the White Citizens Council, a white-supremacist organization. The law enforcers arrested thirty-six young people from FAM, as well as nine white Florida State University students. Brutal police officers and jailers verbally abused the incarcerated protesters. They labeled Florida A&M's White allies "nigger lovers." They kept jail conditions deliberately torturous. For example, the authorities kept seventeen students locked in a six-foot by six-foot cell from Saturday until Monday. They turned off the lights, leaving the students in constant, absolute darkness. They served food that obviously was not fresh, having been prepared the previous day. The police violated students' rights, as illustrated by one student's assertion to Judge John Rudd that he had not been allowed to make a single telephone call during the entire time he was in jail.

Other Florida A&M students decided not to let this situation go unchallenged. On March 12, seven hundred individuals gathered on the FAM campus where they formed three lines and proceeded to march down three different routes into downtown Tallahassee. One jailed student later mentioned his comfort at knowing his fellow students were protesting the incarcerations. He learned of the action when he overheard one police officer telling another, "The niggers are on the march."

The police then provoked violence. March leaders had instructed the students to return to the FAM campus if the police ordered them to do so. But, as the third group was turning around to make their return in obedience to police directives, the supposed lawmen began throwing tear gas into their ranks. Several female students, blinded by the gas, ran forward. Immediately, the police began chasing the students and throwing gas. Several young people were hospitalized for burns, and one received eye injuries.

The NAACP undertook to defend the Black students involved in the earlier demonstrations who belonged to our organization. First, we brought attorney G. E. Graves in from Miami to represent them. Local citizens worked to obtain bonds for the arrested students and kept the press abreast of developments in the case. The eleven students were tried and convicted. They faced sentences of a $300 fine or a sixty-day jail term. Eight elected to serve the time, one of whom was C. K. Steele's eldest son. Another was CORE field secretary Patricia Due. Two other students involved I knew well because they were from Tampa. Arthenia Joyner, an NAACP youth council member whose father owned the Cotton Club Lounge, was arrested. Alton White, whose father owned the Cozy Corner Restaurant, cooked and served meals for the jailed students. Ultimately, Gloster Current arranged for Volusia County bail bondsman Charles Cherry to post bonds still pending, a memory that remains fresh in Cherry's mind as I write.

Other FAM students also faced Tallahassee justice. A second group, composed of six individuals, underwent trials. The accused, upon conviction, were given the same sentencing option as the NAACP student members; that is, a $300 fine or sixty days in jail. We appealed all the sentences to a higher court, but the judgments were confirmed by white judges. In the circumstances, the NAACP felt compelled to pay the fines.

As this series of incidents suggests, the financial cost of the fight against racism ran high. This especially was true in Tallahassee where hundreds of students participated regularly in civil rights protests. Beyond the costs that flowed from these activities, local branch members confronted a constant dilemma in raising enough funds for local demonstrations. Fortunately, NAACP attorneys often worked more out of a sense of loyalty and dedications to the cause than for salary. The NAACP could not pay attorney Graves for his services in Tallahassee until the following year, even though his fee ran a mere $400 for all of his work.

In the case of the FAM students, I asked entertainers to perform at NAACP fundraisers in the hopes of attracting more contributions. One weekend I ran into blues musician B. B. King at a motel in Jacksonville. I boldly asked him to help the NAACP raise necessary funds to pay the students' fines and other costs. This fine man agreed to do three shows for us. Held in Lakeland, Orlando, and Tampa, the events assisted us tremendously in reaching our goals.

The strength of the Tallahassee Black community, resulting from the commitment of its members to kill Jim Crow, impressed me greatly. I can proudly claim credit for the NAACP for the most successful single protest in the capital city, but local civil rights groups and their leaders designed countless other successful demonstrations. Indeed, I was most impressed by the brave Florida A&M and Florida State students who refused to be intimidated by police and the legislature, who stood up to police as they were doused with tear gas, and who withstood police brutality as they were incarcerated for weeks and even months. The Civil Rights Movement could not have been successful without committed individuals and organizations such as these.

Local civil rights activists and Florida A&M students continued to hold demonstrations and protests in Tallahassee during the 1960s. This is one of their efforts to integrate a downtown motion picture theater. Their efforts sometimes resulted in arrests, but they persisted and eventually integrated our capital city.

The Tallahassee NAACP branch shared office space and many goals and interests with the Inter-Civic Council, another active civil rights group led by Rev. C. K. Steele.

Father David Brooks, Episcopal priest and president of the Tallahassee branch, was another tireless activist.

Rev. C. Kenzie Steele speaks to members of the NAACP and Inter-Civic Council in church in Tallahassee. Rev. Steele remained a catalyst for change within the city, and his account of the Tallahassee Bus Protest is printed later in this book as Appendix One.

Rev. King Solomon DuPont discusses voter education priorities in Tallahassee and North Florida with Johnnie Brooks (back to camera) at the Tallahassee branch office.

Rutledge Pearson, state conference president, addresses the gathering following a 1962 march.

Dr. James Hudson, a faculty member at Florida A&M University, was a stalwart during the Tallahassee Bus Protest. Johns Committee members unsuccessfully attempted to pressure Dr. George W. Gore, FAMU's president, into firing Hudson and others on the faculty.

Carrying a sign, Rutledge Pearson joins striking municipal workers in Jacksonville, c. 1964.

10
Jacksonville: The Model Branch

In the 1940s under Harry T. Moore's leadership, Florida had pioneered the concept of a state NAACP conference to provide coordination, planning that was more far-ranging, and larger fundraising potential than was possible for individual local branches. Still, the local branches constituted the lungs that breathed life into NAACP activities. From them emerged the foot soldiers in the war against discrimination, and with them we were afforded the ability to challenge the Jim Crow system in all parts of the state at the same time. As would be expected, the health of some branches rose and fell over time, a fact that made it all the more important that some branches provided solid and sustained commitment to our cause. Those in Tampa and Miami, among many, deserve mention, while that at Jacksonville offered a model for numerous others to emulate.

During time that I spent in Jacksonville working on membership and fundraising drives, as well as on civil rights initiatives, I learned a great deal about the local branch's history from two very special individuals. The first, Theodore Redding, was a retired postal employee. Redding occupied a superb position to gain such knowledge, since he had presided as branch president from 1942 to 1949 and remained active thereafter for many years. Also, Charles Vaught, another postal employee, provided me with insight. He took over as president in 1953, energizing the branch through his example. When he assumed the job, he faced enormous challenges. Most importantly, the branch's membership had sunk to fewer than 100 persons, reflecting the fears that pervaded the African American community in the wake of Harry T. Moore's assassination.

The story of how Charles Vaught and others rebuilt the branch bears telling. With his leadership and with the assistance that I could afford as state field secretary, we began to recruit younger, active people into the NAACP. Among them were attorney Earl M. Johnson, Rutledge Pearson, Glen Washington, Dr. Arnett Giradeau, Dr. Hunter Satterwhite, and brothers Emanuel and Reginald Eaves. This group eagerly desired to increase membership, raise funds, and free the branch from political influences, especially influences emanating from the mayor's office.

These political influences evidenced themselves as soon as we kicked off the 1953 membership drive. Our New York headquarters had assigned Gertrude Gorman, a member of the national field staff, to assist me in coordinating the drive. Local branch officers had suggested a very influential Black fraternal and civic leader Joe James as drive chairman, and his acceptance initially cheered Gertrude and me. Quickly, though, our enthusiasm waned as politics intervened. We convened an organizational meeting in the office of F. Henry Williams, a real estate broker who served as chairman of the Jacksonville branch's executive committee. The site was on the second floor of the Masonic Temple on Broad Street. Its selection for the meeting came as no accident. As Ruby Hurley once remarked to me, Williams at that time ran the NAACP like he ran his office. He was in full control.

I have wandered a little away from my point about political influence, so I will get right to the matter. The meeting in Williams's office appeared to go well, until we were dispersing. Gorman happened to be walking near James and Williams, when she overheard James declare that he could not do what the NAACP expected of him. Should he do so, he insisted, he might jeopardize his influence with city hall. This kind of problem hurt us in many towns and cities in the state. Some Black businessmen felt greater sensitivities to the profits stemming from contracts with local governments or for political favors and insider information than for an end to racial discrimination. In James's case, Gorman and I were forced to accept the setback. All we could do was commit ourselves to work harder to recruit people who were loyal to the organization.

On the subject of politically related scandals in Jacksonville, I recall another incident. It involved a Black man named Amos President, who had been known to sell illegal alcoholic beverages. Suddenly, President moved away from the city under mysterious circumstances. I undertook an investigation which revealed that members of the Jacksonville police department had been receiving kickbacks from President's profits. Some dispute about the payoffs had led to his departure.

That was not the end of the story. Several years after leaving Jacksonville, President, by then suffering from tuberculosis, returned to the city. Within two days police arrested him at his home. That night he died from a wound to the back of his skull. Police reports claimed that he fell backwards, striking his head on the floor or some hard object. Immediately, attorney Rutherford McGriff, who was a local branch executive committee member, and I began to look into the death. On our visit to President's widow, we learned that one of the police officers threatened her husband, warning President that he would not live to see another day. We returned to the house a few hours later intending to get a signed affidavit from the widow, but her house had been abandoned. A neighbor told us that she was afraid of retaliation from the police and left without leaving a forwarding address.

Soon thereafter politics once again touched the heart of Jacksonville's NAACP organization. McGriff and I felt that we should bring the matter of President's death and his wife's disappearance to the attention of the full executive committee. At our request, F. Henry Williams agreed to hold a special meeting in his office. When we arrived at the office, we found that the doors were locked and that none of the other executive committee members were present. The implications appeared plain. I should mention that many members criticized this state of affairs. I particularly recall the forthright stand of executive committee member Sam Jones, whose leadership I want to acknowledge here. A close friend of A. Philip Randolph, Jones deserves credit, as well, for organizing the Porters Club and the Railroad Voters League.

McGriff and I were unwilling to leave the matter unresolved.

On January 28, 1960, I appealed in writing to Jacksonville mayor Hayden Burns, who would preside as Florida's governor for two years beginning in 1965, for an investigation. "It is the belief of our informant that Mr. President died as a result of police brutality," I informed Burns. "We have also been informed that after the beating, he was not allowed to receive medical treatment nor did he telephone relatives or other persons who may have been able to help him."[1] I do not recall that I ever received a response from Burns. The case quickly died from lack of action by the local branch. I will always believe that city hall ordered the branch to "forget" the incident.

Although "downtown" political pressure intimidated the Jacksonville branch at first, it became a model branch for other local branches because the new leaders refused to buckle under. It took a number of years, but the weaker officers eventually were weeded out. Glen Washington presided in the mid-1950s, and I believe that Earl Johnson followed him in 1956. J. H. Goodson served until 1960. Then, Rutledge Pearson achieved election as president. With new leadership came renewed community support. Dentists, physicians, educators, and other professionals courageously and openly endorsed the NAACP.

A key element in the revival of the Jacksonville branch involved organization of a youth council. Rutledge Pearson, a gangling young man who suffered from discrimination on a local interracial baseball team, advised the eager youths. The young people rallied around the energetic, charismatic teacher. Mostly they were high school students and coeds from Edward Waters College. They enjoyed the autonomy that youth councils were permitted under the NAACP umbrella. Even though a member of the senior branch advised the council, its members made their own decisions.

Unfortunately, the youth council's activities rankled some senior branch members. The older members felt that the young people should not do anything without branch executive committee approval. The senior branch, for example, opposed the youth council's participation in anti-segregation demonstrations. They criticized Pearson and the group in 1960 for organizing a sit-in, arguing that sit-ins were not appropriate protest measures. Nevertheless, the determined young people demonstrated each afternoon during July and August in certain designated downtown stores, challenging Mayor Burns's proclamation that there would be no desegregation in Jacksonville.

The defiance of Jim Crow and the mayor's will almost culminated in bloodshed when Ku Klux Klan members confronted the young people. The event occurred on August 26, 1960. As was the custom, the demonstrators met that morning at a Presbyterian church under the call of council president Rodney Hearst. At such meetings, the members would hold a short prayer service, then a senior branch member would counsel them on how to conduct themselves during peaceful demonstrations. On that Saturday, Pearson warned the group that rumors had reached him of Klan plans to attack the demonstrators. I was then attending a youth retreat in Augusta, Georgia. Pearson contacted me there to find out if I could ask Mayor Burns to give the youth council extra police protection. It turned out that Mayor Burns had absented himself from the city that day, and I was not able to arrange the needed protection. The brave members of the council decided to go ahead as planned.

Events quickly led to confrontation. Following their morning meeting, the youth council members left the church and proceeded downtown to several targeted stores, including Cohens Department Store, Woolworth, and Sears. Meanwhile, Klansmen were issuing baseball bats to their constituents at Hemming Park. As the young demonstrators continued their march, attackers suddenly descended upon them swinging their bats. The youths broke and ran toward Brush and Ashley Streets in the heart of Jacksonville's Black business community. Alerted to the attack, a group of courageous youths advanced toward the Klansmen, preparing to counterattack if necessary. Fortunately, before any additional violence arose, the Klan members retreated back to the park. Understandably, the incident incensed the Black community. Unfounded rumors that a youth had been killed helped to fan the flames.

Renewed determination grew out of the incident, as the youth council members pressed their cause, at times prompting arrests and provoking the police to overreaction. One important instance happened the next year, on August 21, when four young people were arrested for picketing the Berrier Ice Cream Parlor. One of them, Roderick Freeman, received a thirty-day sentence. Local courts ordered Quillie Jones, Detry Lang, and Albert Williams to pay $50 fines. They were released from confinement on bonds pending appeals to be filed by attorney Earl Johnson.

The Berrier Ice Cream Parlor story actually had its roots in events that occurred several days earlier. Youth council members had begun picketing the establishment only after learning that its owners discriminated against Black patrons. That knowledge came about when council members asked owner J. R. Berrier if he had made up his mind to hire colored employees. When Berrier responded that he had not given the matter any further thought and that he did not intend to hire additional colored employees, one of the members threatened, "Well, we'll see about that."[2]

The youth council members started picketing. About one week afterward, according to Berrier's claim, a member contacted him asking, "Well, now are you ready to hire colored people?" The owner insisted, "No, I am not going to give in." He added, "I suppose that you are going to try to put me out of business." The activist confirmed, "Yes, that's the way it's got to be." Subsequently, Berrier applied for an injunction against the youths to bar them from congregating in front of the business or detaining customers. Berrier asserted that the youths intimidated his Black customers. He claimed that, on one occasion, customers feared to leave the store and that he had to contact the police to escort them. He also alleged that, on at least one occasion, council members provoked a fight with customers. On September 14, Judge W. A. Stanley issued the injunction.[3]

The Berrier Ice Cream Parlor case posed something new to Jacksonville's White residents, as they were not used to Blacks opposing discrimination so adamantly. The case also focused attention from within the Black community and prompted enhanced support from Rutledge and the youth council. Although the injunction barred youths from demonstrating at the ice cream parlor, it did not stop efforts to improve employment opportunities for Black people in Jacksonville. Despite disapproval from some members of the senior local branch of the NAACP, threats from Ku Klux Klansmen, and police arrests, the youth council's young people had proven themselves valuable assets in the civil rights struggle at Jacksonville.

The results from NAACP branch and youth council initiatives at Jacksonville could be seen clearly by 1962. I can recall vividly speaking that year to a mass rally in the city. I began by reading a letter from Bishop Steven Gill Spotwood, the chairman of the NAACP's national board of directors. My delight shown through as I conveyed Spotwood's words to the affect that he was "immensely proud of the type of leadership" evidenced in Jacksonville.[4] By then the Jacksonville branch had become a model for NAACP units throughout the nation. I fully believe, and I hope it will not be forgotten, that Jacksonville earned that honor in large part due to the persistence of its youth council members.

As an addendum let me mention that Pearson went on to become president of the Jacksonville branch and that the local unit continued to be a very strong and active one. Pearson's leadership abilities, which were so essential to that success, grew partly out of family support. His brother Lloyd worked as chairman of the voter registration drive and in the membership program. Pearson's wife Mary Ann also participated actively, serving as a hardworking member of the local branch and of the state conference. Pearson's achievements came at a price, though. Authorities often targeted his livelihood by threatening his teaching position. Three known Ku Klux Klan organizations harassed him. Several local and state agencies conducted personal investigations of him. Eventually, Pearson went on to a greater role by becoming state conference president and achieving election to the NAACP's national board of directors. I will never forget Rutledge Pearson because he was an outstanding leader and was truly dedicated to the NAACP and to the civil rights cause.

The Jacksonville branch's story did not evolve neatly and without setbacks, frustrations, and difficult challenges. Numerous influences worked to undermine its effectiveness, and key officers succumbed to human frailties. Still, the commitment of individuals to change and reform, coupled with incredible persistence, revitalized a floundering organization into a national model. On a lesser scale, so it was elsewhere. Notwithstanding the repressive tactics of the Johns Committee, state and local governments, and the Ku Klux Klan, the NAACP accomplished a tremendous goal simply by keeping body and soul together after Harry T. Moore's death. Growing stronger and winning many civil rights goals in later years rewarded us, but in an institutional sense it simply was icing on the cake.

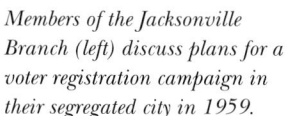

Members of the Jacksonville Branch (left) discuss plans for a voter registration campaign in their segregated city in 1959.

The photos at right and below were taken shortly before the Klan started handing out baseball bats in Jacksonville's Hemming Park for use against sit-in segregation protests at Cohens, Sears, and Woolworth's staged by the NAACP Youth Council on August 26, 1960. Fortunately, violence was averted.

JACKSONVILLE: THE MODEL BRANCH

Rutledge Pearson (center) emphasizes a point as he and Rev. Taston meet with Jacksonville Mayor Lou Ritter July 20, 1966.

Rutledge Pearson (center front), newly elected as president of the Jacksonville NAACP branch, stands in front of Bethel Baptist Institutional Church with members of the Jacksonville Ministerial Alliance who strongly supported him, c. 1960.

Residents in North Pinellas County met to organize a Tarpon Springs Branch in 1956.

11
The NAACP at Home: Local Organizations and Activities

In these pages I have spoken often of the activities of local branches, including the previous chapter's examination of the Jacksonville branch. It would constitute a tremendous slight if I did not at least mention activities, challenges, and personalities in other areas of the state that affected the progress of our cause and the successes and disappointments that eventually came to us.

Escambia County

As already mentioned, the NAACP in the late 1950s and into the 1960s began to secure footholds in many of the state's smaller counties; still, the area of the Florida Panhandle proved a tough challenge. The region extends from Escambia County in the west to beyond Tallahassee in the east, and resistance to any form of organized effort to improve the status of Black Floridians came more intensely there than in just about any other part of the state. Escambia County's principal city of Pensacola offered one notable exception, for there Black leaders worked free from serious threats of economic reprisals.

Pensacola and Escambia County's freer climate contributed greatly to our cause, partly from the fact that two very important suits with origins there resulted in major civil rights victories. The first action, filed by the Reverend R. A. Cromwell in 1944, eventually led to the end of the White Democratic primary in Florida.

Also, the case of *Abraham Tolbert* v. *Escambia County Board of Public Instruction* established an important precedent. Prosecuted on behalf of several Black parents of school-aged children, it constituted the first suit filed in a Florida federal court to mandate desegregation of an entire school system. Thurgood Marshall's name was listed as the attorney of record in *Tolbert*, but Constance Baker Motley and Charles Wilson argued the case before United State District Judge Harold Carswell. The plaintiffs enjoyed a breakthrough when Carswell ordered the school board to submit a plan for desegregation within ninety days. The decision's statewide impact evidenced itself when segregationist Governor Farris Bryant publicly admitted that "in effect, the Court was telling the School Board to use the Pupil Placement Law even if it meant that some Negroes would attend White schools."[1]

Okaloosa County

It is no understatement to say that Okaloosa County was not as progressive as was Escambia, nor was its NAACP local branch as active. People there were very much intimidated by the White power structure, a fact that resulted in fewer NAACP successes there than in many other places. By 1961 little had changed in the Okaloosa branch, unlike say Jacksonville's, where a younger generation had shaken off White political and economic pressure. In Okaloosa, the older members remained in control. Though the allegiance of these individuals to the NAACP involved a sincere commitment, they were not willing to challenge their White oppressors by demanding change. For the most part young people who lived in Okaloosa County did not participate in NAACP activities for fear of some form of reprisal.

Several persons nonetheless performed valuable services. Marcus Davis, a local principal and a graduate of Tampa's Middleton High School, together with his wife who also taught, emerged as key spokespersons at Crestview, one of the county's small towns. Marcus desired change and promised me that he would attempt to recruit younger, aggressive members. His successes were tempered, though, by his caution in light of the severe opposition of some local White residents to the NAACP. No white man exerted more influence in that regard than Congressman Bob Sikes, a die-hard segregationist. Marcus feared that active promotion of NAACP membership would put segregationists on guard, prompting them to begin threatening those who already belonged to our organization.

Interestingly, Crestview offered the site of one civil rights trial that achieved some fame during the 1950s. In that action, the state of Florida sued as plaintiff, with First Lieutenant Robert L. Williams of the United States Air Force named as defendant. The affair had begun with Williams making his way to report to his unit for eventual relocation to Korea. As events turned out, it did not matter at all that he wore the uniform of the United States Air Force. What would matter was that he was a Black man who had bought a ticket on a Trailways bus, sat in the front seat, and, when asked to move to the rear, refused to do so. For his insolence authorities arrested the lieutenant. Released on bond, Williams departed the country for Korea.

Florida's law enforcement authorities, who had sworn an oath to protect and defend the Constitution of the United States, decided to try Lieutenant Williams for violating the state's Jim Crow law that required Black passengers to sit from the rear seats of all buses. Attorney Charles F. Wilson, the same lawyer who pursued Abraham Tolbert's school desegregation suit in Escambia County, represented Williams. The case received a fair amount of publicity because it challenged intra-state segregation policies. It excited Okaloosa County's Black residents principally because they had never seen a Black lawyer practice in the courts. I encouraged them to attend the hearing to show their support for Williams, but most feared the consequences. Nonetheless, attorney Wilson drew a large following from Pensacola, and, in the end, most of the courtroom seats were filled. With the lieutenant already overseas, the court sentenced him "in absentia" and fined him. To compound the tragedy, Williams gave his life for his country when his plane was shot down in Korea.

Bay County

The Bay County (Panama City) branch impressed me. Its officers were aggressive and were more than willing to challenge racial discrimination. I recall meeting with the local officers in January 1961, when the branch boasted a new president in the person of Timothy Youngblood, a young minister and insurance manager. Youngblood arranged for me to meet with a biracial group of ministers. It pleased me indeed, for a meeting of this type in the Florida Panhandle remained virtually unprecedented.

Six White and eight Black ministers attended the forum and discussed with me racial discrimination as it affected Bay County residents. Members of both races spoke frankly and acknowledged that former NAACP branch presidents had suffered from intimidation and had been afraid to provide civil rights leadership. They additionally acknowledged that, in 1959 during the heat of the legislative investigative hearings held by the Johns Committee, the NAACP program failed to materialize in Bay County because some branch leaders found themselves reluctant to challenge the status quo. For example, when the local press and legislative committee investigators questioned the local branch president about race relations, he replied to the effect that everything was fine in Panama City. His assertion came in the face of several complaints received by the NAACP from Black Air Force personnel alleging racial discrimination on the local base and despite the fact that all public buildings in Panama City remained racially segregated.

Happily, the Panama City situation began to change. Local activists compelled the branch president's resignation, and Youngblood soon had organized a group of youths to initiate the first efforts to picket Panama City's restaurants. Youngblood also launched a court action that led to the end of racially segregated schools in Bay County. Without question, the young man's accomplishments before he moved away from Bay County deserve commendation.

After the energetic Youngblood departed Panama City, the Reverend Jackson E. Jones assumed the reins of leadership. He

THE NAACP AT HOME: LOCAL ORGANIZATIONS AND ACTIVITIES

National conventions offered local delegates the opportunity to attend workshops, share strategies, renew friendships, and reaffirm values. Excellent speakers and programs often left us feeling united and inspired. Here Senator Hubert Humphrey speaks to the national convention in Minnesota in 1959, while Arthur Spingarn, the prominent NAACP attorney, listens at the left of the podium.

West Palm Beach Branch President Louise E. Buie and Bay County (Panama City) Branch President Rev. Jackson E. Jones share a moment of enthusiasm during the program of the NAACP national convention in 1962.

James Austin, a spirited leader for the NAACP in Lake Wales and Polk County, examines a national convention display that features Black entrepreneurship, c. 1966. Austin served as president of the Lake Wales chapter for thirty-two years. He was the first Black person in Polk County history to run for public office in 1963. He was elected to the City Commission in 1963 and became the city's first Black mayor in 1989 at age 70.

199

proved just as effective as had Youngblood. Reverend Jones loved the NAACP. Dedicated to the organization's objectives to eliminate all vestiges of racial discrimination, he had first moved from Pensacola to Fort Walton Beach where he succeeded in bringing together that city's splintered Black community. When he relocated to Panama City, he received appointment as pastor of the largest Baptist church in town. Under Jones's guidance, local NAACP memberships increased and activities attracted more young people in our organization. Jones worked closely with me and state conference officials. He always kept me abreast of branch activities. It sometimes seemed that he never slept. I remember him calling me in the middle of the night on any number of occasions to report problems in Bay County and to seek advice as to how to solve them.

Holmes County

My principal recollection concerning Holmes County relates to an incident that occurred in July 1965. On that occasion local school officials notified ten Black teachers at Bonifay that they would no longer be needed after schools were racially integrated. The officials justified their action by arguing that Holmes County would be closing down all Black schools and sending Black students to the former White schools. Some of the Black teachers possessed extensive experience after more than twenty years' service.

Fortunately, the state conference already had established a "watch dog" committee in anticipation of unfair practices such as clearly was the case with the Bonifay teachers. Upon learning of the discrimination, I called the Reverend Jackson E. Jones of our Panama City branch and asked him to accompany a local lawyer to investigate the situation. They and another branch member traveled to Bonifay where they talked with the teachers. Meanwhile, representatives of our watch dog committee met in Tallahassee met with Thomas E. Bailey, the state superintendent of schools. Sadly, state officials refused to respond to our entreaties. As I recall, the teachers were let go. At least they and their community members learned, though, that someone outside their county cared about what happened to them.

Leon County

When discussing Escambia County, I mentioned that United States District Judge Harold Carswell ordered some integration of public schools in Pensacola and surrounding areas. The judge, who would later be denied a seat on the United States Supreme Court due to his own segregationist past, also ruled on a case calling for the desegregation of the Leon County school system. The plaintiffs in that case were the Reverend C. K. Steele, R. L. Anderson, and a Dr. Stevens. Actively supporting the litigation were African Methodist Episcopal church presiding elder K. S. DuPont and Dan Speed, a local businessman. Later Speed presided over the NAACP's Tallahassee branch.

That good man K. S. DuPont deserves greater mention. Also a businessman, he hailed from an upper middle class family that owned extensive property in Gadsden County and other areas of the Panhandle. A mountain of a man, he pastored Tallahassee's A.M.E. church. DuPont supported the NAACP with strength and determination. He often traveled with me when I was organizing in rural areas such as Gadsden, Jackson, and Liberty Counties. I stand in that courageous man's debt for his willingness to carry the cause outside the bounds of his own county.

Marion County

In the early Sixties, F. George Pinkston drove from Ocala to Tampa shortly after he returned from Virginia Union College. He wanted to talk with me about Jim Crow practices in Marion County and see if the NAACP would give support to an organized effort to end racial segregation in Ocala.

Young Pinkston was sincere. We discussed such subjects as Howard Academy, the school founded by White individuals concerned about advancing education of Black students; we talked about the role of Edward D. Davis, an educator who—like Harry T. Moore and Noah Griffin and his wife—were fired from teaching positions in Pinellas County; and we sypathized especially with John Gilbert, who lost his job in Brevard County when he volunteered to become the plaintiff in a teacher equalization suit against the county. We also talked about the role of the Central Life Insurance Company, which provided employment to the victims of reprisals brought by school boards.

On one very cold Friday night, the two of us sat with fishing poles on the Courtney Campbell Causeway. The site is now the location of a Red Lobster Restaurant. That night we settled on a plan of action to include organizing an NAACP Youth Council, reorganizing the Marion County NAACP branch, and moving to protest racial discrimination against Black citizens by all businesses. Several meetings were held in Ocala at the Cunningham Funeral Home and at the office of Dr. N. A. Jones, a medical doctor.

Meanwhile, protests were growing in St. Augustine where students from Florida Memorial and Industrial College were supporting Dr. Robert Hayling, a local dentist, in demanding that St. Augustine end its tacit approval of what was becoming increasingly vicious opposition to peaceful protest. My request that Pinkston be allowed to work in St. Augustine was accepted by Gloster B. Current. Gloster permitted me to bring Pinkston to New York at NAACP expense and we spent almost a week at national headquarters. Hearing a full report of events in St. Augustine convinced Gloster that it would be advantageous for young Pinkston to assist the local branch, so after returning briefly to Ocala, he went on to St. Augustine to help. There four young protestors had been arrested and were being held with juvenile delinquency charges pending. Pinkston led protest marches at the jail and rallied the community. His leadership was a dynamic catalyst for change, and it set the stage for the increasingly visible civil rights demonstrations to come, including the one in which Martin Luther King, Jr., was arrested. These are described in greater detail in the next chapter. You can read of some of them in Pinkston's own words in Appendix Two.

After about two months of concentrated work in St. Augustine, Pinkston returned to Ocala and resumed the almost nightly planning sessions with friends and fellow NAACP members. They remained determined to find the means to end racial discrimination in Marion County.

One effective strategy was a boycott of Ocala stores organized by Pinkston and carried out with pickets from the Youth Council. Pinkston himself was one of those arrested during the downtown marches. At the same time, voter registration efforts in Marion County that he helped to organize led to the arrest of approximately one hundred or more invuduals, mostly on charges of giving false information to the registrar. Among the dubious questions asked was one about whether or not they had ever been arrested. Given the large numbers of arrests for protests, it was easy to trip someone up with that question. Attorneys offering to represent these individuals were Joseph Hatchet, Earl Johnson, and Francisco Rodriguez. One of our stalwart and generous NAACP members, Charles Cherry, a teacher at Bethune-Cookman in Daytona, was called upon to provide bonds for those arrested.

Public meetings in support of these actions were held regularly at Mt. Moriah Baptist Church, where Pinkston served as assistant pastor to his father. On one visit there, baseball great Jackie Robinson expressed amazement at the strong unity within the community. In the face of escalating efforts to intimidate Black citizens, the people summoned forth the increasing solidarity that Robinson noted. For example, when persons claiming to belong to the Ku Klux Klan fired into Pinkston's house, church officers volunteered to stand guard and put an end to the hooliganism.

Orange County

My first trip to Orlando came shortly after my 1952 appointment as state field secretary, and I learned quickly that the place to bring myself up to date on current affairs there was John Frazier's Luncheonette. On that initial trip attorney Paul Perkins, then working on the Groveland Case, met me at the cafe. Over some of John's scrambled eggs, grits, and sausage, Paul introduced me to a cross section of Orlando's Black citizenry.

The get-together also allowed me a better acquaintance with Paul. We shared a tie in that his uncle Daniel W. Perkins had joined my grandmother in civil rights activities at Tampa before World War One. By 1952 Daniel enjoyed fame as a Jacksonville lawyer, with almost everyone in the Black community calling him Colonel Perkins. The colonel later represented many plaintiffs who sued for equal pay and voting rights in Florida. Getting back to Paul, I learned that he operated at Orlando out of a building owned by a retired medical doctor, I. S. Hankins. Paul's civil rights practice received a great deal of financial and other support from Dr. Hankins, who was an NAACP life member. At that time Dr. Hankins, unlike Paul, was not actively working with the local branch, but Paul informed me that the NAACP could always depend on him for financial support.

Landlords such as Dr. Hankins could mean a great deal to civil rights activists, given their ability to support or frustrate initiatives. Frazier's restaurant, for instance, was located in a building that I believe was owned by another influential Black resident, Z. L. Riley. Riley had the attention of downtown politicians. An officer in Orlando's Negro Chamber of Commerce, he served as a liaison between the Black community and White city officials. I remember one occasion when we asked the mayor to put up a banner advertising an NAACP meeting. The word that came back to us essentially told us to go through Mr. Riley. Since he was not an elected public official, we refused to conduct business through him. We had no argument with the Negro Chamber of Commerce, but we objected to the manner in which the city determined the Black leadership.

The Orlando branch enjoyed good fortune in the person of its 1952 president, Dan Ware. At that time Black citizens personally feared for their safety in the aftermath of Harry T. Moore's assassination, and at Orlando many also felt threatened with economic reprisals for civil rights activism. Nonetheless, Ware undertook every effort to obtain support from Orlando's Black community. Working with him were Azalie McCloud and Taylor Snead. Mrs. McCloud served as branch secretary, while Mr. Snead was one of the branch's most loyal and active members. I learned that Snead accepted responsibility for bringing at least five new members to each branch meeting. The efforts earned him the nickname "membership man." The team of Ware, McCloud, and Snead worked hard with real dedication to the cause of freedom. They helped to bridge troubled waters at a treacherous time, a fact which permitted the evolution of one of the best organized branches in Florida.

Other individuals performed remarkable service at Orlando. Berneice Wheeler offers a fine example. The trait that commended her most strongly to me was that she was very dependable, a quality the importance of which should not be underestimated. I could always count on Berneice to contact key NAACP members, to work with Taylor Snead on our membership drives, and to argue affirmatively for civil rights programs when others in the Black community were afraid to or were just not interested. Marie Palmer worked diligently with Ware and McCloud, as well. She later became secretary and president of the Orlando branch and treasurer of the state conference. Allie Smith often hosted me when I visited Orlando, generously assisting and guiding me.

Allie Smith led me to a friendship with Lylah Hankins, a person who made a major difference for our work at Orlando. When I met Mrs. Hankins (she was Dr. Hankins's wife), she was relatively new to Florida, having moved to Orlando from New Jersey after her marriage. As I visited with her that first time, I asked if she would participate in the Orlando branch membership drive that year. I explained that we had set a goal of 150 new members. Lylah expressed surprise at such a modest goal, mentioning that she had actively participated in her local branch in New Jersey. Already aware of how important the NAACP was to improving the lives of African Americans, she recognized the need for a thriving organization with active members. She did not immediately commit to helping, however, preferring to discuss matters with Dr. Hankins. Fortunately for the NAACP, she called a few days later and agreed to lead the drive.

What a whirlwind hit us with Lylah Hankins. Almost singlehandedly, she set out to organize the 1952 membership drive. Her goal was 1,000 new members, six or seven times as many as I had suggested! Dr. Hankins supported her efforts 100 percent. With his help, she recruited workers from the local medical and dental groups, Greek letter organizations, churches, masonic orders, and other organizations with large Black memberships. As a direct result of her efforts and at a crucial time for us, Orange County's drive exceeded even her goal. With more than 1,800 new members that year, the Orlando branch drew plaudits from the state conference and was honored at the annual NAACP national convention. In addition to Lylah Hankins, the state conference commended the contributions of Taylor Snead, Mavis Starke, Georgia Woodley, Dr. Robert Hunt, and Freddy R. Johnson, the newly elected branch president and Central Life Insurance Company's Orlando branch manager.

The Orange County branch battled against multiple points of opposition to achieve longlasting success. In the county Ku Klux Klan activity heightened White community reluctance to eliminate racism; fears of economic reprisal haunted Black residents; and the Florida legislature's investigative committee looked over everyone's shoulder in the person of its first chairman, Orange County state representative Henry W. Land. Still, armed with its force of 1,800 members the branch strove to take direct action. Under Freddy Johnson's leadership, for instance, the Orlando NAACP Youth Council organized. The branch successfully closed down a Publix supermarket on Robinson Street and Orange Blossom Trail after Black customers decided to boycott because of racial discrimination. Another protest involved the Winn-Dixie supermarket and resulted in the store's hiring of Black clerks and cashiers. Notable for their contributions in these and other activities as branch officers were Marie Palmer, Dr. Robert Hunt, and the Reverend Toomer. I also recall that Mrs. Woodley, Berneice Wheeler, and Mrs. Palmer served as branch secretaries.

A few sidenotes might be in order. The NAACP youth council in later years staged sit-in demonstrations at Kress and Woolworth department stores. Incidentally, when police arrested four youth council members for peacefully demonstrating, Dr. Hankins posted their bond. A young lawyer, Norris Woolfork, represented the four youths. He also took on the case of several parents who sued the Orange County school board for racially segregating its schools. The plaintiffs included J. P. Ellis, a graduate of Bethune-Cookman College and a parent of several children enrolled in the local public schools; Georgia N. Woodley; Mavis Starke; Emma Goines; and Altamese Prichett.

Pinellas County

Pinellas County's race relations problems have extended themselves well into the present era, with rioting occurring in its largest city as recently as 1997. That community, St. Petersburg, calls itself the "Sunshine City," a nickname given to it many years ago by the local chamber of commerce and newspaper. If the sun did not shine on any day, the paper would be free of charge the next day. For St. Pete's Black residents, the sun rarely shined. As in most southern cities, racial discrimination permeated the air, and, as was the case in many other cities, a large portion of St. Pete's Black community rarely challenged the White power structure's Jim Crow restrictions, softened slightly as they were by an appearance of paternalism.

Unlike many other Florida cities, however, St. Pete held some White leaders and strong-willed Black individuals who were not willing to compromise civil rights. The first name that comes to my mind is that of Noah Griffin, who doggedly pursued equal salaries for Black teachers throughout Florida. Mrs. O. B. McLin, an outspoken and long-time NAACP supporter, also played a prominent role in the Florida State Teacher's Association and local community affairs. She acted, as well, as secretary of the St. Petersburg NAACP local branch.

It should not be forgotten that Whites played a part in creating a helpful dialogue at St. Petersburg. As in true with the modern city, in the 1950s and 1960s the community's White population consisted in good part of retirees from the North. From among

Attorney Malcolm Cunningham became a close friend. I stayed with him whenever I visited the West Palm Beach office.

Robert L. Gilder was an energetic Tampa branch president who advanced fair housing initiatives.

Justice Joseph Hatchett, born in Clearwater, became the South's first Black state Supreme Court Justice when he was named to the Florida court in 1975.

Members of Tampa's Orchid Club presented life memberships in the NAACP in honor of Leon Claxton, a liberal contributor to the Freedom Fund. Left to right are Joyce [last name unknown]; Gwendolyn Claxton, Leon's widow; Helen Saunders, president of the Tampa Branch; Helen Williams; and Authorine Clark, Orchid Club president. They stand beside a portrait of Caxton.

Officers of the newly formed North Pinellas Branch display a poster promoting a Florida appearance of Gloster B. Current at St. Paul A.M.E. Church in Tampa. Current spoke there May 15, 1960, in celebration of the six-year anniversary of the May 17, 1954 Supreme Court ruling striking down the doctrine of "separate but equal" segregated schools.

these newcomers to Florida came persons who accepted responsibility for establishing effective communication between the races. I especially recall several White clergymen, including Ben F. Wyland, Robert H. Gemmer, and Lamar Clements, who helped to integrate local ministerial associations.

The publisher of the *St. Petersburg Times* offered assistance. I first met with Nelson Poynter in the early 1950s at the suggestion of Clarence Mitchell, then director of the NAACP Washington Bureau. Poynter expressed a willingness to help me promote the NAACP and the civil rights cause. We often met in his office where we discussed the NAACP's Florida efforts to implement the 1954 *Brown* decision, outlawing racially segregated public schools. He assigned a Black reporter named Samuel Adams to cover the NAACP. Sam, his wife, and I maintained a close relationship until they moved from Florida. Before their departure, Mrs. Adams occupied the position of secretary of the St. Pete branch.

Black physicians played a crucial role in the effort to improve race relations in St. Petersburg. Ralph Wimbish and Fred Alsup forced integration of the Pinellas County golf course as a result of their suit, *Wimbish and Alsup, et al. v. The Pinellas County Commission and Corps Gold Corporation*. Dr. Alsup also sued to integrate the St. Petersburg beach and other recreational facilities. As a committed NAACP member, he generously provided bonds for youths who protested segregated lunch counters. In addition, Robert Swain and Eugene Rose, former classmates of mine at Bethune-Cookman College, participated in the civil rights movement, as did B. F. Jones, Orian Ayer, and Harry Taliaferro.

Others stepped forward when the call came, and among them were numerous religious leaders. Out of that group, the Reverends Enoch Davis and H. McNeal Harris proved themselves to be stalwarts. They often offered their churches for mass meetings. Davis, a charismatic leader, not only persuaded other Black clergymen to join the struggle but also helped to drive integration of the ministerial association.

Though its membership figures ran only to modest totals during the 1950s and early 1960s, the St. Petersburg branch actively pursued NAACP goals with the assistance of truly committed supporters such as those I have mentioned. The first local president with whom I worked in 1952, F. A. Dunn, typified the leadership. A close associate of Harry T. Moore and Edward D. Davis on the state level and of Fannye Ayre Ponder on the national level, he refused to give up the fight. Ten years later, with Dr. Ralph Wimbish as president and Leon Cox as youth council advisor, the branch remained just as active. Cox successfully persuaded many businesses, such as the Howard Johnson Motel, to lower racial bars. To address those businesses that refused to desegregate (the Florida and Central Theaters were two), he organized a youth council to conduct demonstrations.

To give a feel for the problems faced by these St. Pete activists and their counterparts throughout Florida, let me quote from my January 1962 report to Robert Carter, the NAACP's general counsel. It read, in part:

> On January 14th the group [i.e., members of the youth council] tried to purchase tickets to a showing of *King of Kings*. The manager roped off the entrance, allowing only Whites to enter the theater. He stated that he was operating a private business and that anyone who entered even to purchase tickets would be trespassing.
>
> On January 15th Mr. Cox [the branch president] was called to the office at Gibbs Junior College, where he was employed as an instructor, by Miss Johnnie Ruth Clarke, a secretary at the college. Miss Clarke stated that she was told to tell Mr. Cox that if he continued to organize students, he would be dismissed as of January 16, 1962. She also stated that the Board of Public Instruction did not want students at the Junior College involved in the issue.
>
> On January 16th, Mr. Cox called the Superintendent of Schools, Mr. Floyd Christian, and asked for clarification. Mr. Christian stated that if Mr. Cox was arrested, he would suspend him pending the outcome of his trial. Mr. Cox was still active, however, although he no longer attempted to purchase movie

tickets. As many as 50-60 persons have participated in the effort at one time, and the manager closed the ticket office on several occasions.[2]

Eventually, some members of the youth council were arrested and charged with disorderly conduct. Among those courageous youth were Earl Williams, Eli Williams, Artis L. Livingston, Titus A. Robinson, Arnett T. Doctor, Jimmy L. Swain, Harvey L. Hammonds, Ruby L. Hollins, Vernon Kearns, and Joseph W. Lampkins. When the youths tried to purchase tickets at the Central Theater, the manager posted a foot barrier and designated ushers to "control the crowd." In order to reach the ticket booth, people would have to cross the barricade and pass an usher. Of course, the ushers refused to allow youth council members to purchase tickets. Thus, the young people climbed the barricade whereupon the manager and ushers confronted them. None of the youths verbally or physically assaulted the ushers, but the manager attacked one demonstrator. The police charged the young people with disorderly conduct.

Pinellas County's second city is Clearwater, and the NAACP extended its efforts to that community as well. In 1962, I met with Talmadge Rutledge and others to discuss organizing a local branch there. Though a charter might have existed for a branch prior to that time, I have never seen it. Rutledge emerged as the local's first president. One Clearwater problem that comes to mind concerned a policeman named Leon Bradley. Even though he wore the same badge as a White policeman and carried a gun as a law enforcement officer, he suffered racial discrimination from segregation policies. With our assistance, Bradley persisted and, to his credit, helped to curb some of the racism that existed on the force.

Another Clearwater memory involves one of American's most admired sports figures. On one occasion the Clearwater branch invited Jackie Robinson to speak to a mass meeting. His appearance marked the first time that a nationally known figure had spoken for the NAACP in that city. He delivered his message at a church near the railroad tracks. Ever the gracious gentleman, he expressed no frustration when a local train passed during the speech. Afterward, he offered to sit for an interview with a local radio talk show personality, a broadcast event that offered added notoriety to the Clearwater branch.

The NAACP in Clearwater earnestly demonstrated against signs that marked racial segregation in the downtown business sector. The most effective attack against discrimination came, though, when Officer Bradley joined with several parents to break down the dual school system in Pinellas County. When the school board initially rejected their petition, the NAACP Legal Defense Fund in New York agreed to represent them in a suit against the school board. Attorney James B. Sunderlin was assigned the case, which was filed in May 1964. The following January United States District Judge Joseph P. Lieb ordered compliance with the *Brown* decision and creation of a plan that would desegregate the schools.

Lake County

Perhaps there were rural counties where bigotry and brutality ran more rampant than in Lake County, but I would be hard pressed to name one. Mention the case of *State of Florida* v. *Shepherd*, and most NAACP leaders then and now immediately will think of Lake County and its racist sheriff Willis McCall. Refer to the community of Groveland, and they quickly will tie the word with the riot that occurred there in 1949 after four Black youths were accused of raping a White woman. These stories are legend, but many others lurk in the shadows of memory, neglected but not quite forgotten. I would mention Fruitland Park in that category, a small community that witnessed the framing of two Black men for the rape of a White woman.

Previously in this book I referred to the Groveland case, and I also discussed Sheriff McCall's arrest of Virgil Hawkins's nephew. Readers will remember that the younger man was accused of raping a White woman but was released after Governor LeRoy Collins interceded subsequent to an NAACP request. Those stories having been told, the details of the Fruitland Park incident deserve treatment at this point, for the charges against Jerry Chatman and Robert Shuler and the steps toward their convictions well illustrate how justice cowered by racism resulted in the deaths of many innocent Black men in the South. It goes without saying that Sheriff McCall involved himself deeply.

My first-hand involvement in the Fruitland Park case came somewhat late in the day. Shuler, aged twenty-three, and Chatman, aged twenty-six, already had been convicted and sentenced to die in Florida's electric chair. These events had occurred, respectively, in July 1960 and September 1962. The charges alleged that they had raped a White woman who lived alone in tiny Groveland Park. Both judgments were appealed and upheld. So, when I obtained evidence that they had been framed, both men were sitting on death row awaiting execution.

The information came to me out of the blue. One morning I was working at my office at NAACP headquarters in Tampa when my secretary Margie Johnson told me that a White man wished to speak to me. She said, "He says that it involves the two Black men who are supposed to die in the chair." The man, Noel Griffin, was one of Sheriff McCall's deputies but one with a conscience. He had decided that he could no longer stand idly by and see injustice continued. He confessed that Chatman and Shuler had been accused intentionally and fraudulently and that the convictions had been attained based upon trumped-up evidence. By a stroke of luck, attorney Francisco Rodriguez, who was closely associated with the NAACP and who represented the youths, was in his office when I asked Margie to bring Griffin into mine.

Griffin's story related a tale of corruption and bigotry. The testimony of two sheriffs' deputies, L. G. Clark and James Yates, had laid the foundation for the convictions. These men had submitted plaster casts of shoe prints allegedly made at the crime scene. "But," Griffin told us, "the casts were made by the deputies in Yates's yard." Quickly springing into action, attorney Rodriguez petitioned for stays of execution based upon the new evidence. His initial attempts failed. In the meantime, we were able to spur the Federal Bureau of Investigation to look into Griffin's allegations while the *Tampa Tribune* agreed to cover the story. The *Tribune*'s reporters gave the investigation outstanding coverage, which forced Florida's judicial system to take note of the case.

More was to come. The FBI's report showed that the footprint casts indeed had been taken from Deputy Yates's yard. Thereafter, Judge W. Troy Hall, Lake County's circuit court judge, finally ruled in favor of Rodriguez's petitions. Chatman and Shuler received forty-day stays of execution while the courts investigated further. Among matters to be examined were new charges levied by Rodriguez in his petitions. Basically, he alleged that Gordon G. Odom, Jr., a state's attorney, Sheriff McCall, and Deputies Yates and Clark violated their oaths of office, going so far as to frame the defendants. He further had accused them of obstructing justice and suppressing evidence.

Additional evidence came to light. Particularly, we received a copy of a letter written by the alleged rape victim to Robert Shuler's mother. The author had been confined to a mental institution at Macclenny since the time of the rape. In the letter she declared that she told Sheriff McCall that Shuler was not one of her assailants. She stated, as well, that McCall was the only person to whom she had confided the information. Subsequently, both Yates and Clark were indicted for their crimes.

As the defendants fought for their freedom with NAACP assistance and as new information of criminal conspiracy by law enforcement agents surfaced, I grew increasingly troubled about parallels between the Fruitland Park affair and the earlier Groveland case. In the latter travesty of justice, Deputy Yates also had figured importantly and plaster casts taken by him had been introduced into evidence.

It is worth noting here, since most historians have neglected to give great weight to the subsequent Fruitland Park evidence when examining the Groveland case, the high likelihood that the Groveland evidence likewise had been created fraudulently.[3] I outlined my concerns in a January 1963 letter to NAACP general counsel Robert L. Carter. After mentioning the Fruitland Park situation I added, "In doing research [into the Groveland case], I've been given a clipping from a news article which tells of evidence similar to the above that was denied admission (correction: later admitted so I am told)." My report continued: "I am searching to find out if, when ordered to produce the casts of Walter Lee Irvin and/or the other Groveland defendants, Yates testified that the 'casts had been lost' or destroyed. A question has been raised concerning Irving, who is still in prison, if something can be done to get him released."[4] The NAACP's efforts only slowly helped to bring positive results. Irvin remained in jail for five more years while Farris Bryant and Haydon Burns presided over the state. Republican governor Claude Kirk finally paroled him in 1968.

T. H. Poole stepped into a real hornet's nest when he accepted the presidency of the Tri-City Branch (which encompassed Lake County). Willis McCall was still "King Pin," and the Groveland case was still under investigation, remaining the number one issue. Most of the old NAACP leadership that had worked with and supported Harry T. Moore's voter registration were getting up in age. I had made visits to Mrs. Golia Lang in Fruitland Park and Mrs. Mamie L. Mike in Leesburg. While actively soliciting NAACP memberships, they expressed the need for new and aggressive leadership that would stand up against the likes of McCall and Deputy Yates. Mrs. Mikes was doing what she could to maintain the NAACP image and had convinced several local parents that it was time to attack school segregation in Lake County. I was meeting with them to discuss desegregation strategies when I received a telephone call notifying me that I was being considered for the civil rights position with the Office of Economic Opportunity in the Southeast Region. Fortunately, T. H. Poole, a school teacher and radio technician, was there to take the initiative. As Branch president, he immediately began to deal with the issues that had developed over years of opposition to civil rights. It was said that Lake County was for the first time being forced to deal with the real civil needs.

Volusia County

I felt a special closeness to Volusia County, because, from 1940 until 1942, I had lived there while a student at Bethune-Cookman

College. Even with the college's presence and with the national and international prestige of its president Dr. Mary McLeod Bethune, though, racial segregation created a barrier that was ever present. Our campus represented an exception, somewhat of an oasis of racially integrated society. Mrs. Bethune insisted that students would not be separated by race at her college. Each person was to be treated as an equal, without regard to their race. Occasionally White visitors would attend Sunday afternoon worship services, for example, and were seated without attention to the kinds of designated areas reserved for White people at other places in the county and state.

Mrs. Bethune or "Mame," as we affectionately called her, set for us a strong and enduring example. An avid foe of racial discrimination, she encouraged us never to bow down to this evil. When I returned to Florida as the NAACP field secretary in 1952, I met with her. She told me that she was happy and proud that I had been hired by the NAACP and promised to give support to the organization's efforts in the state. She wanted Daytona to be one of the leading cities in the fight for freedom, but, as I left her office, she predicted, "It will take a great amount of effort at shaking up most of Daytona's Black citizens before the community will move to fight against discrimination."

She hit the nail right on the head. Between 1952 and 1956 the Volusia County NAACP branch's membership stagnated. During the period Horace Reed, a retired railroad worker, served as local president. Like other branch presidents during this time in Florida, Reed remained faithful to the organization but failed to encourage membership as a result of the terror that followed Harry T. Moore's death. Ultimately, the election of restaurant owner Flossie M. Crinton as branch secretary spurred membership growth. For a long time NAACP meetings convened at her place of business on Campbell Street. She motivated some of the new ministers who had moved into the area to assume active roles. She also persuaded a member of the Bethune-Cookman College staff named Charles Cherry to join. Under Cherry's direction the branch began to exert itself on community affairs.

As was true with much of the state, energy surged into Volusia with the involvement of young people and the birth of the sit-in movement in 1960. I can remember meeting on February 24 of that year with branch officers and a group of youths from DeLand, the county seat. The group had initiated protests of segregated facilities at the Woolworth's department store in DeLand. I learned from them that a group of teenagers had organized and was planning to spread the protests in DeLand and to Daytona. This information concerned me somewhat because the local branch had worked diligently to negotiate with the Daytona Council on Human Relations. This was an interracial organization that was scheduled to meet with managers from several businesses within two weeks to discuss desegregation. The council felt that a public protest of any nature at this delicate stage of negotiations would upset plans for the meeting.

As field secretary I was compelled to consider both sides' arguments and alternatives. I decided that, since the Council on Human Relations was scheduled to meet with management in only two weeks, a public demonstration would not be in our best interests. Instead, I opted to hold a public meeting where we would announce that negotiations to end racial discrimination in public facilities were in progress. I suggested that people write letters to the national headquarters of major chain stores. Finally, I suggested to the group that it could organize a buyers' protest, something that had proved to be a very effective tool in other areas. The public meeting, convened on February 29, agreed not to jeopardize the negotiations. Rather, efforts would be focused on letter writing and, where appropriate, business boycotts.

Mrs. Bethune's warning echoed as these and other initiatives were launched in Volusia and Daytona. It remained extremely difficult to energize the local community at large. In the early 1960s, for instance, the Florida state conference of branches held its annual meeting at Daytona. Charles Cherry and a young Baptist minister named Eugene C. Tillman planned and promoted the meeting by encouraging the lethargic community to participate in various workshops. The Sunday afternoon meeting was held in the new gymnasium on the Bethune-Cookman campus. Dr. John

Morsell, assistant to Roy Wilkins and an expert on race relations, gave the keynote speech. In the midst of his talk, however, the students present rose and left the auditorium. They later expressed disgust that only a few community members had attended.

Despite Volusia County's seeming unwillingness to fight Jim Crow in the 1950s and early 1960s, by 1966 Daytona was, as Dr. Bethune had hoped, one of the top branches for civil rights activity. It had initiated a school desegregation program for the county as early as 1961, when two Black students, Paula McMillan and Dietrich Golden, were transferred to a White school at the request of their parents and with the unanimous approval of the local school board. As the branch grew stronger, it became a forceful supporter of activities throughout the state. Its leadership backed demonstrations far removed from the county. Its membership posted bonds and provided money for attorneys' fees during the 1964 protests at St. Augustine. What a difference from the days when Horace Reed singlehandedly struggled to save the branch's charter early the previous decade.

Broward County

In 1952 Broward County's only active branch operated at Fort Lauderdale. Its president was an elderly man named Thomas M. Mandy. We still call this pioneer in the struggle for freedom by the simple name Mandy. When I met him, Mandy appeared close to seventy years in age. He showed pride at his affiliation with the NAACP. But, as I soon learned, his example was not typical. Most of our few members in Broward County, scarred deeply by Jim Crow and its legacies, felt ashamed of their ties with the organization. Beyond that, Fort Lauderdale's Black community was intimidated greatly by the White power structure that enforced strict racial segregation. The city's bus system not only required the races to sit separately but established separate bus stops for passengers based on skin color.

Mandy hoped that I could help him rejuvenate the branch. One of his first actions was to introduce me to Dr. Von Mizell, a

Black physician and activist. As Mandy's right-hand man, Mizell inspired the branch president when he became discouraged. A total of seven persons met that day in the doctor's office. Mandy introduced them to me as the executive board. Apparently these core members were the only active members in the branch.

Important work needed to be done. Since the state conference's annual meeting was to be held in Fort Lauderdale that year, the branch officers naturally felt concern about boosting the membership. They sought direction from me, and I told them that I would happily remain in the community to help them prepare. For one month the branch supporters worked enthusiastically. We met almost every night. The number of members increased as residents became curious and then excited about the NAACP's sudden activity.

We were determined to make the occasion a special one. Edward Davis, the state conference president, would attend the state meeting, which would mark his final days in office. In addition, NAACP executive director Walter White had promised to speak. More than 100 delegates also were expected for the gathering, which would begin Thanksgiving morning and continue throughout the weekend. All delegates would be housed in private homes because segregation laws did not allow for public accommodations. Most conference meetings were to be held at Mt. Herman A.M.E. Church, pastored by the Reverend "Shep" Hunter, Sr. I think back on Shep by remembering the pride he felt when his granddaughter, Charlene Hunter Gault, became the first Black student to attend the University of Georgia.

Just about everything moved as smoothly as we could have expected. By Saturday of the meeting weekend fully 100 delegates had registered. Of course, a few snags cropped up. Particularly, the Reverend Holly, pastor of the Baptist church at which Walter White was to speak, refused to let us use the sanctuary if the Miami Jewish Choir performed. His reasoning was that Jews bore responsibility for Jesus Christ's death. Holly adamantly stood by his decision even when influential local residents stressed to him that Walter White was internationally known and respected and that he had worked hard all his life to end racial discrimination. They tried to make the case to him that Jewish people were perhaps the greatest allies of the Black community.

A resolution of the problem finally arose. Shep Hunter told us that he would open his church if Holly would not bend. Then, late Saturday afternoon I learned that a compromise had been reached. Holly had agreed to allow the Jewish choir to sing under the condition that its members remained behind the pulpit. Sunday afternoon thereafter proved a great success as the Miami singers drew a loud applause from the racially integrated audience. On that occasion, Walter White announced the state conference's new program of activism to end racial discrimination.

The changes that began to appear in the Fort Lauderdale community elated Mandy. He hated to retire as president, but his concerns eased with the knowledge that the organization was expanding and that it was well on its way to beginning the hard fight against discrimination. Mandy knew that all of his labors through the years finally were paying off.

During the tenure of the second person after Mandy to hold the presidency, real and substantive changes occurred in Fort Lauderdale. That person was Eula Johnson, a widow and small businesswoman. With her encouragement and financial assistance, a youth council was formed in 1961. Its members immediately planned a demonstration for the world-famous Fort Lauderdale beach. As they organized they met at Mrs. Johnson's home on a regular basis, where they would discuss the rudiments of effective protesting. Their efforts came none too soon. When I returned to the city to assist with the demonstrations, I found that officials still were enforcing the same racial segregation policies that had existed in 1952.

Thus, desegregation of the beaches carried enormous symbolic importance to the resort city. As the demonstrations commenced, a pattern evidenced itself. The youth council members would march toward the beach, but, when they neared the bridge that connected the beach to the mainland, police officers would meet them and force them to turn back. Nonetheless, each day more people joined the marches as the effort gained tremendous support. Sadly, while most Black community members fully supported the group's initiative, some domestic workers feared that the demonstrations would cost them their jobs. A few Black ministers denounced the demonstrations from the pulpit at a time when residents were reporting threats of violence from the Ku Klux Klan.

The marches went on. They were well advertised on a daily basis since the Fort Lauderdale and Miami newspapers and other media outlets were covering them. When it became obvious to town fathers that the young people were not planning to give up, city officials asked for a meeting with Mrs. Johnson, Dr. Mizell, and me. Attorney G. E. Graves of Miami also attended. The mayor ranted about being upset with us, telling us he assumed that the Fort Lauderdale citizens were marching only because the NAACP wanted to stir up trouble in his community. Never did he mention ending racial discrimination. He demanded instead that we advise the protesters to end their marches. I responded by reminding the man that the youths enjoyed a constitutional right to demand that segregation end. Additionally, we told him that we were concerned not only with ending beach segregation but also with discrimination in employment and public accommodations. Finally, we reminded him that the Fort Lauderdale transport system had not complied with the 1956 Montgomery case that outlawed segregated seating on inter-city transport. The city refused to compromise.

Finally, the struggle moved into the courts. The city sought to enjoin the NAACP from "organizing, conducting, coercing, participating in or urging organized efforts to end racial segregation at the Ft. Lauderdale Beach."[5] It named as defendants Mrs. Johnson, Dr. Mizell, a young law student assisting the NAACP, and me. We were also charged with interfering with the city's right to conduct commerce. Attorneys Frank Reeves (who had appeared in support of the 1954 *Brown* case) and G. E. Graves represented us.

The trial lasted about four days. I believe the turning point came when the mayor took the stand. Reeves questioned him about the city's racial policies. The mayor denied that buses still operated on a segregated basis and that segregation existed in other municipal operations. As he testified under oath that the city did not discriminate against its Black citizens, I noticed that several city officials left the courtroom. I learned later that they had ordered the removal of all signs designating race from municipal operations. After the trial Reeves bragged that this was the first time he had desegregated a community without having to go into federal court. The local judge ruled against the city.

Broward County served as the forum of another important court action, a challenge of Florida's miscegenation law. A Black Jamaican had married a White woman after moving to Broward County. Officials arrested him for his temerity at attempting a mixed marriage. With NAACP backing, attorney Graves sued to have the law overturned. In due time the courts agreed with our position and struck the law from the books.

Brevard County

Thanks to its distinction as being Harry T. Moore's home county, Brevard could have been considered the birthplace of the modern NAACP in Florida. Of course, it also was the site of Moore's tragic murder. As such, affairs there were of special concern to us at the state conference. We monitored events there closely.

During the 1950s two men, Nick Ford and Elmer Silas, constituted the guiding lights of the Brevard NAACP. Both men had worked with Harry T. Moore. Ford served as the long-time president of the Cocoa Beach branch, while Silas acted as branch secretary. By 1959 both men had decided to retire as a result of age and failing health. Ford additionally had grown concerned about his wife's employment as a teacher. As both of them neared retirement age, Ford feared that reprisals from the Florida legislative investigating committee might jeopardize Mrs. Ford's job or else her pension. I could understand their concern because other teachers, including the Moores, had suffered such reprisals.

As Ford and Silas relinquished their positions, new, activist leaders arose within the Brevard community. Soon, an aggressive program emerged. One sign came on December 26, 1961, when about forty members of the Cocoa branch met to discuss initiating a school desegregation effort in the county. Among those present were the Reverend W. O. Wells, Jr., who pastored the largest church in Cocoa Beach, and Rudy Stone, a local funeral director. Wells and Stone would prove themselves as two of the branch's most dedicated members.

The new program at first ran into roadblocks. When the members petitioned the Brevard school board to desegregate the public schools, the board members referred the matter to the state's attorney general. They argued that other Brevard County parents might decide to sue the board. This cowardly move on the part of public officials proved to me that the county was prepared to resist desegregation, especially since the attorney general openly advocated a dual school system.

The setback failed to stop Wells and Stone, however. They worked together to organize the community to protest discrimination in housing, employment, and public accommodations. Stone also began encouraging people to exercise their voting privileges. In 1963 Wells formed a Brevard branch youth council. The young people who joined it quickly began to tackle the all-White lunch counters and other segregated facilities in the downtown area. Sit-ins brought immediate results. The mayor, who owned a large restaurant, agreed to negotiate. When the mayor attempted to name his own gardener as a Black community representative, Wells protested loudly. Finally, merchants accepted the inevitable and desegregated.

Housing discrimination offered another issue for the Cocoa community. It was addressed after Dave Johnson, a Black teacher who worked in Brevard County, filed a complaint against the city, charging that he had been denied the opportunity to purchase a home. Jack E. Wood, the NAACP's national housing director, consulted with the branch. The question merited his involvement since several contractors with the NASA space agency had already employed NAACP assistance to eliminate housing discrimination in Volusia and Brevard Counties. In the end, Johnson's complaint found resolution only after the federal Veteran's Administration and the Federal Housing Authority withheld funds from the builder accused of discrimination.

There was more. Joining forces with an instructor from Brevard County Junior College, Wells and Stone successfully laid the ground work for a grant for Head Start funds. Wells also assisted in organizing a group to test several bus depots between Miami and Valdosta, Georgia, to ensure that they did not discriminate. Dubbed "Florida's Freedom Riders" by the press, the group included Father Theodore Gibson of the Miami branch, the Reverend Eugene Tillman of Daytona Beach, and the Reverend Frank Pinkston of Ocala. Their initiative offered an inspirational example throughout the state.

Charles W. Cherry, president of the Florida State Conference of NAACP Branches, accepts a proclamation from Governor Bob Graham on "NAACP 75th Anniversary Month" in the State of Florida. Mrs. Arnita Davis, president of the Tallahassee NAACP branch, is at the governor's left.

(Below) Baseball great Jackie Robinson was an inspiring role model for Tampa Youth Council members when he visited Tampa in 1956.

(Above) Prominent Tampa educators Lutrell Bing and A. J. Ferrell offered leadership during NAACP voter registration initiatives in the late 1950s and early 1960s. Bing later was elected to the Hillsborough County Commission. (NAACP Papers/Library of Congress)

THE NAACP AT HOME: LOCAL ORGANIZATIONS AND ACTIVITIES

Our Tampa chapter did pioneering work in voter registration. James A. Hammond, chairman, stands at a sound truck used to gather prospective voters. With him are Catherine Harris, office secretary, and William A. Fordham, one of our attorneys. (NAACP Papers/Library of Congress)

Mapping out plans are (left to right) William A. Fordham, unidentified, Jim Hammond, Catherine Harris, and W. C. Patton, southeast voter registration director for the NAACP. (NAACP Papers/Library of Congress)

Members of the Youth Council demonstrate in Tallahassee, c. 1960 (right). Below are three young activists arrested during the Tallahassee Bus Boycott. In the center is Leonard Speed, son of Tallahassee businessman Dan Speed, who is photographed in front of his father's store at right below. (NAACP Papers/Library of Congress)

Protestors in the nation's oldest city made a dramatic statement as they demonstrated near the columns of the old St. Augustine Market in 1964. (AP/Wide World Photos)

12
The Challenge at St. Augustine

During the 1950s and 1960s St. Augustine, the nation's oldest town, also was one of its most racist cities. That fact was brought back to my mind recently when I had the chance to reminisce with the Honorable Leander Shaw, the chief justice of the Supreme Court of Florida. During the Civil Rights era, Justice Shaw was one of the principal Black attorneys who worked with the NAACP in the Ancient City. It is no understatement for me to declare that his efforts contributed substantially to the progress that came eventually, although painfully, to that community.

By way of background, the murders of Harry T. Moore and his wife deeply affected the NAACP's members in St. Augustine, just as they did residents of most Florida cities. As early as my first visit to the town after assuming the job of field secretary in 1952, it appeared clear to me that economic pressures and fears of police brutality would inhibit our desire to rebuild an effective organization there. A local barber and minister named Mr. Wells valiantly presided over the branch. Yet, in the aftermath of the assassinations, he could not rally the community. It struck me that the religious sector offered us little support. An important exception concerned Thomas W. Wright, who in time would serve as branch president.

Over the next decade patience, determination, hard work, and the courage of a number of local residents permitted the NAACP to establish a serious and influential presence in the St. Augustine community. This fact became of major importance in 1963 and 1964, when national and international attention focused on the Ancient City and its racial problems. In the events that led up to the St. Augustine civil rights demonstrations and local White reactions to them, the NAACP and its members involved themselves in crucial ways. Sadly, these contributions mostly have been neglected by students of the Civil Rights movement.[1] I hope that the following discussion will begin the process of rectifying this unfortunate situation.

Let me begin the tale by mentioning a part of the conversation that I had with Justice Shaw. We recollected one particular meeting between the local branch members and St. Augustine city officials. The March 12, 1963, session was called to discuss racial injustices. That day Black residents and students from Florida Memorial and Industrial College filled the audience. A tense atmosphere pervaded the room as these men and women, tired of years of oppression and intimidation, stood ready to demand decent treatment as befitted United States citizens.

The session commenced when the city manager, Charles Barrier, stood and asked for attention. He then announced that persons wishing to speak would be required to give their names and addresses and to identify any organization that they represented before they would be allowed to express their concerns. Leander and I were sitting next to each other. I turned to him and asked if I should protest Barrier's obvious intimidation tactics. Today's reader may ask why such a simple request constituted intimidation. The fact was that local White racists could target named individuals with threats or, worse, carry out such threats against them. In any event, Shaw urged me to act. I thereupon asserted that, due to potential economic reprisals and police brutality, those present would decline to reveal such information. Barrier abruptly adjourned the meeting.

Barrier's actions failed to surprise us. City officials were not aware that, the previous evening, I had received a telephone call from an unidentified White woman. She warned me that the municipal officials had no intention of providing an open forum within which people could express themselves freely. In fact, she told me that certain public officials would avoid the session entirely. Thus, I knew ahead of time that the meeting was a sham.

Nonetheless, we needed to call their bluff in order to begin the arduous process of compelling St. Augustine to honor the United States Constitution. The farce played out, we set in motion a series of protests that would continue until passage of the 1964 Civil Rights Act. This is how it all started.

The important year came in 1961, and the individual who initially served as catalyst was Dr. Royal W. Puryear. He presided over St. Augustine's Florida Normal and Industrial College, which was one of the oldest centers for Black higher education in the state. The White community's discriminatory treatment of Black students and faculty angered the good doctor. Already he had begun quietly to support the NAACP's strategies to end the climate of passivity so common in Black neighborhoods. Because he held the position of college president, Dr. Puryear walked a tight rope, hoping to advance the cause while not disrupting what little financial support the college received. Then, in 1961, he bravely allowed the NAACP to hold meetings on campus. A college chapter also organized.

For two years the efforts pushed by Dr. Puryear continued, resulting in a solid core of NAACP support. Then, on February 6, 1963, our Southeast Regional Director Ruby Hurley and I met at the college with a group of the local branch officers. We convened to discuss strategies that would improve the branch's capabilities to bring about change and to consider plans to pressure the city to end racial discrimination. Among those present were Dr. Robert Hayling, a local Black dentist, and several employees of the nearby Fairchild Stratos Corporation. Earlier I had filed on behalf of the Fairchild employees a complaint with the President's Equal Opportunity Committee alleging employment discrimination.

At this meeting, we decided that the city's planned quadricentennial celebration—St. Augustine was founded in 1565—could prove quite advantageous to us. Branch members and Dr. Hayling suggested that Ruby and I ask Roy Wilkins, our national executive director, to call Vice President Lyndon B. Johnson. Since the vice president was scheduled as key-note speaker for an upcoming quadricentennial dinner to be held at the town's Ponce de Leon Hotel, Hayling thought that we should ask him to cancel his speaking engagement because no Black citizens had been invited to the affair. Surely, the thinking went, the vice president could not be aware of the discrimination.

A second initiative commenced when Dr. Hayling subsequently met with Rutledge Pearson, the Jacksonville branch's former president, who recently has been elected head of the NAACP's state conference. Hayling inquired whether the Jacksonville branch would picket in St. Augustine during the vice president's visit. I later reinforced Hayling's appeal to Pearson. I mentioned that, should Johnson insist on coming to St. Augustine despite the city's refusal to end discriminatory practices, then Jacksonville branch members should be prepared to picket. We knew that we could count on the larger branch for a successful protest since most members were veterans of the 1960 desegregation efforts in which they bravely had faced Ku Klux Klan members armed with baseball bats.

Meanwhile, other meetings and a series of protests by Black citizens who were outraged that no Blacks had been invited to participate in planning the quadricentennial celebration seemed to be creating a measure of progress. Dr. Puryear reported to me about one such conference. It had involved local branch officers and someone named Bill Peak, who said that he represented United States Senator George Smathers. Puryear also informed me that he had been appointed to the vice presidential welcoming committee. Most importantly, he told me that tickets would be made available for African Americans and that the vice president promised to correct all discriminatory practices at the Fairchild plant.

As the events unfolded, another part of the equation began to take form. A local NAACP church committee formed to aid in desegregation efforts. The Reverend J. H. McKissick served both as the state NAACP church committee chairman and as the St. Augustine chairman. He, along with the Reverends Thomas Wright, Goldie Eubanks, Thomas DeSue, and others, participated in several meetings over the span of five days between the local branch and Bill Peak. The latter individual asked Fannie Fulwood, the new St. Augustine branch president, to invite the vice president to the city and to assure him that the NAACP welcomed his visit. Mrs. Fulwood agreed at first. However, when Peak returned to pick up the letter he found himself met by a refusal from the local branch. Rather, its officers told him that they wanted him to arrange a meeting with the city commissioners to address discriminatory practices. They called for all signs designating race to be removed from all areas of public accommodation, for non-discriminatory employment practices, and for racially integrated lunch counters and restaurants.

By Sunday, March 10, new information came to hand. Roy Wilkins called me about his contact with Vice President Johnson. He reported that the vice president had moved to correct all conditions of racial discrimination over which the federal government possessed jurisdiction. Wilkins also stated that Johnson had promised to try to persuade city officials to end discriminatory policies. We agreed that, if the vice president acted upon his promises, it would be possible for some measure of progress to occur in St. Augustine.

A series of events ensued with sometimes frustrating results. First, the Jacksonville branch opted not to picket the dinner at which Vice President Johnson would speak. They came to their decision based upon the city's assurance that ten seats would be reserved for Black guests. The Jacksonville branch's decision disappointed Dr. Hayling, especially after he learned additional details. Particularly, as he informed me, Blacks would be permitted no more than ten seats, tickets had to be purchased, and the Black guests likely would be forced to sit at one or two tables designated for them. Dr. Hayling bought a ticket and planned to attend but changed his mind before the dinner.

By the banquet day I felt compelled to press the matter personally. In the circumstances I attempted to contact Senator Smathers's man Bill Peak. He did return the call and, in doing so, let me know that the vice president's party was departing Jacksonville by helicopter on its way to St. Augustine. He promised to call me again when they arrived and otherwise to keep me informed.

Peak also introduced me on the telephone to Johnson's administrative assistant George Reedy. We discussed the fact that Black citizens' approval of the vice president's appearance had been conditioned upon the promise of Johnson's influence being brought to bear to end racial discrimination in St. Augustine and St. Johns County. I told him that Black citizens were dissatisfied with the availability of only ten tickets to the dinner. Further, he learned from me that, since each table would seat only six persons, we expected the whole seating arrangement to follow racially segregated patterns, with Black persons in attendance forced to segregate themselves. Reedy assured me that he personally would see to it that there was no racial segregation, even if it meant that he had to sit at one of the tables reserved for Blacks. We also discussed avenues for fulfilling the vice president's promises. Reedy stated that Johnson had asked him to provide a record of a meeting on the subject to be held the following Tuesday in the city manager's office.

Having now the benefit of Reedy's input, I contacted local branch officials. I informed Mrs. Fulwood that afternoon about the conversation and stressed the importance of members' attendance at the meeting arranged for March 12. When we all arrived at the appointed time and place, no one was there to greet us save Barrier and his secretary. Neither George Reedy nor the city commissioners attended. We, of course, noted their absences carefully. This was the meeting that I mentioned earlier, the one that Barrier adjourned so abruptly when we protested revealing names and addresses of NAACP members.

The NAACP could not let the snub by St. Augustine's city officials go unchallenged, and so we protested by contesting the town's generous budget for the quadricentennial celebration. Millions had been spent renovating some historic sites, including the Ponce de Leon Hotel. I learned that the city had applied for a grant totaling more than $300,000 for additional funding to promote and support the upcoming festivities. With Mrs. Fulwood, Dr. Hayling, and others, I assisted in drafting a formal letter opposing the grant. Mrs. Fulwood signed on behalf of the local branch.

As days and weeks passed following the vice president's visit, it became more and more evident that local officials had "forgotten" Johnson's promises, as well as several of their own commitments to us. We dispatched complaints to Washington but received no replies. White House officials appeared more involved with events in other parts of the South, as the eyes and ears of the world especially looked toward the protest marches and activities led by Dr. Martin Luther King, Jr., and his Southern Christian Leadership Conference. Rebuffed on the federal level, I resorted to an approach to Florida's racist governor Farris Bryant. The meeting lasted no more than ten minutes. The governor told me that he would not intervene in St. Augustine's situation because it was a local matter. Beyond that, I did all the talking.

I am sure that Governor Bryant wished the situation to be resolved simply, but the NAACP would not be shunted aside so easily. Over the course of several meetings with Mrs. Fulwood, Elizabeth Hawthorne, Dr. Hayling, Reverend Eubanks, and others, we reviewed the city officials' reluctance to end racial discrimination and to address the issues that our organization had raised. By consensus, it was agreed that the NAACP would step up the pace of demonstrations. At my request, assistance arrived from the national NAACP headquarters when Director of Branches Gloster Current agreed to hire the Reverend G. Frank Pinkston of Ocala to work with the St. Augustine branch and to coordinate activities of its youth council. Pinkston had just returned from Virginia Union College where he had attended workshops on nonviolence and participated in protest activities. Within a short span of time, the young man and I flew to New York to meet with Gloster to develop strategic plans.

An incident occurred during that summer of 1963 that proved the value of Pinkston's presence in St. Augustine. One of my regular letters to NAACP General Counsel Robert L. Carter, dated July 27, described the situation:

> We are involved in several cases here in the state covering the arrests of youth[s] between the ages of 14 and seventeen years and in one or two cases, who have been declared "Juvenile Delinquents" because of a refusal of the youths and the parents to sign papers stating that they (the youths) would not participate in demonstrations aimed at protesting racial discrimination in this state. . . .
>
> Attorneys Leander Shaw and Earl Johnson, both of Jacksonville[,] represented the juveniles. Shaw has requested that some one from New York come in to Jacksonville to help them with the case because they do not want to make any errors. I heard the Judge say also that there had been a "directive" come down on how to handle juveniles in sit-ins. He would not divulge the source. But we take cognizant of the fact that there have been arrests of youths in many communities within the past week on the same charges.[2]

The St. Augustine incident concerned four youths who were detained in the St. Johns County jail while a local judge decided whether to declare them juvenile delinquents. The battle to free them raged back and forth. Some people believed that they were being held as pawns by the state as a warning that similar actions would be taken, not only in St. Augustine but across the entire state, should sit-in demonstrations continue.

In the circumstances, our young organizer went to work. Pinkston strove full time to put together protest demonstrations while instructing participants in methods of nonviolence. At first he and Dr. Hayling worked well together. Then, as White segregationists pressured protesters, Pinkston increasingly saw Hayling as a difficult partner. On his own part, Pinkston faced threats of arrest while organizing pickets outside the county jail.

The availability of money to finance such activities posed a chronic challenge. To help meet it, I made a point, whenever I visited to Miami, to brief the Reverend J. A. Finlayson, president and elder statesman of the Florida Baptist Association, on the conditions in St. Augustine. I told him how difficult it was for the

NAACP to raise funds to continue organized protests. Always eager to assist, Finlayson would request donations at each state Baptist convention meeting.

The financial urgency grew in intensity during that summer of 1963, as St. Augustine began to witness mass arrests. On the day that the largest number of individuals were jailed, a special train of delegates happened to be traveling to the national Baptist convention. Pinkston and I agree to call upon the Baptist Association to contribute toward the tremendous expense of representing the protestors, most of whom were students from Florida Normal and Industrial Memorial College, a Baptist institution. I telegraphed the Reverend Finlayson, who was on the special train. My message read:

> Since your organization supports Florida Memorial College in this City, we ask that you call your executive Board together to consider action to protect rights of students attending your institution against such acts as use of dogs and electric prods yesterday and refusal to serve Negroes at Lunch Counters. [I] also [ask that this group join in] protest[ing] [the] confinement of four youths as Juvenile Delinquents for refusing to give up Constitutional rights to protest against racial discrimination. We ask you to organize all Baptist churches under your direction in Florida to back this fight.[3]

My plea to Reverend Finlayson received no immediate response, although I knew that he received the telegram when his train arrived at Jacksonville. We also did not hear back from an appeal that Pinkston made to the Baptist Association, even though he was a Baptist minister and his church belonged to the association. Accordingly, I dispatched an urgent follow-up letter to Finlayson:

> Several weeks ago following an incident in St. Augustine, Florida where nearly forty Negro citizens were arrested for praying on the Slave Mart, I wired you requesting that the Baptist

General State Convention take a stand on the situation in that city. I felt that this was necessary especially since the Convention does support the Florida Memorial College and that the students at the school are Negroes.

As of this date, and almost a month later, I have not heard from you nor have I seen any announcement made publicly as to the position that your group assumes. Since the police of St. Augustine used cow prods and police dogs to assist in making the arrests, I felt that this would be enough to prod the Baptist Convention and its leadership into giving active support to the demands of Negroes of that city.

But it appears that this leadership is not willing to speak out and to be heard. Nor is it willing to give for Freedom in our home state. For this reason, and because many of the nation's news media are interested in knowing what your stand is going to be, I am again requesting that you give your immediate attention to the original request.[4]

These messages and the pleas from St. Augustine's citizens, as well as the Florida Memorial College students who also were victims of police brutality, still brought no response.

By that time other events had caught up with us. In early September Dr. Hayling had shown me a handbill advertising a Ku Klux Klan gathering to be held behind a local bowling alley on U.S. Highway 1 on Saturday night, September 18. Connie Lynch, a rabid segregationist preacher from California and a founder of a group called the National States Rights Party, was promoting this hate rally. Hayling mentioned that he intended to drive down to the area to see what was going on. I cautioned him against doing so. I knew the danger of attending such a demonstration without police protection. Hayling, in turn, called me a chicken. He argued that, since U.S. 1 was a federal highway, he, just like any other citizen, had the right to travel it to see what was happening. I returned to Tampa the Friday evening before the event.

Word of the results of Hayling's actions came to me that Sunday. Roy Wilkins called at about 5:00 a.m. and asked if I was aware

The Challenge at St. Augustine

of a Klan rally at which four Black men, one of whom was Dr. Hayling, had been badly assaulted. I told him no but that I was preparing to travel to St. Augustine in one hour. Roy asked that I go straight to the hospital to get statements from the men and to tell them that the NAACP would pay their medical and legal expenses.

My journey got me to St. Augustine before noon, and there I learned the rest of the story. When I walked into the hospital, a horrible sight confronted me. Dr. Hayling's face was puffed, apparently his jaw had been broken, and several of his teeth were missing. I could tell that he was suffering pain. I tried to talk to him about the evening before. He related to me that he, Clyde Jenkins, James Hauser, and James Jackson drove down the highway and prepared to turn around. They drove their car up a dirt road, intending to return to the highway for a better view of what was happening. Then, out of nowhere it seemed, a car pulled up behind them. One of the passengers in that car yelled at them to pull over to the side of the road so that his car could pass. But, instead of passing, the car stopped alongside Dr. Hayling's, and several Klansmen in the car pointed guns at the four civil rights activists. The Klansmen demanded that the men get out of their automobile. They frisked their captives and ordered them to continue to the rally as they followed.

The violence came at the rally site. When the frenzied crowd saw the four men, they began to yell "niggers" repeatedly. Then, one Klansman recognized and identified Dr. Hayling as one of the leaders of the St. Augustine protest. The mob beat the men severely and might have killed them had it not been for Art Chaney, an official of the Florida Human Relations Council who had infiltrated the Klan to help destroy it. Chaney called Sheriff L. O. Davis who rescued the men. As I listened to their statements, I could not help but wonder to myself what might have happened to me if I had joined Dr. Hayling.

The vicious beating demanded legal response. The NAACP appealed to Governor Bryant and to United States Attorney General Robert Kennedy for an investigation and the apprehension of those responsible. I have in my personal papers a clipping from the *Daytona Beach Morning Journal* that tells the results. Its headline reads, "Four White Men Arrested As Aftermath of Klan Session."[5] The racist bullies all came from Jacksonville. Their names were Clarence O. Wilson, Harmon Davis, Lawrence A. Bessent, and DeWitt W. Springfield. They ranged in age from twenty-nine to forty-nine. Authorities released them pending trial on $100 bonds.

Otherwise, the St. Augustine scene continued to be a troubled one. Attorney Earl Johnson persevered on behalf of the four youths who had refused to waive their rights to picket and protest against racial discrimination. Their parents consented to filing suits with NAACP assistance to force desegregation of the Marianna School for Boys where two of the young men had been assigned. As far as the city's leadership was concerned, it had been put on notice that Black citizens wanted changed. Yet, city officials failed to take advantage of many opportunities provided through peaceful protests and petitioning to even discuss needed and lawfully required change. Developers and financiers were too busy investing in what they believed would be a major attraction for White tourists. Even the vice president's warning that all racial discrimination must end fell on deaf ears. The police chief and the sheriff allowed their employees to perform acts of indecent and often violent means to stem protests. Elected officials, who overtly condoned brutal attacks, backed them up.

And so St. Augustine's White community cast the die for itself. It set a scene that made it easy for the Southern Christian Leadership Conference to move into the city. Dr. King commanded attention because he had the support of the media that followed him. SCLC and Dr. King did indeed come to St. Augustine. While the Klansmen and other pro-segregationists vowed to get King, the resistance they promoted only helped to fuel the Civil Rights Movement. The NAACP continued to work in the community during the SCLC's presence in the town and long after the passage of the 1964 Civil Rights Act. Even with the many marches and jailings, change came only with legal action. At NAACP urging, the federal courts forced St. Augustine finally to accept Blacks as citizens.

THE CHALLENGE AT ST. AUGUSTINE

Rev. F. George Pinkston was an eloquent speaker and a tireless leader for the NAACP in the nation's oldest city. His energy and advice were always a pleasure to me, and he understood the problems of racism in his city and county better than anyone. His address to the state conference is a good overview of the issues and problems we faced in the critical years of the 1960s, and it is printed in full in Appendix Two at the end of the book. (The Pinkston Family)

Meeting in this church in St. Augustine, Rev. F. George Pinkston addresses an attentive crowd. To the far left on the front row is Dr. Robert Hayling, the St. Augustine dentist who was one of the "spark plugs" of our local NAACP branch there. (The Pinkston Family)

On June 11, 1964, Rev. Ralph Abernathy and Rev. Martin Luther King, Jr., were photographed in a St. Augustine jail cell following their arrest during the march organized by the Southern Christian Leadership Conference. (UPI/Corbis-Bettman)

Dr. Robert Hayling was a courageous leader in St. Augustine whose civil rights activism helped change the city.

Robert Hayling, Rev. Frank Pinkston, and the St. Augustine NAACP Youth Council deserve tremendous credit for challenging Jim Crow racism in the nation's oldest city. When Rev. King showed up to encourage young pickets on June 10, 1964, he brought the national spotlight with him, but our attention had been there for some time, and the results of our efforts were starting to be known. (AP/Wide World Photos)

THE CHALLENGE AT ST. AUGUSTINE

Attempts to integrate the public beach at St. Augustine Beach encountered forceful resistance from police in June 1964. (AP/Wide World Photos)

Demonstrations continued. During a night march on June 25, the protestors were attacked, and some of them injured. Andrew Young helps one of the victims move out of harm's way. (AP Wide World Photos)

Chief Justice Leander Shaw of the Florida State Supreme Court clearly remembers the days of struggle to end segregation in St. Augustine. He was one of the NAACP attorneys defending the civil rights of the protestors and was one reason that the constitutional principles of freedom and justice were affirmed in the end.

Ruby Hurley could command attention with her energy, experience, and conviction. Here she is standing to speak while Medgar Evers (left) and Gloster Current listen attentively. Evers had just been recently appointed as the first full-time field director for the NAACP in Mississippi.

Ruby Hurley, her back to the camera and partially hidden, conducts an early morning NAACP caucus at the Southeast Regional NAACP conference, c. 1957. These meetings have been an important feature of each NAACP conference and convention, and Ruby's skill at leading them can be read on the attentive faces of the participants.

13
Ruby Hurley, Youth, and the NAACP

By now, the reader will understand clearly that the Civil Rights Movement in Florida owed a great debt to the energy, drive, enthusiasm, and determination of young people. This especially proved true in overcoming the climate of fear that rendered so many individuals helpless in the aftermath of Harry T. Moore's murder. Fortunately, the NAACP had in place a mechanism, called the youth council, that permitted us to channel youthful passions in positive directions. I cannot think of our youth councils without also thinking of that great organizer and nurturer Ruby Hurley, who did so much to foster our programs for young people. For these reasons I think it fitting and proper to close this book with a closer look at Hurley's contributions and of the results as seen in the work of our youth councils.

I would like to begin with Ruby. She was born on November 7, 1909, in Washington, D.C. The only child of Alice and Edward R. Ruffin, she received her education in the public schools of our nation's capital. Later Ruby attended Miners Teacher's College and Robert H. Terrell Law School. A tall, beautiful woman with a slightly freckled, tan complexion, she caught the eye of William Hurley, who soon became her husband. Just as Ruby endeared herself to William Hurley, so she would endear herself to many of us in the movement. The list of persons could go on and on who recognized her great merit as a leader, organizer, and fine human being. I think immediately of Florida's Edward D. Davis, of whom I have written in this book, and of the Reverend Vernon Dahmer of Mississippi (Klansmen would take his life). To their names I would add those of Rosa Parks of Montgomery, Alabama; Aaron Henry of Mississippi; and many, many others.

Ruby Hurley devoted thirty-five years of her life to working for the NAACP. In 1943 she received appointment as director of the association's Youth and College Division. Eight years later our executive secretary Walter White sent her to Birmingham, Alabama, on special assignment to coordinate membership campaigns in five southern states. Despite stepped-up racial violence and racially based attacks on Black citizens in Alabama and the other southern states, Ruby overcame the challenges to her leadership potential. Due in great part to her efforts, the NAACP successfully organized the southeast region. Hurley became its first regional director.

The NAACP's successes in Alabama forced Ruby to relocate in 1955. The state was attempting to outlaw the association. So, at the NAACP national convention in San Francisco, Roy Wilkins, the new executive director, instructed Hurley to by-pass Birmingham on her return to the southeast. The sudden transfer of operations forced Ruby to leave many of her valuable possessions behind in Alabama. Fortunately, Atlanta offered a excellent new home base for her work.

During the mid-1950s Hurley began receiving long-overdue recognition for her achievements. I know, for instance, that in 1956 *Look* magazine published an article entitled, "Ruby Hurley's South." The story told of the many miles and hours Ruby spent working in the South, especially of her role in untangling the story behind the murder of young Emmett Till in Mississippi. Evidencing tremendous courage, Ruby had slipped into the vicinity of the lynching dressed as a farm worker. The conversations that ensued provided key details and insights into the tragedy. Langston Hughes, the internationally known poet, lauded her accomplishments in a book on the NAACP published in 1962. By the time of her retirement in 1975 the Southeast Region itself stood as a testament to her leadership. It had become the largest and most-productive part of the NAACP organization.

Beyond the NAACP, Ruby always found time to honor her religious convictions. An active church member, she affiliated with Birmingham's St. Paul Methodist Church before joining the Warren Memorial United Methodist Church in Atlanta. For several years she served as the president of the United Methodist Women. Her contributions for the U.M.W. extended to membership on its Pastor-Parish Relations Committee and discharge of the position of Christian social involvement mission coordinator for the North Georgia Conference. In 1977 Atlanta mayor Maynard Jackson appointed her to serve on the city's license review board.

Ruby began to touch my life in 1946, when I met her while she was visiting Tampa. I can recall thinking during that and subsequent meetings about how she always dressed fashionably and well. On that occasion she was touring Florida to offer assistance to the local NAACP branches. Her special mission was to develop youth programs. Up to that time, most organizational energies aimed at ending discrimination and segregation had been expended on programs of interest only to adults. Harry T. Moore had seen the error in this and had organized a youth council in his Brevard County home area of Mims and Titusville. He also encouraged the growth of a college chapter at Florida A&M University in Tallahassee, which became one of the nation's largest such groups. Of the early pioneers of the youth council movement, I remember Ruby speaking of the outstanding work of Mrs. Mary Grooms, the adult advisor at Pompano Beach.

When I lived in Detroit during the late 1940s and early 1950s, our paths crossed again. Hurley actively assisted in the work of a college and youth group, of which I became president. My respect for Ruby grew deeper during that period of time, as she helped to spur my own commitment to the civil rights cause. I would mention, by the way, that we named our group after Ruby's NAACP friend and colleague Gloster B. Current, a native of Detroit and former executive director of the local NAACP.

Once in Birmingham, Ruby's headquarters became a focal point for young activists from all over the southeastern region. She located her first office in the Masonic temple. At least twice each year, NAACP southeast staff members would gather there to plan regional meetings and to coordinate activities. Once it became known that the NAACP office had opened in Birmingham, threatening calls and other efforts to intimidate Ruby were not long in coming. Eugene "Bull" Connor, Birmingham's infamous police chief, and Ruby soon found themselves at odds. On one occasion "Negro dolls" with sliced throats and red fingernail polish were left at her home. A tremendous number of vile and obscene phone calls forced Ruby to keep her telephone number unlisted for a time.

Responsibility for so large an area as the entire southeast did not keep Hurley from coming to Florida to work with us "in the trenches." She spent nearly ninety days with me in Jacksonville following the incident I have mentioned earlier when baseball bats were distributed by the Ku Klux Klan for use against protesters. I already have discussed the series of events that led up to this incident. Here, let me just state that it was all that Ruby and I could do—working with Rutledge Pearson, the youth advisor, and other community leaders—to bring about a solution to the community's dilemma.

I shall never forget her experience meeting with Jacksonville gang leaders, after midnight, in a cemetery. Those young men, from that experience, developed a mountain of respect for and devotion to Hurley. The gangs' members, in some respects, even became our protectors. They gathered in front of and inside the NAACP office, although I will acknowledge that their dress did not, at first, suit the occasion. When Ruby asked them to wear more presentable attire, all of them left. When they returned one hour later, they wore suits and ties. Their attitude had changed because they now considered themselves acceptable and a part of the NAACP movement.

This hands-on assistance was repeated in many areas of Florida. By way of example, Ruby was with me in St. Augustine at the time I met with NAACP members at the Florida Memorial and Industrial College. As I explained in the previous chapter, we heard pleas on that occasion from a group which included Robert Hayling, a young dentist, for us to call on Roy Wilkins to ask Vice President Lyndon Johnson to cancel his scheduled speaking engagement at the city's Ponce de Leon Hotel. That contact, once made, constituted the real beginning of the effort to end what became a vicious conspiracy to destroy the fight to end Jim Crow in the state of Florida. Ruby stood with us every step of the way.

As was suggested at the beginning of this chapter, Ruby's contributions in Florida found themselves repeated throughout the southeast. Think of those great names in the Civil Rights Movement who labored alongside her. Among the individuals who worked with Hurley as NAACP staff could be counted Medgar Evers of Mississippi; Charles McClain, North Carolina; the Reverend I. D. Quincy Newman, South Carolina; W. C. Patton, who organized voter registration drives in the southeast; Vernon Jordan, Georgia; Dr. Judy Wright, South Carolina; and Hazel Lamb of Tennessee. While these persons served with the NAACP at different times, all found their dedication to the cause enhanced by Ruby's presence and influence.

Not enough is said today about Ruby Hurley. Not enough credit is given to her for her leadership during really tough times. Today, many persons claim credit for their civil rights exploits, but few deserve credit more than does Ruby. She inspired a majority of the young men and women from the South who have occupied leadership positions in the recent past and continue to do so in the present. And, beyond that, she did so much more.

The name of Mrs. Mary Groom already has arisen in connection with Ruby Hurley and Florida's youth councils. Perhaps as much as anyone she deserves recognition for pioneer efforts at organizing effective youth councils in this state. Such work desperately was needed. During the late 1940s, thanks to Ruby's initiatives, college chapters operated at Florida A&M College in Tallahassee, Bethune-Cookman College in Daytona Beach, Florida Normal and Industrial Memorial College in St. Augustine, and Edward Waters College in Jacksonville. Then came the murders of Harry T. Moore and his wife on Christmas Day 1951. By the following September only one college chapter, that at Florida A&M, remained active. Even there, very little emphasis was placed on youth work.

Just as Ruby had inspired the college chapter and some local youth councils, she also inspired Mrs. Groom. Mary developed her interest in youth work in 1945-1946 after meeting with Ruby. Because of widespread publicity given to a number of NAACP legal initiatives, including the *Chambers* case, Mrs. Groom recognized the importance of our organization. Working against criticism and failure of support from individuals in Broward County whose economic ties depended heavily on the school system, she became the youth advisor for the Pompano Beach council. Ruby praised her effectiveness, especially when she brought a representative group to several state and national NAACP meetings. Mary Groom is gone now, having died in August 1961 after nearly twenty years of work with the NAACP and its youth councils in Florida. If she were alive today, I know that she would look proudly on the work of Black and White youth whom she inspired during the fight to desegregate eating establishments, institutions of higher education, and other significant places in the state.

My own experience with the NAACP's approaches to youth while I was growing up in Tampa mirrored the rest of the state's experience. There simply were not many such approaches to be found. Harry T. Moore's success at nurturing youth councils came mostly in Brevard County, his home area. The fact was that the NAACP aimed the principal thrusts of its initiatives at adults and the goals of combatting segregation and Jim Crow practices. Similarly, the mostly male, adult-oriented Florida State Conference—and its branches—focused on adult-oriented issues such as political action, police violence, and discrimination against Black teachers.

Just before Moore's death, he and Hurley did attempt to expand the presence of youth councils in the state. The call issued for the state conference's eleventh annual meeting, to be held at Daytona Beach in November 1951, sounded the theme. It specified:

> Since both Mrs. Hurley and Mr. [Walter] White will be with us, it has been decided to hold the State NAACP Youth Meeting in Daytona Beach on these same dates [as the state conference meeting]. Mrs. Hurley served as youth secretary for several years,

and it is felt that she will be able to give the young people some helpful suggestions relative to their work. And it will certainly be a great inspiration for our people to see Walter White, the famous leader of the NAACP and one of the most outstanding Negroes of modern times.

The young people will hold their business session on the campus of Bethune-Cookman College. All will meet jointly in two mass meetings. Youth Councils and College Chapters are urged to send delegates to this meeting. And branches that do not have Youth Councils are invited to send some of their youth members, as they might be inspired to go back home and help to get Councils organized. Please send the name of your youth delegates to Mr. Henry Finley, state youth president, Florida A&M College, Tallahassee. For room accommodations, youth delegates should write to Herman Morris, president of Bethune-Cookman College Chapter, Daytona Beach.[1]

Unfortunately, as detailed in the first chapter, this meeting proved a tumultuous one, and, about one month afterward, Harry Moore lay slain.

As a result, a dismal picture that resulted confronted me when I assumed responsibilities as field secretary in 1953. Following my appointment, I conducted a tour of the state. It disclosed a void of activity except, as I mentioned, at Florida A&M. With support and guidance from Dr. Emmett Bashful and Daisy Young, a staff member, the FAM chapter constituted one of the largest in the southeast region. Monroe Mack would represent its members at the 1953 national convention. When I spoke with Mrs. Groom at Pompano Beach, she told me of the pressures and lack of support from community leaders. In fact, the Pompano Beach council, despite her best efforts, had become inactive. At the first state conference planned by me and held in Fort Lauderdale, not more than fifteen youth delegates participated.

Real interest in youth council work began to grow only after the 1954 United States Supreme Court decision in the *Brown* school desegregation case. The continuing rejection of Black students by the University of Florida also generated interest among several young adult groups. Then, Tallahassee provided a series of events that helped to galvanize efforts. They included the rape of a Florida A&M coed and the subsequent convictions of four white men. Also, the Tallahassee bus protests in 1956 and 1958 spurred organization building as more college students became active. Patricia Due helped establish a chapter of the Congress of Racial Equality at FAM which some White students from Florida State University also joined. The NAACP chapter at FAM grew into the largest NAACP college unit in the country. Pressures from the legislature, White citizens councils, the Ku Klux Klan, and Tallahassee law enforcement officers (including local courts) failed to break the groups' determination. A fuller discussion of these events has appeared earlier in this book.

Then, the stage was set for the true send-off of youth involvement that came in 1960 with the birth of the sit-in movement. Thereafter, NAACP youth groups staged protests in every major city in Florida. I have mentioned numerous examples previously, but would call special attention to youth efforts in Tallahassee, Tampa, Jacksonville, Fort Lauderdale, St. Augustine, St. Petersburg, West Palm Beach, and Ocala. Significantly for today, much of the current NAACP leadership developed from these local units.

By the 1960s, of course, Florida's NAACP already was entering its third generation of leadership. We needed and welcomed youth, and how privileged I felt to see them demanding change. I had lived by then for long enough to have known state NAACP founders, some of whom had been public officials in the Civil War's aftermath. Within my lifetime the worst aspects of Jim Crow had come and gone, and here were these fine young people taking up the cause as their own. No greater reward could I have asked.

Baseball great Jackie Robinson with Ruby Hurley at a mass meeting in Tampa at St. Paul A.M.E. Church.

Rev. A. Leon Lowry, state president, talks with Mrs. Ruby Hurley during a visit to Tampa in 1962.

My good friend and colleague Roy Wilkins made me feel more than welcome in my new role as civil rights coordinator for the southeast under the Office of Economic Opportunity. It began a new chapter of challenge and achievement in the building of bridges to cross the great chasms of hatred and inequality that remain both deep and wide.

Afterword

How can I summarize what fourteen years of service as Florida's NAACP field secretary meant to me? I can only say, *just about everything*. As I reflect back, I cannot comprehend how I was so fortunate as to have the opportunity. The faces of so many outstanding men and women appear in my mind as their voices continue to echo in my ears. I can declare proudly that I was there with those fine people to push the fight after the terrible tragedy of Harry and Harriett Moore's deaths. It was my honor to stand with them. We made a difference.

Do not be fooled, though, into thinking that the fight is over. Racism fools just as does cancer. It might slip into remission after treatment is applied, but often it quietly resumes its tragic course when attention has shifted away. I can tell you that Florida's NAACP will be there when it is needed. It will not back down from confrontation nor falter in the face of apathy. It will continue in the twenty-first century to serve as the conscience of Florida just as it did for the final eighty-five years of the twentieth.

A very few last words about me. As has been mentioned earlier, I departed the field secretary's job in March 1966 to serve the federal government through the civil rights office of the Office of Economic Opportunity's southeastern region. After a decade or so, I returned to Tampa where I accepted the position of Hillsborough County's civil rights compliance head. In 1988 I finally retired. We still live in Tampa, where, God willing, we will remain for years to come.

Tampa, Florida
May 2000

APPENDICES, NOTES, BIBLIOGRAPHY, AND INDEX

Reverend C. Kenzie Steele in front of his church in Tallahassee.

APPENDIX ONE

The Tallahassee Bus Protest Story

A Speech by the Rev. Charles Kenzie Steele Delivered at the 17th Annual Session, Florida State Conference of Branches, National Association for the Advancement of Colored People, St. Paul A.M.E. Church, Tampa, Florida, October 26, 1956

The Tallahassee Bus Protest story concerns a town that has for more than ninety years taken pride in being the only unconquered state capital of the Old Confederacy. Therefore, the customs, traditions, and prejudices that have grown up out of the seed bed of such racial pride and unfairness have caused our town to move forward with a snail's pace until within the last fifteen years.

Southeast Georgia is twenty miles northeast of us. Southeast Alabama is less than ninety miles northwest of us, but in spite of Tallahassee's fortunate or unfortunate location it has made some marked progress within the last fifteen years—progress that has been occasioned by the influx of new people and new ideas brought in to a large measure by the expansion of Florida State University (white) and Florida Agricultural and Mechanical University. Here was a progress of which many people of both races were totally unaware.

Therefore, it was to the horrible shock of some, and to the pleasant surprise of many of us, that on May 26, 1956, an incident occurred that brought to focus the fact that *Old Tallahassee is not what she used to be.* For it was on this day that two young women students of Florida A and M University were asked to stand rather than occupy the only available seat on a city coach. They were ordered to stand on this crowded bus simply because a white woman was on the other end of the seat. The white lady did not object, but the bus driver insisted that it would be an unpardonable sin for these neatly clad college women of color to share a seat with a white woman.

But it so happened that these young ladies from A and M had too much of this new Twentieth Century Negro blood in their veins to pay their fare for segregated services. The driver would not refund their money; instead, he had them arrested and carried to police headquarters, where they were charged with placing themselves in the position of starting a riot. On Saturday night a cross was burned in front of their residence. This was purposed to frighten the young women and make of them an example for the rest of the students as well as for all Tallahassee Negroes. But thank God! Instead, it had the opposite effect. It rang a bell that pealed for the robust truth that *Old Tallahassee is not what she used to be.*

On a Monday following the cross burning, the entire student body of more than two thousand met in Lee Auditorium and voted unanimously that they would register their protest by staying off of city buses. They came out of their meeting with passions running high and spirits that were so fiery and contagious that their protest captured the imagination of the entire Negro community. On Tuesday night, citizens from all walks of life in our city met at the Bethel Baptist Church and heard the unfavorable report from the City Manager, and the manager of the bus company. It was then that we voted in mass that until riding conditions on city coaches were amended, improved, and made democratic that Negroes would avoid them. Wednesday morning, the next day, found Tallahassee city buses empty, for fifteen thousand Negroes had decided that they had suffered and endured enough humiliation, injustice, and unfairness at the hands of a company kept in business primarily on money from Negro patrons. From this heartfelt conviction the Inter-Civic Council was born. By this time many of us knew that *Old Tallahassee is not what she used to be.*

Many and varied have been our experiences through the past *four* months of our protest. There have been mountains of laughter and joy, and there have been valleys of tears and sorrows. There have been long, weary nights of disappointments and there have been sunshiny days of knowing ourselves to be in the great and unconquerable *Will of God*—Yes, thank God that on the darkest night we have been able to see the star of being right, the brilliance of which no cloud has been able to hide and no darkness has been able to put out.

Nearly every two weeks since the beginning of our movement we have faced a crisis of one kind or another—a crisis created by our prejudiced city officials or the "Uncle Toms" in our midst. There is quite a difference in the Uncle Toms that resulted from the period of re-construction and the Uncle Toms of the Twentieth Century and now. The old Uncle Toms stooped, bowed, and conducted themselves to the end of obtaining favors for the race. They felt their conduct was necessary in an age of fear for the people of color in America. But the new Uncle Toms stoop, grin, and talk out of both sides of their mouths to feather their own nest, and to sell their own people down the river. I really don't know which group has been the most alarmed by our movement in Tallahassee—the White city officials, or the new Uncle Toms. They have both learned the hard way that *Negro Tallahassee is not what she used to be.*

There is power in oneness. It took the Negroes in Tallahassee thirty-three days to put the bus company out of business. Yes, it took us thirty-three days to demonstrate to the world that Tallahassee Negroes had been keeping alive a company and business that had no appreciation whatever for our patronage—for it was only thirty-three days after the beginning of our protest that the bus company declared itself dead—killed by "rabble rousing suitcase newcomers" to the city, and *I happened to be one of them accused.*

With the pending collapse of the Bus Company in Tallahassee, the Inter-Civic Council was faced with the crisis of having to decide between the rising dignity of a downtrodden race and the perpetuation of a segregated transportation system. The officials of the city (City Commissioners and others) sought to take advantage of the religious nature of our people by showing them how evil, sinful, and awful it would be to deprive a capital city of a transportation system. They further pointed out how we would suffer and how handicapped we would become without buses to ride. It was then that Tallahassee Negroes decided that it is far better "to walk in humble dignity, than to ride in shameful humiliation." Thus for some thirty-odd days there were no city buses running in Florida's Capital City simply because Negroes would not ride them.

If the collapse of the bus company was a crisis and a time of testing of the Inter-Civic Council, then the resurrection and return of them to the streets was even more so. They returned with courtesy promised, with Negro drivers on routes predominantly serving Negro communities, but with the sworn policy that never would a Negro and a white person share seats side by side. This, of course, meant that there would always be the possibility of someone having to stand while there were still vacant seats available. With this, the Inter-Civic Council could not and would not agree. The people themselves without the prodding of leadership, turned all of these half-measure proposals down—and in some cases in spite of the fact that there were some few leaders who advocated them....

Whereas the NAACP did not start our protest, they came to our help as soon as the news got out that we were having trouble in Tallahassee. They have been with us every step of the way. Even now they have supplied us with a lawyer to help us in our defense. I cannot exaggerate the meaning of this militant organization to us.

> A. They have the lawyers equal to any organization in the country.
>
> B. They don't have all the money they ought to have, but no organization makes better use of what they have than our own NAACP.
>
> C. I would be a member of the NAACP for no other reason than they are feared by the Southern white man. Why else would he try to outlaw it from the states?
>
> D. Ladies and Gentlemen, I am somewhat like the little boy was about being a Baptist. If I were not a member of the NAACP I would be ashamed of myself.

The Southern white man has the police force, the city, state, and even the national representatives of legal powers. The one organization that Negroes have is always out there in the battle, and the Southern politicians are so little, unfair, and afraid until now they want to destroy the NAACP, etc. The Inter-Civic Council is indeed thankful for what the National Association for the Advancement of Colored People has meant to Tallahassee.

Ladies and Gentlemen, the time has now come when Negroes throughout America must stand up and be counted. Please don't misunderstand me—for whereas I am positive that love will win, I know that nowhere must we stoop, bow, or cry before the idle god of racial prejudice and exclusiveness of any kind and within anyone. We must push our fight on non-violence and legal procedure, not only to the city halls, but to the Governors' offices, and to the White House if need be. To do this, we must be prepared with prayer, love, and faith in our hearts, the techniques of non-violence in our heads, and the ballot in our hands.

The white man here in America has great respect for Dollar Bills, lead bullets, and paper ballots. We don't have the bullets, tanks, guns, and ammunition with which to fight our battles. If we did have them, I would not advocate the use of them; violence is unwise and immoral and carries upon its head the fading crown of death and hell. So violence is for us of all things, both impractical and immoral. Moreover, we don't have the money with which to altogether wage our fight, but what little we have can go a long way toward helping us come to the place of first class citizenship. Somewhere and at some time, we must come to the maturity of knowing that sugar from a Negro store is as sweet as that from a white store, and that Negro inssurance money will spend in the same places as the money that comes from a white company. Castor oil or aspirins prescribed and filled by Negro doctors and druggists will have the same affects as if given by white doctors and druggists (gas and oil). Ladies and gentlemen, I am trying to say that we must put our money together and when possible, use it to advance our race. Economically, we must adopt the practice of the early Christians. They *worked honestly, lived simply,* and *saved carefully.* By so doing, they soon became the most powerful force within all the confines of the Roman government. It is to this end that I have humbly asked that we would avoid getting into debt and not to loiter in town on Central and Scott Streets. We must, like the early Christians, make ourselves indispensable to the good and well-being of our city, state, and nation . . . .

Guns are powerful, money is effective, but I know of nothing that the American white man is more afraid of than the ballot. The Southern white man is afraid of the ballot. Do you know why Negroes are by the pwers that be, frightened away from the polls in Gadsden County? I'll tell you—it is because the white man is afraid that if the Negro votes he may take over the affairs of County and City governments. Do you know why all the registrars in Tuskegee, Alabama, resigned? Well, I'll tell you—it's because the white man in Macon County is afraid that the Negroes there will wake up and really make use of their united power at the place of voting. *All politicians know that a voteless people is indeed a hopeless people.* So I am pleading that we will each and all register and vote in all elections. Remember every vote counts one. Your vote will carry the same weight as any white vote. Listen, even President Eisenhower's vote can count no more than yours. If we fail now to register and vote, we are of all people most pitiable. The test of one's worthiness to first-class citizenship is his appreciation of the *Ballot.* Listen, in the voting booth, every man is a *king* and every woman a *queen.*

Ladies and Gentlemen, there is a better day for the American Negro now rapping at the door of Now. We must with love, faith, and prayer, force that door open in the name of Christ. God has no brakes nor speed limit on the coming of freedom, fraternity, and the Kingdom of God. Our God has promised this world the Kingdom and it must come. It has not come yet but it's still a-coming.

Yes, it's still a-coming in spite of the Eastlands and the Talmadges. Yes, it's still coming in spite of the Ku Klux Klans and the White Citizens Councils. Yes, thank God, the day of freedom is still a-coming in spite of hell and high water. There are some things that even God can't give us until we get ready and worthy of them. Listen, God is waiting on the right spirit, interest, love, and appreciation in us, and then and not until then will the day of full freedom dawn for the Black man of America. Until then we must work and fight, trusting our God for happy and heavenly results.

Now a word about the nature of our fight in Tallahassee. We are a committee waging our battle against evil principle and not against people; therefore, we must be non-violent, and motivated by love. Whereas we hate segregation, racial prejudice, and injustice, we are committed to not losing our white friends. We know that they are victims in need of rescue from the poisonous fangs of racial customs and traditions that have grown up out of the hotbed of ignorance and prejudice. Love is the most powerful force in the world. It is an agreement between means and ends. Protesting in love is not easy. It requires prayer and faith, [patience and hope, constancy and vision, humility and courage].

Another very important factor in our struggle has been the sense of worth and dignity that goes along with the conviction that you are right. All along we have been confident that we are economically right, socially right, politically right, and above all, morally right and in line with Divine teachings.

Right cannot be destroyed.

    Crushed to the ground, it will rise.

    On a scaffold, it will sway the world.

    I watched them mishandle right in Jerusalem, and I saw it triumph there for all eternity.

    If you are right God through Jesus has promised, "and lo I am with you always even until the end of the world."

He has never left us alone:

I've seen the lightning flashing,
And heard the thunder roll;
I've felt sin's breakers dashing,
Trying to conquer my soul:
Telling me still to fight on,
He promised never to leave me,
Never to leave me alone.

The world's fierce winds are blowing
Temptations sharp and keen;
I feel a peace in knowing
My Savior stands between;
He stands to shield me from danger

When earthly friends are gone;
He promised never to leave me,
Never to leave me alone.

When in affliction's valley
I'm treading the road of care,
My Savior helps me to carry
My cross when heavy to bear,
My [way] entangled with briars,
Ready to cast me down,
My Savior whispers His promise:
"I never will leave thee alone."

He died for me on the mountain,
For me they pierced His side,
For me He opened that fountain,
The crimson, cleansing tide;
For me He's waiting in glory,
Seated upon His throne:
He promised never to leave me,
Never to leave me alone.

Appendix Two

Freedom Now

An Address by Rev. Frank Pinkston, President, Marion County Branch, NAACP Florida State Conference Meeting at First Baptist Church, Winter Haven, Florida, November 7, 1963.

President Lowry, Field Secretary Saunders, Distinguished Participants, Officers of the State Conference, Chapters, Auxiliaries, Members, Ladies and Gentlemen: I am deeply grateful and honored to have the privilege of addressing this Twenty-Fourth Annual Session of the Florida State Conference of Branches.

A few years from tonight, the audiences of eternity will applaud the closing of one of the greatest dramas ever enacted upon the stage of life: the Negro and his struggle for total freedom in a democratic America. With the rising of the curtains of injustice and discrimination in 1619, the Negro, bound by chains, made his entrances on the stage of a newly found country. With the backdrop of cotton, he began picking his way to freedom in an encounter with segregation which had already consumed over two hundred years.

The scene is continuously changing, but the plot to keep the Negro in "his place" remains the same. However, it is becoming increasingly apparent that the new Negro and the understanding white man have picked up the eraser and the pencil with the purpose in mind of erasing injustice, discrimination, and segregation, and rewriting the plot to the tune of Brotherhood.

We have gathered here tonight from the four corners of Florida with our minds set on changing the plot and rewriting the script in every segregated city of Florida.

We have gathered here tonight to revitalize our efforts with a renewed determination to cut the strings of injustice, so that the curtains of justice might fall, enabling us to live happily ever after.

We have gathered here tonight because we are sick and tired of being second class citizens in a rocket-ship age.

We have gathered here tonight because the seats of satisfaction can't hold us any longer, because we want freedom, not ten years from now, not five years from now. We want freedom, now!

This past year, the segregationists, using the pliers of injustice and intimidation, have tightened the bolts of hard core resistance in many Florida cities. This resistance on the part of intelligent illiterates has given birth to violence and police brutality in St. Augustine, Ocala, and other cities.

In St. Augustine, on various occasions, Youth Council members have been cursed, pushed, and challenged to "end everything" in the alley by officers of the law. Four Negroes have been beaten severely by Klansmen with a verdict in the Klan's favor; four young high school students have been sentenced to Correctional Institutions because they refused to give away that to which the Constitution entitles all Americans, because they refused to stop protesting the evils of a segregated society.

In Ocala, peaceful picketers were arrested in mass because they protested the illegal arrest and whipping of freedom fighter Zev Aelong in the Marion County jail. They were arrested in mass again when peacefully picketing and charged with the ancient charge of improper identification.

In Bay County and other counties there have been similar charges.

This opposition to peaceful protest is indicative of the need for strong legislation guaranteed to protect the right to peaceful protest and the pursuit of happiness of all Americans without regard to color.

Yet, we know that many political leaders in Florida and some members of the press have openly voiced opposition to passage of Civil Rights Legislation. This becomes a most questionable issue, in that, if legislation can be passed for the health and welfare of hogs and cattle, why not pass legislation for human beings?

Certainly this cannot be the home of the brave nor the land

of the free where more thought and attention are given to hogs and cows than to nearly twenty million loyal Negro citizens.

Could it be that these sparks of violence, intimidation, and mass arrests have made an overseas orange salesman out of your friend and my "homeboy" Governor Bryant? If my "homeboy" really believes that Florida has no segregation problems, that everything is "lovey dovey," then I invite him to come on down home, because things have gone wrong there. The Governor cannot help being aware of the re-activating of the Ku Klux Klan and White Citizens' Council in Florida.

In Ocala and Marion County, the Chief Deputy Sheriff and the president of the White Citizens' Council practically run the town. It has become increasingly apparent that whenever political leaders do not speak out against these evils of segregation and injustice, they are just as guilt as those who commit the acts of violence and intimidation.

Many merchants were once willing to open their facilities, but pressure from the White Citizens' Council changed their minds. When this happened, they realized that the white man is not free to make his own decisions. It then becomes our task to free the white man as we free ourselves. Again, this points to the need for strong legislation.

School desegregation has moved at a slow pace. Some fifty or more counties have no desegregation whatever.

Voter registration workers have been active throughout the state and in particular, Orange and Marion Counties, where a big job has already been done.

In employment, there have not been enough Negroes in white collar jobs nor technical skills. In many instances this has resulted from the closed doors of many apprenticeship programs. There has been token employment in Tampa, thanks to the Merchants Association.

In many cities, stores belonging to national chains have desegregated, while most local owners have not for fear of reprisal and intimidation. KKK stickers have been put on the doors of those who opened their lunch counters in Ocala, as well as inside a post office, which is owned by the federal government.

The enactment of Civil Rights Legislation would also protect the right of a man to do business.

During the past year, the NAACP stepped up its program of desegregation in Florida. The NAACP is responsible for a major part of the one-fourth of 85,000 registered voters mentioned by Secretary of State Tom Adams. The NAACP, realizing that fair employment practices make up a part of that freedom which we are seeking, has stepped up its efforts to bring an end to discrimination in employment.

When the U.S. Supreme Court upheld Father Gibson's stand in not revealing the membership roll of the NAACP, a victory was won which has inspired us to push for kinder legislators.

And active stand has been taken against brutality in Bay, St. John's, and Marion Counties, as well as other Florida communities.

What can we do to get freedom now? In this struggle for human dignity and brotherhood, W. D. Weatherford has said that "the church is running behind schedule." This is a strange place for the church to find herself when the rest of the world is in a social revolution.

There is a need for a deeper and more sincere belief in God. Every minister and worshipper ought to instill in his life a more Christ-like Spirit which would enable him to cry out in the midst of darkness and danger, "Yea, though I walk through the valley of the shadow of death, I will fear no evil, for Thou art with me." The cry of the church out to be, we know the way to freedom, we will show the way to freedom, and we will do it now.

This comes as a challenge to every organization—Masons, Elks, Pall Bearers, Lily Whites, Fraternities, Sororities, and all others—to rise up from the "pool of ease," to take off the boots of "standstill," and to put on the shoes of "do something," for the cry of every Negro and organization ought to be, we want freedom, we want freedom, and we want it now.

In 1964, the balance of political power will be determined by the Negro who votes. We must do everything possible to increase our registration to 450,000 in the state.

Every Branch, Youth Council, College Chapter, and Woman's Auxiliary will be called upon and urged to take a part in this all-important task. We must see to it that all registered persons are voting persons. The NAACP is non-partisan and does not endorse candidates nor parties. This enables us to stay loose from the skirts of conservatives and liberals, and puts us in better position to do the best job possible in voter registration.

Gubernatorial candidates who are talking about deserting their sworn obligations as Democrats [in order] to support a conservative Goldwater need to take note, that the Negro knows that there is power in the vote. Republicans who seek power in the state of Florida and who are so readily willing to desert the principles of their founding fathers, need consult the "ghost of Lincoln" and march with a progressive America.

All sheriffs, mayors, and all other elected persons need take note, when we say "freedom now," we don't only mean through court decision but also through the use of the ballot. For it has appeared that in many places in Florida, the Negro needs protection from elected officers who hide behind the pen, the badge, and the gavel to enforce their prejudiced concepts. We would have them know, that this new Negro is determined and knows that right inevitably wins over injustice, that we want freedom, and we want it now.

If it is essential for the Negro to block vote, then let us block vote to defeat those who would block our constitutional rights. We shall press for equal employment and fair hiring practices in Florida. To accomplish this, we may use the method of selective buying, which teaches the Negro how to spend his dollar wisely. The Selective Buying Program is like an institution of higher learning, it teaches so many things in so many ways.

The Selective Buying Program in Ocala, Florida, has be ninety-five percent effective. Negroes have paid out bills, saved more, and now have more than ever before. One merchant in Ocala who didn't have enough hindsight to see that he was losing his foresight said that "business is booming." The Negro there has made up his mind that he will sit back and see how long it's going to boom without his dollar. The truth of the matter is that so much booming has gone on that business has practically boomed away two shopping centers. Yet, we do not want to put anybody out of business; we want to put employment in business. It's not that we want to eat hot dogs, for we have been "hot-dogging" long enough. It is the principle of the thing that matters. It is not that we want freedom of employment, not tomorrow, but we want it now.

This calls for stepped-up programs, demands, and actions to employ more Negroes in the State, County, and City Governments who merit such; the elimination of segregation in hotels, theaters, and all other places of public accommodations.

The passage of a Civil Rights Bill which does not include businesses catering to the general public and which are not in interstate commerce will not stop us from our move to obtain state action for the ending of racial discrimination. If we are to put up the signs of brotherhood, we must take down the racial signs of segregation in Winter Haven, Leesburg, and every city in the state of Florida. We must step up activity and desegregation of schools in more counties. All counties should desegregate their schools voluntarily without being taken to court. But if going to court is what it will take, the NAACP will not hesitate to back any parent who petitions the organization for such help. We know that anything [that] is separate cannot be equal; therefore, we want to use the same schools, the same books, the same lessons, the same education, and the same crystal water that flows from every fountain that we are entitled to as American citizens.

There is no need in worrying about the Negro being subversive, for he is too loyal and black to be communist and red. As a matter of fact, we have been so loyal that we have been pushed back, shoved around, kicked, slapped down, and even *lynched*, and the Negroes have lived and died being patient. But the blood of brave children and men like Medgar Evers has been rising from the ground telling us about freedom. This same blood of love and determination has given the Negro a new thrust; he doesn't act like he used to, for he is the new Negro. This new Negro has said, "John, things aren't going to be like they used to, and I want you to tell Ann the same." As a matter of fact, the new Negro is changing things. He has rewritten the poem, "Old Black Joe." We used to say, "I'm coming. I'm coming, and my head is bending low. I hear the gentle voices calling Old Black Joe." Now we say, "I'm coming. Yes, I'm coming, and my head isn't bending low. I'm stepping high and striding wide, 'cause I'm the New Black Joe." This New Black Joe wants freedom.

Every Branch ought to want freedom, every College Chapter ought to want freedom, every Youth Council ought to want freedom, every NAACP member ought to want freedom, every true Christian ought to want freedom, every American ought to want freedom. And finally, when this drama of the Negro's struggle shall have ended, when the audience of eternity shall have made its final applause, we shall then know fully that freedom comes to those who seek her; we need to know now this is still my father's world, I'm just passing through, my treasures are laid up, somewhere beyond the blue, and the angels beckon me to heaven's open door, and I can't feel at home in this world anymore; that we are strangers and sojourners in a society seeking freedom and brotherhood.

I challenge you tonight to go back to your cities to demonstrate, to work together, to picket together, to sit-in together, to stand together, to wade-in together, to crawl-in together, to struggle together, to sing together, to shout together, to pray together, to arouse the people from their seats of satisfaction and their rocking chairs of contentment, and to work together, children, and don't you get weary for there is going to be great day in the Promised Land.

WE WANT FREEDOM AND WE WANT IT NOW!

Abbreviations

FSA
Florida State Archives, Tallahassee

LC
Library of Congress, Washington, D.C.

NA
National Archives, Washington, D.C.

PKY
P. K. Yonge Library of Florida History, University of Florida, Gainesville

SLF
State Library of Florida, Tallahassee

USF
University of South Florida, Tampa

Notes

Chapter One

[1] United States Census Office, *Census Reports, Volume 1, Twelfth Census of the United States*, 13; Department of Commerce, Bureau of the Census, *Negro Population in the United States 1790-1915*, 51; Maxine Jones, "The African-American Experience in Twentieth Century Florida," 379-83.

[2] McRae, W. A., *The Fourth Census of the State of Florida Taken in the Year 1915*, 15, 70.

[3] Jane Landers, "Gracia Real de Santa Teresa de Mose: A Free Black Town in Spanish Colonial Florida"; James W. Covington, "The Negro Fort"; Canter Brown, Jr., "The 'Sarrazota, or Runaway Negro Plantations': Tampa Bay's First Black Community, 1812-1821."

[4] Daniel L. Schafer, "'A Class of People Neither Freemen nor Slaves': From Spanish to American Race Relations in Florida, 1821-1861"; Canter Brown, Jr., "Race Relations in Territorial Florida, 1821-1845"; idem, *Florida's Black Public Officials, 1867-1924*, 43-54; Barbara Ann Richardson, "A History of Blacks in Jacksonville, Florida, 1860-1895: A Socio-Economic And Political Study"; Richard A. Martin, *The City Makers*; James B. Crooks, *Jacksonville After the Fire, 1901-1919, A New South City*.

[5] Walter T. Howard, *Lynchings and*

Extralegal Violence in Florida; Robert P. Ingalls, *Urban Vigilantes in the New South: Tampa, 1882-1936*, 1-115; Brown, *Florida's Black Public Officials*, 55-64.

[6] Canter Brown, Jr., "African Americans in the Tampa Bay Area to World War I"; Leland M. Hawes, "Blacks made headway in 1915."

[7] Leland M. Hawes, "Booker T. Washington slept here"; *New York Age*, March 14, 1912.

[8] W. E. B. Du Bois, *The Souls of Black Folk*, 36-50; David Levering Lewis, *W. E. B. Du Bois, Biography of a Race*, 263-64, 273-77, 286-88.

[9] Brown, *Florida's Black Public Officials*, 81, 86; Jacksonville *Florida Times-Union*, June 16, 1891.

[10] Lewis, *W. E. B. Du Bois*, 316-23.

[11] Ibid., 386-407; Charles Flint Kellogg, *NAACP: A History of the National Association for the Advancement of Colored People, Volume 1 1909-1920*, 9-45; Jacqueline L. Harris, *History and Achievement of the NAACP*, 17-36.

[12] *New York Age*, December 31, 1914, April 1, September 2, 1915; Brown, *Florida's Black Public Officials*, 118; Maxine D. Jones and Kevin M. McCarthy, *African Americans in Florida*, 101.

[13] *New York Age*, June 10, 24, 1915; Tracy E. Danese, "Disfranchisement, Women's Suffrage, and the Failure of the Florida Grandfather Clause."

[14] Walter T. Howard and Virginia M. Howard, "The Early Years of the NAACP in Tampa, 1915-1930," 42-43.

[15] *The Crisis* 11 (March 1916), 261; Leland M. Hawes, "A special day for blacks."

[16] Wayne Flynt, *Cracker Messiah: Governor Sidney J. Catts of Florida*; *New York Age*, May 4, 1916.

[17] Kellogg, *NAACP*, 133-35; James Weldon Johnson, *Along This Way: The Autobiography of James Weldon Johnson*, 314-15; *The Crisis* 14 (May 1917), 18-19.

[18] Howard and Howard, "Early Years," 46-47.

[19] Report of the Field Secretary, January 6, 1919, Part 1, Reel 4, NAACP Papers; Flynt, *Cracker Messiah*, 190-92.

[20] Lewis, *W. E. B. Du Bois*, 579-80; John Hope Franklin and Alfred A. Moss, Jr., *From Slavery to Freedom: A History of African Americans, Seventh Edition*, 349-52.

[21] Brown, *Florida's Black Public Officials*, 68-69; Wayne Flynt, *Duncan Upshaw Fletcher: Dixie's Reluctant Progressive*, 134; Audrey Thomas McCluskey, "Ringing Up a School: Mary McLeod Bethune's Impact on Daytona," 213-14; report of the secretary, June 1920, and report of the acting secretary, November 1920, Part 1, Reel 4, NAACP Papers.

[22] Report of the acting secretary,

November 1920, and report of the secretary, December 1920, Part 1, Reel 4, NAACP Papers; Jones and McCarthy, *African Americans in Florida*, 81-82.

23 Brown, *Florida's Black Public Officials*, 68-69; report of William Perkins for November 1921, Part 1, Reel 4, NAACP Papers; *The Crisis* 23 (January 1922), 115.

24 Maxine D. Jones, Larry E. Rivers, David R. Colburn, R. Thomas Dye, and William W. Rogers, "A Documented History of the Incident Which Occurred at Rosewood, Florida, In January 1923."

25 Report of Department of Branches for May [1923] Board Meeting, Part 1, Reel 4, NAACP Papers; Leedell W. Neyland and John W. Riley, *The History of Florida Agricultural and Mechanical University*, 72-73; *The Crisis*, 29 (March 1925), 213, 31 (March 1926), 232-33, 32 (September 1926), 230.

26 Howard and Howard, "Early Years," 48-49.

27 Ibid., 50-51.

28 *The Crisis* 47 (July 1940), 206-207.

29 Ibid., 47 (March 1940), 81; J. Clay Smith, Jr., *Emancipation: The Making of the Black Lawyer, 1844-1944*, 280-81.

30 On the Claude Neal case generally, see James R. McGovern, *Anatomy of a Lynching: The Killing of Claude Neal*.

31 Roy Wilkins, *Standing Fast, The Autobiography of Roy Wilkins*, 132-36.

32 On the Florida State Teachers Association, see Gilbert L. Porter and Leedell W. Neyland, *The History of the Florida State Teachers Association*. See also, Edward D. Davis, *A Half Century of Struggle for Freedom in Florida*.

33 Porter and Neyland, *History of the Florida State Teachers Association*, 64-65; Davis, *Half Century of Struggle*, ii-iii, 133-34.

34 Caroline Emmons Poore, "Striking the First Blow: Harry T. Moore and the Fight for Black Equality in Florida," 22; Porter and Neyland, *History of the Florida State Teachers Association*, 64-66; *Pittsburgh Courier*, February 8, 1941; *The Crisis*, 49 (February 1952), 77-78.

35 Porter and Neyland, *History of the Florida State Teachers Association*, 66-71; *The Crisis* 49 (February 1952), 77-78.

36 Emmons, "Striking the First Blow," 22; Franklin and Moss, *From Slavery to Freedom*, 437.

37 *St. Petersburg Times*, October 19, 26, 1941.

38 Franklin and Moss, *From Slavery to Freedom*, 433-60; Catherine Fere, "Crime and Racial Violence in Tampa During World War II"; Tampa *Florida Sentinel*, January 12, 1946, October 25, 1947; Gary R. Mormino, "GI Joe Meets Jim Crow: Racial Violence and Reform in

World War II Florida."

[39] *The Crisis* 49 (February 1952), 78-79; Davis, *Half Century of Struggle*, 143-48.

[40] Poore, "Striking the First Blow," 37; James C. Clark, "Civil Rights Leader Harry T. Moore and the Ku Klux Klan in Florida," 170.

[41] Tampa *Florida Sentinel*, January 26, February 16, March 23, 1946, December 17, 1949.

[42] *Pittsburgh Courier*, June 1, 1946; Kermit L. Hall, *The Magic Mirror, Law in American History*, 322-33; John Egerton, *Speak Now Against the Day, The Generation Before the Civil Rights Movement in the South*, 413-15.

[43] Tampa *Florida Sentinel*, June 15, 1946, January 18, October 25, December 13, 1947.

[44] Poore, "Striking the First Blow," 60.

[45] *Miami Times*, November 12, 26, December 24, 1949, February 11, 1950; Tampa *Florida Sentinel*, February 11, 1948, January 14, 28, 1950; *St. Petersburg Times*, November 26, 28, 1948.

[46] There are many sources available on the Groveland case. See particularly, Steven F. Lawson, David R. Colburn, and Darryl Paulson, "Groveland: Florida's Little Scottsboro."

[47] Ibid.; Poore, "Striking the First Blow," 92.

[48] Tampa *Florida Sentinel*, December 9, 1950, January 13, 1951, January 5, 1952; *Miami Times*, November 25, December 9, 1950; Poore, "Striking the First Blow," 84.

[49] *Miami Times*, October 13, 20, November 17, 1951; Poore, "Striking the First Blow," 87-92.

[50] Poore, "Striking the First Blow," 92; Clark, "Civil Rights Leader Harry T. Moore," 176.

[51] Poore, "Striking the First Blow," 4-11.

Chapter Two

[1] On West Tampa, see Sanchez, "West Tampa and the Cigar Industry: A Photographic Essay."

[2] On Christina Meacham, see Hawes, "'Miss Tina' spurred students for 40 years."

[3] *Tampa Tribune*, August 7, 1898.

[4] Grismer, *Tampa*, 302.

[5] Brady, *Things Remembered*.

[6] Brown, "Politics, Greed, Regulator Violence, and Race in Tampa"; Ingalls, *Urban Vigilantes in the New South*.

[7] Ingalls, *Urban Vigilantes*, xvii.

[8] Howard and Howard, "Early Years," 51-52.

[9] Ingalls, *Urban Vigilantes*, 166-68.

[10] Howard, "Hillsborough County Tragedy."

[11] Ingalls, *Urban Vigilantes*, 182-83.

[12] Ibid., 150-52.

[13] While the white Tampa newspapers failed to cover DePriest's appearance, the *Tampa Daily Times* noted his imminent arrival in its issue of January 18, 1932.

[14] Richard Cornish Martin to the author, November 22, 1988, collection of the author.

[15] On Charles "Charlie Moon" Vanderhorst's death, see *Tampa Daily Times*, January 15, 17, 1944, *Tampa Tribune*, January 16, 1944, and Tampa *Florida Sentinel*, March 16, 1946.

[16] *Tampa Tribune*, January 16, 1944.

[17] *Tampa Daily Times*, November 23, 25, 1935.

[18] *Tampa Tribune*, January 16, 1944.

[19] *Tampa Daily Times*, April 10, 1944; Tampa *Florida Sentinel*, March 23, 1946.

Chapter Three

[1] Tindall, *America*, II, 1158-80.

[2] Ibid., 1170-73; Franklin and Moss, *From Slavery to Freedom*, 435.

[3] Jones and McCarthy, *African Americans in Florida*, 60-63. See also, Halasa, *Mary McLeod Bethune*.

[4] Tampa *Florida Sentinel*, April 13, 1946.

[5] Franklin and Moss, *From Slavery to Freedom*, 356, 411-12.

[6] Tampa *Florida Sentinel*, September 20, 1952.

[7] Ibid., October 4, 1952.

Chapter Four

[1] *Miami Times*, October 4, 1952.

[2] Tampa *Florida Sentinel*, October 4, 1952.

[3] *Miami Times*, December 27, 1952.

[4] Tampa *Florida Sentinel*, January 31, 1953.

[5] Ibid., August 8, 1953.

[6] Ibid., August 15, 1953.

[7] *Miami Times*, June 20, 1953.

[8] Tampa *Florida Sentinel*, November 7, 1953.

[9] Hughes, *Fight for Freedom*, 141.

[10] Tampa *Florida Sentinel*, May 9, 1953.

[11] *Miami Times*, May 8, 1954.

[12] Ibid., June 26, 1954.

[13] Ibid., March 12, 1955.

[14] Ibid., September 4, 1954.

[15] Colburn and Scher, *Florida's Gubernatorial Politics*, 76.

[16] *Miami Times*, August 28, 1954.

[17] Ibid., June 11, 1955.

[18] Ibid.

[19] Ibid., July 23, 1955.

[20] Ibid., October 1, 1955.

21 Ibid., January 28, 1956.

22 Jacksonville *Florida Star*, January 14, 1956.

23 *Miami Times*, March 17, 24, 1956.

24 Colburn and Scher, *Florida's Gubernatorial Politics*, 77.

25 *Miami Times*, June 16, 30, 1956; Jacksonville *Florida Star*, June 16, 1956.

26 Jacksonville *Florida Star*, June 16, 1956.

27 *Miami Times*, July 7, 1956.

28 Tampa *Florida Sentinel*, July 28, 1956.

29 Jacksonville *Florida Star*, August 4, 11, 18, 1956; Schnur, "Cold Warriors in the Hot Sunshine: USF and the Johns Committee," 10.

30 *Miami Times*, August 18, 1956.

31 Ibid., August 25, 1956; Jacksonville *Florida Star*, September 1, 15, 1956.

32 Jacksonville *Florida Star*, October 6, 1956; *Miami Times*, November 3, 1956; *Tampa Daily Times*, October 30, 1956.

33 Jacksonville *Florida Star*, November 17, 1956.

34 *Miami Times*, October 20, 27, November 3, 1956.

35 Jacksonville *Florida Star*, January 19, 1957.

36 *Miami Times*, March 16, 1957.

37 Ibid., October 26, 1957.

38 Jacksonville *Florida Star*, April 13, 20, 1957; *Miami Times*, May 25, 1957.

39 Tampa *Florida Sentinel*, May 18, 1957.

40 Franklin and Moss, *From Slavery to Freedom*, 492-94; *Miami Times*, August 31, 1957; Tampa *Florida Sentinel*, October 5, 1957.

41 Jacksonville *Florida Star*, December 20, 1958.

42 Ibid., June 13, 1959.

43 Franklin and Moss, *From Slavery to Freedom*, 495-97.

44 Jacksonville *Florida Star*, May 21, 1960.

45 Colburn and Scher, *Florida's Gubernatorial Politics*, 78-79.

46 Ibid., 227-28.

47 Ibid., 228.

48 Saunders, "Profile of School Desegregation," 73.

49 *Tampa Daily Times*, March 15, 1963.

50 Colburn, *Racial Change and Community Crisis*, 32.

51 Hughes, *Fight for Freedom*, 183.

52 Garrow, *Bearing the Cross*, 357-430; Franklin and Moss, *From Slavery to Freedom*, 507-13.

53 Colburn, and Scher, *Florida's Gubernatorial Politics*, 80-82, 228-29.

Chapter Five

[1] On Harry T. Moore generally, see Poore, "Striking the First Blow: Harry T. Moore and the Fight for Black Equality in Florida" and Green, *Before His Time*.

[2] Harry T. Moore to "Co-workers," November 15, 1945, Part 4, reel 6, NAACP Papers.

[3] Ibid., H. T. Moore to Florida house of representatives members, May 16, 1947, Part 4, reel 6.

[4] Ibid.

[5] On the Groveland case, see Lawson, Colburn, and Paulson, "Groveland."

[6] Poore, "Striking the First Blow," 70-72.

[7] Ibid., 72-73.

[8] *Miami Times*, October 20, 1951.

[9] Current, "Martyr For A Cause."

[10] H. T. Moore to Fuller Warren, December 2, 1951, Administrative File, Governor Fuller Warren papers, RG 102, series 235, FSA.

[11] See also Davis, *Half Century of Struggle*, 127.

[12] Fuller Warren statement quoted in Poore, "Striking the First Blow," 7.

Chapter Six

[1] Portions of this chapter have appeared in Saunders, "Synopsis of the Civil Rights Struggle in Tampa."

[2] On local follow-up to the 1949 agreement, see Saunders, "Profile of School Desegregation," 75.

[3] Madison E. Jones to William H. Gordon, uncatalogued, Saunders Papers.

[4] Ibid., 1961 Tampa branch statement on housing and urban renewal.

[5] See, for example, Jack Wood to Robert W. Saunders, June 12, 1961, section 1, box 3, Saunders Papers.

[6] Ibid., Robert W. Saunders to Jack Wood, June 15, 1961.

Chapter Seven

[1] Morris, *Florida Handbook*, 342-44; Colburn and Scher, *Florida's Gubernatorial Politics in the Twentieth Century*, 288.

[2] Clipping in Ruth Perry Papers, USF.

[3] Ibid.

[4] Robert W. Saunders to LeRoy Collins, February 10, 1956, uncatalogued, in Saunders Papers.

[5] Telephone interview, Gloria Hawkins Barton by the author, January 10, 1998 (notes in collection of the author).

Chapter Eight

[1] Schnur, "Cold Warriors in the Hot Sunshine," 10-11; Colburn and

Scher, *Florida Gubernatorial Politics*, 75-76.

[2] Henry Land to Roy Wilkins, et al., February 1957, uncatalogued, Saunders Papers.

[3] Ibid., Virgil Hawkins testimony to Florida Legislative Investigative Committee.

[4] Ibid., Edward D. Davis testimony to Florida Legislative Investigative Committee.

[5] Ibid., Virgil Hawkins testimony.

[6] Ibid., Shirley Wayne Curtis testimony to Florida Legislative Investigative Committee.

[7] Transcript of testimony of Robert W. Saunders before the Florida Legislative Investigation Committee, March 14, 1957, M81-17, carton 2, FSA.

[8] Florida *House Journal* (1957), 2094.

[9] Ibid., 2095.

[10] Ibid.

[11] Jacksonville *Florida Star*, April 13, 1957; *Miami Times*, May 25, 1957.

[12] The Jacksonville *Florida Star* recorded Herrell's statement as declaring those who refused to answer the committee's questions to be "not fit to be citizens of this state." Jacksonville *Florida Star*, March 1, 1958.

[13] My recollection differs slightly from some news accounts of this incident. See, for example, Jacksonville *Florida Star*, March 1, 1958.

[14] On the Johns Committee's activities at the University of South Florida, see Schnur, "Cold Warriors in the Hot Sunshine."

Chapter 9

[1] Clipping in Ruth Perry Papers, USF.

[2] Robert W. Saunders to Roy Wilkins, March 1960, uncatalogued, Saunders Papers.

Chapter Ten

[1] Robert W. Saunders to Hayden Burns, January 28, 1960, uncatalogued, Saunders Papers.

[2] Ibid., Berrier Ice Cream Parlor case materials.

[3] Ibid.

[4] Ibid., Robert W. Saunders speech, Jacksonville, December 9, 1962, box 5, file folder 5.

Chapter Eleven

[1] Clipping in Escambia County desegregation materials, uncatalogued, Saunders Papers.

[2] Ibid., Robert W. Saunders to Robert Carter, January 1963, uncatalogued.

[3] See Lawson, Colburn, and Paulson,

"Groveland."

⁴ Robert W. Saunders to Robert L. Carter, January 24, 1963, box 1, folder 9, Saunders Papers.

⁵ Ibid., Fort Lauderdale desegregation materials, uncatalogued.

Chapter Twelve

¹ See, for example, Colburn, *Racial Change & Community Crisis.*

² Robert W. Saunders to Robert L. Carter, box 1, file folder 9, Saunders Papers.

³ Ibid., Saunders to J. A. Finlayson, September 1, 1963.

⁴ Ibid., c. late September, 1963.

5 *Daytona Beach Morning Journal*, September 20, 1963.

Chapter Thirteen

¹ Call for Eleventh Annual Meeting, Florida State Conference of Branches, November 1951, uncatalogued, Saunders Papers. See also *Miami Times*, October 13, 1951.

Bibliography

Manuscripts

Clippings File. Tampa-Hillsborough County Public Library, Tampa.

National Association for the Advancement of Colored People. Papers. LC.

Perry, Ruth. Papers. USF Special Collections.

Saunders, Robert W. Papers. USF Special Collections.

Warren, Fuller. Papers. RG 102, series 235, FSA.

Public Documents and Records

Department of Commerce, Bureau of the Census. *Negro Population in the United States 1790-1915.* Washington, DC: Government Printing Office, 1918.

Florida. *House Journals.*

Florida Legislative Investigative Committee Records. M81-17. FSA.

Jones, Maxine D., Larry E. Rivers, David R. Colburn, R. Thomas Dye, and William W. Rogers. "A Documented History of the Incident Which Occurred at Rosewood, Florida, in January 1923." Typescript, Tallahassee, 1994.

McRae, W. A. *The Fourth Census of the State of Florida Taken in the Year 1915.* Tallahassee: T. J. Appleyard, State Printer, 1915.

United States Census Office. *Census Reports, Volume 1, Twelfth Census of the United States, Taken in the Year 1900.* Washington, DC: Government Printing Office, 1901.

Newspapers and Periodicals

The Crisis, 1916-1952.

Daytona Beach Morning Journal, 1963,

Jacksonville *Florida Star,* 1956-1966.

Jacksonville *Florida Times-Union,* 1891.

Miami Times, 1948-1966.

New York Age, 1912-1916.

Pittsburgh Courier, 1941-1951.

St. Petersburg Times, 1941-1949.

Tampa Daily Times, 1935-1963.

Tampa *Florida Sentinel,* 1946-1966.

Tampa Tribune, 1898-1996.

Secondary Sources

Brady, Rowena Ferrell. *Things Remembered: An Album of African Americans in Tampa.* Tampa: University of Tampa Press, 1997.

Brown, Canter, Jr. "African Americans and the Tampa Bay Area to

World War I." An historical introduction to *Things Remembered: An Album of African Americans in Tampa* by Rowena Ferrell Brady.

_____. "Bishop Payne and Resistance to Jim Crow in Florida During the 1880s." *Northeast Florida History* 2 (1994), 23-40.

_____. "Carpetbagger Intrigues, Black Leadership, and a Southern Loyalist Triumph: Florida's Gubernatorial Election of 1872." *Florida Historical Quarterly* 72 (January 1994): 275-301.

_____. *Florida's Black Public Officials, 1867-1924*. Tuscaloosa: University of Alabama Press, 1998.

_____. "Politics, Greed, Regulator Violence, and Race in Tampa, 1858-1859." *Sunland Tribune* 20 (1994): 25-30.

_____. "Prelude to the Poll Tax: Black Republicans and the Knights of Labor in 1880s Florida." In *Florida's Heritage of Diversity: Essays in Honor of Samuel Proctor*. Ed. by Mark I. Greenberg, William Warren Rogers, and Canter Brown, Jr. Tallahassee: Sentry Press, 1997.

_____. "The 'Sarrazota, or Runaway Negro Plantations": Tampa Bay's First Black Community, 1812-1821." *Tampa Bay History* 12 (Fall/Winter 1990): 5-19.

_____. "'Where are now the hopes I cherished?' The Life and Times of Robert Meacham." *Florida Historical Quarterly* 69 (July 1990): 1-36.

Cannon, Poppy. *A Gentle Knight: My Husband, Walter White*. New York: Rinehart & Company, 1956.

Clark, James C. "Civil Rights Leader Harry T. Moore and the Ku Klux Klan in Florida." *Florida Historical Quarterly* 73 (October 1994): 166-83.

Colburn, David R. *Racial Change and Community Crisis: St. Augustine, Florida, 1877-1980*. New York: Columbia University Press, 1985. Reprint ed., Gainesville: University of Florida Press, 1991.

Colburn, David R., and Jane L. Landers, eds. *The African American Heritage of Florida*. Gainesville: University Press of Florida, 1995.

Colburn, David R., and Richard K. Scher, *Florida's Gubernatorial Politics in the 20th Century*. Tallahassee: Florida State University, 1980.

Cooper, Algia R. "Brown v. Board of Education and Virgil Darnell Hawkins Twenty-eight Years and Six Petitions to Justice." *Journal of Negro History* 64 (Winter 1979): 1-20.

Covington, James W. "The Negro Fort." *Gulf Coast Historical Review* 5 (Spring 1990): 79-91.

Crooks, James B. *Jacksonville After the Fire, 1901-1919, A New South City*. Gainesville: University Press of Florida, 1991.

Current, Gloster B. "Martyr for a

Cause." *The Crisis* 49 (February 1952): 73-81, 133-34.

Danese, Tracy E. "Disfranchisement, Women's Suffrage and the Failure of the Florida Grandfather Clause." *Florida Historical Quarterly* 74 (Fall 1995): 117-31.

Davis, Edward D. *A Half Century of Struggle for Freedom in Florida.* Orlando: priv. pub., 1981.

Davis, Jack E. "'Whitewash' in Florida: The Lynching of Jesse James Payne and Its Aftermath." *Florida Historical Quarterly* 68 (January 1990): 277-98.

Du Bois, W. E. B. *The Souls of Black Folk.* Chicago: A. C. McClurg and Company, 1903.

Edmonds, Rick. "LeRoy Collins: Journey to the Selma Bridge." *Florida Humanities Council Forum* 18 (Winter 1994/1995): 30-33.

Egerton, John. *Speak Now Against the Day, The Generation Before the Civil Rights Movement in the South.* New York: Alfred A. Knopf, 1994.

Fere, Catherine. "Crime and Racial Violence in Tampa During World War II." *Tampa Bay History* 17 (Spring/Summer 1995): 65-82.

Flynt, Wayne. *Cracker Messiah: Governor Sidney J. Catts of Florida.* Baton Rouge: Louisiana State University Press, 1977.

_____. *Duncan Upshaw Fletcher: Dixie's Reluctant Progressive.* Tallahassee: Florida State University Press, 1971.

Franklin, John Hope, and Alfred A. Moss, Jr. *From Slavery to Freedom: A History of African Americans, Seventh Edition.* New York: McGraw-Hill, 1994.

Gannon, Michael. *The New History of Florida.* Gainesville: University Press of Florida, 1996.

Goldman, Roger, and David Gallen. *Thurgood Marshall, Justice for All.* New York: Carroll and Graf Publishers, Inc., 1992.

Green, Ben. *Before His Time: The Untold Story of Harry T. Moore, America's First Civil Rights Martyr.* New York: Free Press, 1999.

Halasa, Malu. *Mary McLeod Bethune: Educator.* New York: Chelsea House Publishers, 1989.

Hall, Kermit L. *The Magic Mirror, Law in American History,* New York: Oxford University Press, 1989.

Harris, Jacqueline L. *History and Achievement of the NAACP.* New York: Franklin Watts, 1992.

Hawes, Leland. "Blacks made headway in 1915." *Tampa Tribune,* February 12, 1995.

_____. "Booker T. Washington slept here." *Tampa Tribune,* February 7, 1993.

_____. "'Miss Tina' spurred students for 40 years." *Tampa Tribune,* February 25, 1990.

_____. "A special day for blacks." *Tampa Tribune,* February 4, 1996.

Howard, Walter T. "A Hillsborough County Tragedy: The 1930 Lynching of John Hodaz." *Tampa Bay History* 11 (Fall/Winter 1989): 34-51.

―――. *Lynchings and Extralegal Violence in Florida.* Selingsgrove: Susquehanna University Press, 1995.

Howard, Walter T., and Virginia M. Howard. "The Early Years of the NAACP in Tampa, 1915-1930." *Tampa Bay History* 16 (Fall/Winter 1994): 41-56.

Hughes, Langston. *Fight for Freedom: The Story of the NAACP.* New York: Berkley Publishing Corporation, 1962.

Ingalls, Robert P. *Urban Vigilantes in the New South: Tampa, 1882-1936.* Knoxville: University of Tennessee Press, 1988.

Johnson, James Weldon. *Along This Way: The Autobiography of James Weldon Johnson.* New York: Viking Penguin, 1933. Reprint ed., New York: Penguin Books, 1990.

Jones, Maxine D. "The African-American Experience in Twentieth Century Florida." In *The New History of Florida*, ed. by Michael Gannon.

Jones, Maxine D., and Kevin M. McCarthy. *African Americans in Florida.* Sarasota: Pineapple Press, 1993.

Kellogg, Charles Flint. *NAACP: A History of the National Association for the Advancement of Colored People, Volume I 1909-1920.* Baltimore: Johns Hopkins University Press, 1967.

Kimmel, Elinor. "Hillsborough County School Desegregation Busing and Black High Schools in Tampa, Florida, April 1971-September 1971." *Sunland Tribune* 18 (November 1992): 37-43.

Landers, Jane. "Gracia Real de Santa Teresa de Mose: A Free Black Town in Spanish Colonial Florida." *American Historical Review* 95 (February 1990): 9-30.

Lawson, Steven F., David R. Colburn, and Darryl Paulson. "Groveland: Florida's Little Scottsboro." In *The African American Heritage of Florida*, ed. by David R. Colburn and Jane L. Landers.

Lewis, David Levering. *W.E.B. Du Bois, Biography of a Race 1868-1919.* New York: Henry Holt and Company, 1993.

Martin, Richard A. *The City Makers.* Jacksonville: Convention Press, Inc., 1972.

McCluskey, Audrey Thomas. "Ringing Up A School: Mary McLeod Bethune's Impact on Daytona." *Florida Historical Quarterly* 73 (October 1994): 200-17.

McDonogh, Gary W. *The Florida Negro: A Federal Writers' Project Legacy.* Jackson: University Press of Mississippi, 1993.

McGovern, James R. *Anatomy of a*

Lynching: The Killing of Claude Neal. Baton Rouge: Louisiana State University Press, 1982.

Mohlman, Geoffrey. "Bibliography of Resources Concerning the African American Presence in Tampa: 1513-1995." Masters thesis, University of South Florida, 1995.

Mormino, Gary R. "GI Joe Meets Jim Crow: Racial Violence and Reform in World War II Florida." *Florida Historical Quarterly* 73 (July 1994): 23-42.

Neyland, Leedell W., and John W. Riley. *The History of Florida Agricultural and Mechanical University.* Gainesville: University of Florida Press, 1963.

Pepper, Claude Denson, with Hays Gorey. *Pepper, Eyewitness to a Century.* San Diego: Harcourt Brace Jovanovich, 1987.

Poore, Caroline Emmons. "Striking the First Blow: Harry T. Moore and the Fight for Black Equality in Florida." Masters thesis, Florida State University, 1992.

Porter, Gilbert L., and Leedell W. Neyland. *The History of the Florida State Teachers Association.* Washington, DC: National Education Association, 1977.

Richardson, Barbara Ann. "A History of Blacks in Jacksonville, Florida, 1860-1895: A Socio-Economic and Political Study." Doctor of Arts dissertation, Carnegie-Mellon University, 1975.

Rivers, Larry E., and Canter Brown, Jr. "African Americans in South Florida: A Home and a Haven for Reconstruction-era Leaders." *Tequesta* 56 (1996): 5-23.

Sanchez, Arsenio M. "West Tampa and the Cigar Industry: A Photographic Essay." *Tampa Bay History* 13 (Spring/Summer 1991): 44-62.

Saunders, Robert W. "On the Trail of a Near-Lynching." *Florida Humanities Council Forum* 18 (Winter 1994/1995): 35-36.

_____. "A Profile of School Desegregation in Hillsborough County." *Sunland Tribune* 18 (November 1992): 73-79.

_____. "A Synopsis of the Civil Rights Struggle in Tampa and the Role of the Tampa Branch of the National Association for the Advancement of Colored People." *Sunland Tribune* 17 (November 1991): 51-61.

Schafer, Daniel L. "'A Class of People Neither Freemen nor Slaves': From Spanish to American Race Relations in Florida, 1821-1861." *Journal of Social History* 26 (Spring 1993): 587-609.

Schnur, James A. "Caught in the Cross Fire: African Americans and Florida's System of Labor During World War II." *Sunland Tribune* 19 (November 1993): 47-52.

_____. "Cold Warriors in the Hot Sunshine: USF and the Johns Committee." *Sunland Tribune* 18 (November 1992): 9-16.

Smith, J. Clay, Jr. *Emancipation: The Making of the Black Lawyer, 1844-1944.* Philadelphia: University of Pennsylvania Press, 1993.

Tindall, George Brown. *America: A Narrative History.* 2 vols. New York: W. W. Norton & Company, 1988.

Wilkins, Roy. *Standing Fast: The Autobiography of Roy Wilkins.* New York: Viking Press, 1982.

Index

A

Abernathy, Ralph 240
Adams, Mrs. Samuel 209
Adams, Neal 121
Adams, Samuel 209
African Methodist Episcopal church 71, 201
activist ministers 128
Afro-American Civic League 5
Afro-American Life Insurance Company 132, 162
Air Force
racial discrimination 198
Akerman, Alex, Jr. 22, 163
Alabama
legislation to outlaw NAACP 76
Albury, Mrs. Vernell 144
Albury, Vernell 161
Alexander, Luther, Sr. 2
Alsup, Fred 209
American Benevolent Association 8
American Civil Liberties Union 29
Anderson, Bill 38
Anderson, Marian 37
Anderson, R. L. 201
Andrews, C. Blythe, Sr. 42, 54, 124, 126, 139
Archie, Dr. E. O. 125
Archie, Mrs. Jewel 125
Arrington, Henry H. 74
Arrington, Ruby 74
Artest, Edwin 127
Atlanta Life Insurance Company 132
Atlanta University 6
Austin, James 199
Ayer, Orian 209

B

Bahama Islands 27
Bailey, Thomas D. 73, 200
Baker, Ella 125
Banfield, Warren 128, 139
Baptist Association 235
Baptist church 30, 128, 200, 219, 235
activist ministers 128, 200
Baptist Convention 236
Barrier, Charles 228, 232
Barrio de Elinche 26
Bates, Daisy 79
Bates, L. C. 87
Bay County 198-99
Bay Queen (boat) 26
Beasley, Thomas 175
Belafonte, Marguarite 62
Bell, William "Big Bill" 43
Berrier Ice Cream Parlor 190
Berrier, J. R. 190
Berry, Frankie 37
Berry, Theodore 145
Bessent, Lawrence A. 238
Bethel Baptist Institutional Church 193
Bethel Metropolitan Baptist Church 18
Bethune, Mary McLeod 12, 50-51, 62-63, 94, 216-17
and Central Life Insurance Company 62
and Eleanor Roosevelt 50, 52
receives Spingarn Prize 50
Bethune-Cookman College 43, 50, 53, 56, 61, 63, 207, 209, 215, 217
Beulah Baptist Church 82, 128, 139
Bing, Lutrell 52, 224
Black, W. J. H. 21
Blake, Howard W. 37
Blocker, Mary White 18
Blood, Olga Rolfe 37
Blountstown 13, 149
bolita 39
bombings 83
Bonifay 200
Booker T. Washington High School 18, 36-37, 41
Boy Scouts 33-34, 57
boycotts 217
Bradley, Leon 211-12
Brady, Rowena Ferrell 29
Branch, Edna 138
Braxton, Mazie 99
Brevard County 111, 222
Brevard County Junior College 224

287

Brinson, G. B. 37
Brooks, David 100, 182
Brooks, Johnnie 89, 100, 183
Brotherhood of Sleeping Car Porters 131
Broughton, Anna 37
Broughton, E. E. 124
Broward County 218, 222
Brown, Lorenzo 139
Brown v. The Board of Education of Topeka, Kansas 21, 58, 71, 127-28, 159-60, 169, 209, 212
Browning, Albert A. 12
Bryant, Farris (Florida governor) 85, 196, 215, 233, 237
   approval of Tallahassee March route 177
   one target of March on Tallahassee 174
Buie, Louise E. 199
Bunche, Ralph 63
burnings 151
Burns, Hayden (Florida governor) 88, 215
   absent during Klan attacks 189
Burts, Frank 21
Bushwell, Byron 139

C

Caldwell, Millard F. (Florida governor) 23, 114
Calhoun, W. H., 139
Camp Blanding (Fla.) 48, 52
Carley, Henry 139
Carr, George 42
Carswell, Harold 196, 201
Carter, Robert L. "Bob" 76, 91, 210, 214, 233
   and Johns Committee 160
Casellas, Vicki 62
Cassidy, Lola 16
Catts, Sidney J. 9, 10
Central Avenue (Tampa) 39-40, 55
   as border from the "Scrub" 126
   impact of urban renewal 133, 137
   NAACP state office 60
"Central Avenue Buckshot" 55

Central High School 82
Central Life Insurance Company 37, 62, 80, 124, 127, 132, 206
Central Park Village Housing Development 126
Central Theater 39, 211
Central Theater (St. Petersburg) 210
Chambers, Isiah 14
Chambers v. *Florida* 14-15, 17
Chaney, Art 237
Charles, Ray 38
Chatman, Jerry 212, 214
Cherry, Charles W. 121, 146, 180, 216-17, 224
Choate, Emett C. 83
Christian, Floyd 210
civil rights acts 83
   of 1957 79
   of 1964 85, 87, 128, 138, 238
civil rights commission 21, 59
Civil Rights Era 173, 227
civil rights legislation 144
Civil Rights Movement 238
civil rights movement 181, 228
   first martyrs 24
Clara Frye Hospital 38
Clark, Authorine 208
Clark, L. G. 213
Clarke, Johnnie Ruth 210
Claxton, Gwendolyn 208
Claxton, Leon 79, 208
Clearwater 211, 212
Clements, Lamar 209
Cleveland *Call and Post* 55-56
Clinton, Joe, Jr. 32
Clinton, Joseph N. ix, 6, 11, 30
   and Tampa NAACP chapter 10
Clinton, Red 32, 38
Cocoa Beach 222
Cocoa Junior High School 17
Cohens Department Store 189, 192
Coleman, Faith McQueen 38
Collins, LeRoy (Florida governor) 72-76, 83, 87, 107, 146-57, 212
   and Jesse Woods case 155
   common ground with NAACP 148
      Sheriff McCall case 156
   defeats Charley Johns for governor 159

failure to respond in Liberty County 151
NAACP concern over policies 149
named director of Community Relations Service 157
radio address against racism 174
segregation policies 148
staff investigation of Woods incident 153
staff member in Jacksonville 148
stands against racism 174
support for NAACP 151-52
Colored Board of Trade (Jacksonville) 8
communists
  attempts to associate NAACP with 72, 74, 77, 81
  Johns Committee 168
Community Relations Board (Tampa) 139-40
Community Relations Service 87, 157
Cone, Fred P. 112
Congress of Racial Equality (CORE) 19, 86, 175, 180
  conflict with NAACP
  March on Tallahassee 177
Cookman Institute 51
  See also Bethune-Cookman College
Cotton Club Lounge (Tampa) 180
Cox, Leon 210
Crawford, Fred 30
Crestview (Fla.) 141, 196-97
Crinton, Flossie M. 216
The Crisis 7, 9, 11, 14-15, 17
Cromwell, R. A., 195
Cubans 123
  and bolita 40
  in Roberts City 30
Cunningham, Malcolm 208
Current, Gloster B. 58, 69, 75, 91, 208, 233, 242
  arranges Tallahassee jail bonds 180
  praised by Hughes 87
Currinton, Flossie 90
Curtis, Shirley Wayne 164

D

Dade County 20
DaValt, C. J. 128
Davis, Albert 121
Davis, Benjamin O., Jr. 53
Davis, Charlie 14
Davis, Edward D. ix, 17, 62-63, 112, 127, 147-48, 162, 210, 219
  and hiring of Saunders 60, 69
  opening of NAACP state office in Tampa 65
  presidency of Florida State Teacher's Association 17, 21
  questioned by Johns Committee 162-63
  target of Johns Committee 161
  work with Harry T. Moore 112
Davis, Harmon 238
Davis, Marcus 196
Davis, Mrs. Arnita 224
Davis, Enoch 209
Davis, L. O. 237
Daytona Beach 13, 23, 212-14, 216-18
Daytona Beach Morning Journal 238
Daytona Council on Human Relations 217
Daytona Normal and Industrial Institute for Negro Girls 51. *See also* Bethune-Cookman College
Democratic party 112-13, 151
Democratic primary
  open to Blacks 20
    Supreme Court decision 58
Dennison, Arrabella 63
Depression 35-36
DePriest, Oscar (congressman) 32
desegregation 73, 75, 83
  first school system lawsuit 196
  in Little Rock, Arkansas 79
  NAACP lawsuits attacked by Johns Committee 167
  of St. Augustine 230-32, 238
  of Bay County schools 198
  of Dade County school system 76
  of Fort Lauderdale beaches 220-21
  of Miami buses 83
  of movie theaters 139, 210

of public schools
   Brevard County 223
   Volusia County 218
of Tallahassee buses 76
of Tampa public transportation 76
support from Collins 156
University of Florida lawsuit 161
DeSue, Thomas 230
Detroit Institute of Technology 56
Dixon, Howard W. 72
Doctor, Arnett T. 211
Dodd, Wilson 139
Dominguez, E. *See* E. Dominguez Wholesalers
Double-V 19
Douglas, Maxine 100
Douglas, Mildred 79
Downing, Alvin "Al" 53
Du Bois, W. E. B. 6-7, 10-11
   contact with Tampa 8-9
Due, Patricia 180
Dunbar Elementary School 32
Dunbar, Paul Laurence, Literary Society 5
Dunmore Town (Bahamas) 27
Dunn, F. A. 210
Dupont, Charles F. ix, 6, 9
DuPont, Rev. King Solomon 158, 183, 201
DuPree, Linnell 36
Durham, Charley 14
Dyson, Clifton 88

E

E. Dominguez Wholesalers 44
Eaves, Emanuel 186
Eaves, Reginald 186
economic reprisals 228
Edward Waters College 188
Eisenhower, Dwight D. 70, 82
Ellinger & Co. Cigar Factory 26
Ellis, J. P. 207
Emancipation Day 2
Emmanuel Temple A.M.E. Church (Tampa) 35
employment
   discrimination against Blacks in 229

opportunities 132
Equal Employment Opportunity Commission 87
Equal Opportunity Committee 229
Ervin, Richard 72, 83
Escambia County
   organizing efforts 195
   Tolbert lawsuit 197
Eubanks, Rev. Goldie 230, 233
Evers, Medgar 70-71, 90, 242
   gunned down in Jackson, Miss. 87
Executive Order 8802 18

F

Fair, Eleanor 77
Fair Housing Program 138
Fairchild Stratos Corporation 229-30
FAMU (Florida Agricultural & Mechanical College) 13
Federal Bureau of Investigation (FBI) 155
   Fruitland Park case 213, 214
   location of Jesse Woods 156
   work with Johns Committee 160
Federal Housing Administration 136, 138
Federal Housing Authority 224
Fernandez, Aurillio 127
Ferrell, Andrew Jackson, Jr. 127
Ferrell, Andrew Jackson, Sr. 33-34, 224
"Fight for Freedom" 124
Finlayson, Rev. J. A. 234-35
First Baptist Church 128
Fisk University 55
Florida
   as refuge for runaway slaves 4
   population 3
      racial and ethnic mix 3-4
Florida A&M College 34, 43
Florida A&M University 13, 84, 141, 172-73, 176, 181, 183
   CORE activities on campus 86
   faculty called before Johns Committee 161
   President George Gore 175
   student NAACP chapter 179

students sentence in Tallahassee protest 180
Florida Association for Constitutional Government 159
Florida Baptist Association 234
Florida Collegians 38
Florida Elks
   Black lodges 68
Florida Human Relations Council 237
Florida National Guard
   integration 86
Florida Normal and Industrial College 74, 228-29
   students in St. Augustine demonstrations 236
Florida Normal and Industrial Memorial College 235
Florida Sentinel 20, 42, 54, 60, 125
Florida Sentinel-Bulletin 125
Florida Capitol 158
Florida State Fair
   "Colored Day" 42
Florida State Teacher's Association 17, 161, 205, 207
   investigated by Johns Committee 164-65
   law suit for equal pay 17
Florida State University 179
   student protestors 181
   white students arrested 179
Florida Supreme Court 208, 241
Florida Theater (St. Petersburg) 210
Florida Times-Union 13
Florida's Freedom Riders 224
Ford Motor Company 56
Ford, Nick 222
Fordham, Evelyne 79
Fordham, Leugenia 79
Fordham, William A. 66-68, 73-74, 79, 127, 161, 225
Fort, Clarence 139, 143
Fort Homer Hesterly Armory 127
Fort Lauderdale 218-20
Fort Lauderdale branch 144
Fort Pierce 66
Fort Walton Beach 200
Fort Walton branch 130
Fowler, Cody 139
Frazier, John 203

free-Black settlements 4
Freedom Fund 152, 208
Freedom House 59, 70
Freeman, Roderick 190
Fruitland Park 212
Fruitland Park case 213
   trumped-up charges 213
Ft. Lauderdale Beach 221
Fulwood, Fannie 231-33

G

G.I. Bill 54, 56, 127
Garcia & Bros. cigar factory 45-46
Gasparilla Festival (Tampa)
   bars Black bands 38
Gault, Charlene Hunter 219
Gemmer, Robert H. 209
George S. Middleton High School (Tampa) 37, 42, 126, 196
   Saunders protests at 43
Gibbs, Cary, Bishop 71
Gibbs High School (St. Petersburg) 17
Gibbs, Jonathan C. ix
Gibbs Junior College (St. Petersburg) 210
Gibson, W. H. 121
Gibson, Theodore R., Sr. ix, 79, 154, 157, 169-71, 175, 224
   and the Johns Committee 157, 168-70
Gilbert, John 17-18, 169
Gilder, Robert L. 128, 138, 208
Giradeau, Arnett 186
Goines, Emma 207
Golden, Dietrich 218
Gonzalez, B. V. 9
Goodson, J. H. 188
Gordon, William H. 134
Gore, George 141, 175-76, 183
Gorman, Gertrude 186
Graham, Bob 224
Graham, Edward T. 169, 175
Grant, W. T. department store 122, 139
Graves, G. E. 77, 85, 169, 171, 180-81, 221
Gray, Robert W. 74

Greater Bethel A.M.E. Church (Miami) 80
Green, Chris 34
Green, Cyrus T. 34
Green, Ellen 79, 127-28, 136
Greenberg, Jack 69, 91
Greene, Z. D., "Col." 39, 124
Greenlee, Charlie 120
Greenwood (Fla.) 16
Gregory, Matthew 125-26, 131
Greyhound bus company 140
Griffin, Benjamin D. 127
Griffin, Noah 17, 207
   files equal pay law suit 17
   fired as Gibbs principal 17
   hired as FSTA executive 17
   serves as first NAACP state conference president 18
   work with Harry T. Moore 112
Griffin, Noel 213
Groveland (Fla.) ix, 71
Groveland case 22-23, 60, 115, 116-17, 120, 203, 212, 214-15
Groveland Defense Fund 116

H

Haisley, J. C. 128, 139
Hall, Juanita 80
Hall, W. Troy 214
Hammond, James A. 140-41, 225
Hammond, Lucille 79
Hammonds, Harvey L. 211
Hampton, Lionel 69
Hankins, I. S. 204-207
Hankins, Lylah 205-206
Hannibal, Christine E. 29
Hannibal, Shadrach 29
Harbour Island (Bahamas) 27
Hard Rockers (orchestra) 38
Hargrett, James, Jr. 139
Hargrett, James T., Sr. 37, 126
Harlem Academy 5
Harlem Elementary School 36
Harris, Catherine 225
Harris, Ozepher 79
Harris, Patricia 145

Harris, H. McNeal 209
Harvey, Perry, Sr. 131, 139, 152
Hatcher, Reuben 120
Hatchett, Joseph 208
Hauser, James 237
Havana-American Company 26
Hawes, Mark 158-66
Hawkins, "Banjo Boy" 38
Hawkins, Dee, 149-51
Hawkins, G. W. 74
Hawkins, Melvin, Jr. 156
Hawkins, Melvin, Sr. 156
Hawkins, Virgil ix, 161, 163, 212
   brother of Melvin Hawkins 156
   denied admission to UF law school 74
   and Johns Committee 161-64
Hawthorne, Elizabeth 233
Hayes, George E. C. 99
Hayling, Robert 229-34, 236-37, 239-40
   assaulted by KKK 237
Head Start 224
Hearst, Rodney 189
Hemming Park (Jacksonville)
   Klan attack with baseball bats 189
Hendry, J. Marion 77
Henry, Aaron 145
Herlong, A. S., Jr. (congressman) 81
Herrell, Cliff 169
Higgins, Miss (teacher) 32
Hill, Herbert 91
Hill, Horace 22
   called before Johns Committee 161-63
Hillsborough County
   school desegregation 85
Hillsborough County Commission 224
Hodaz, John 30
Hollins, Ruby L. 211
Holly, Reverend 219
Holmes County 200
Holmes, Reverend 90
Holsey Temple C.M.E. Church (Tampa) 125
housing 134, 138
   Fair Housing Program 138
   Tampa NAACP housing committee 134
   urban renewal and segregation 135-37

housing discrimination
　Volusia and Brevard counties 223
Howard Johnson Motel (St. Petersburg) 210
Howard University 127
Hudson, Henry 125
Hudson, James 175, 183
Hughes, Langston 87
　praises southern NAACP courage 87
Humphrey, Hubert 199
Hunt, Robert 206
Hunter, J. W. 115
Hunter, "Shep," Sr. 219
Hunton, Addie W. 13
Hurley, Ruby 66, 73, 82, 90-91, 177, 186, 229, 242, 251
　begins southeast regional NAACP conferences 71

I

Ingram, Sam 126
integration 223
　in Cincinnati 56
　in New York schools 35
　NAACP lawsuits 167
　of Florida beaches 84, 209
　of Florida schools 72, 200
　of Pinellas County golf course 209
　of public accommodations 138, 148
　of Tampa schools 143
　See also individual headings in this index
Inter-Civic Council 182
International Longshoreman Association 152
Interstate highway construction
　impact on Blacks 133
Irvin, Walter Lee 69, 116-18, 120, 215
Italians 123
　and bolita 40
　in Roberts City 30, 34

J

Jackson County ix
Jackson, Harold 127
Jackson, James 237

Jackson, Mr. 35
Jacksonville 10, 12, 76, 124, 185-193, 204, 230, 234, 238
　demonstrations 148, 184, 192
　Ku Klux Klan 139, 148, 238
　mass meetings over Moore bombing 118
　NAACP branch 9-10, 13, 131, 185-193
　　1953 membership drive 186
　　conflict with KKK 189
　　influence from mayor's office 186, 188
　　KKK attack with baseball bats 189
　　model branch 188, 191
　　model for national action 192
　　police abuse of President 187
　　youth council demonstrations 190-91
　organizational efforts in 8, 186
James, Chappie 53
James, Joe 186
Jenkins, Clyde 237
Jim Crow ix, x, 67, 75, 119, 124, 148, 207, 218, 240
　and LeRoy Collins 148
　Broward County 218
　eroded by Collins 148
　and Johns Committee 159
　NAACP challenge to 185
　policies in Tampa 125
　resistance to in Tallahassee 181
　segregated train cars 35
　Williams Trailways case 197
job discrimination 131
Johns, Charley E. (acting Florida governor) 67, 72, 159, 171
　committee to investigate NAACP 76
　See also Johns Committee
Johns Committee 76, 81, 90, 144, 158-71, 175, 183, 192, 198, 222
　challenge to NAACP 168
　　March on Tallahasee 173
　chilling effect on NAACP donors and causes 170
　extension of investigation 168
　hearings 158
　investigation of Florida State

Teacher's Association 164
    purpose of 160
Johnson, Art 59
Johnson, Dave 223
Johnson, Earl M. 186, 188, 190, 234, 238
Johnson, Eula 220, 221
Johnson, Freddy R. 206
Johnson, James 100, 125
Johnson, James Weldon
    ix, 8, 11, 25, 94
    appointed NAACP organizer 9
    organizes Tampa NAACP branch 9
    tours southeast 9
    visits Tampa 10
Johnson, K. S. 21
Johnson, Lyndon B. 87, 157, 229, 231, 233
Johnson, Margie 213
Johnson, Mrs. Eula 144
Johnson, Robert 29
Jones, B. F. 209
Jones, Florene 127
Jones, Jackson E. 130, 198-200
Jones, Madison E. 133, 135
    visit to Tampa 133
Jones, Quillie 190
Jones, Sam 187
Joyner, Arthenia 139
    sentenced in Tallahassee protest 180
Joyner, Henry 132
Joyner, Marjorie 63
Julius Ellinger & Co. Cigar Factory. *See* Ellinger & Co. Cigar Factory

K

Kearns, Vernon 211
Kennedy, John F. 129, 145
Kennedy, Robert 237
Key West 6, 9, 13, 27, 29
King, B. B. 181
King, Martin Luther, Jr. ix, 76, 178, 233, 240
    and Meredith case 174
    in Tampa 127, 145
    St. Augustine protests 238
Kirk, Claude (Florida governor) 88, 215
Knights of Pythias 8, 16
Kress department store 42, 206
Ku Klux Klan 12, 59, 65, 68, 102, 130, 149, 221, 230
    banned from Florida demonstrations 83
    bombing of Moore home 23
    Jacksonville 139, 148, 191-92
    response to youth council sit-ins 189, 191
    law to unmask 159
    Orange County 206
    St. Augustine 236
    assault on Hayling and others 237
    assault on Kingston and others 237-38
    threats in Liberty County 150

L

Lacey, Norman E. 125
Lake County 212
Lake Wales branch 199
Lakeland (Fla.)
    fundraising concert by B. B. King 181
Lampkins, Joseph W. 211
Land, Henry W. 160-61, 206
Lane, Julian (Tampa mayor) 136-37
    appoints Blacks to urban renewal board 137
    asks Saunders to withdraw NAACP complaint 137
    establishes biracial committee 137
    police protection for demonstrators 139
Lang, Detry 190
Lazarus, Michael, Sr. 125
Legal Defense Fund. *See* NAACP
Leon County branch 201
Lester, Herbert E. 8, 11, 32, 124
Lester, Susie 32
Liberty City (Fla.) 121, 154, 165
Liberty County (Fla.) 91, 149-51
Lieb, Joseph P. 212
Lincoln University School of Law 127
Little Rock, Arkansas 82

Livingston, Artis L. 211
Lockhart, J. W. 37
Lowry, A. Leon 80, 90, 128-29 139, 142, 151, 251
   called before Johns Committee 161
   opposition to hotel and motel segregation 137
   telegram to Gov. Collins 84
Lynch, Connie 236

lynchings 4, 10, 12, 20, 29, 111, 113
   in Key West 6
   laws to prevent 16
      work of Harry T. Moore 116
   in Polk County 12
   of Neal in Greenwood 16
   Woods incident 152

M

MacDill Air Force Base 19, 137
MacFarlane Elementary School 85, 143
Maddox, Luther 125
Malloy, Dan 125
A Man Called White 59
Mandy, Thomas M. 218, 220
March on Tallahassee 173-78
   chaired by Rev. Steele 175
   CORE decision to withdraw 177
   number of participants 177
   statement of principles 178
   success of 178
   support from FAM's Gore & students 178
March on Washington 87, 178
Marianna School for Boys 238
Marion County 174
Marshall, Cecelia 91
Marshall, Thurgood 25, 60, 69-70, 80, 91, 99, 163, 196
   and Chambers case 15
   and Dade County school desegregation 76
   appointed to U.S. Supreme Court 88
   and Johns Committee 160
   named U.S. solicitor general 88
Marti-Maceo Cuban Club (Tampa) 62

Maryland Avenue Project 136
Mays, Benjamin 79
McAden, Pearl 40-42

McCall, Willis 22, 212-14
   and Fruitland Park case 214
   and Groveland case 22, 116, 117, 120
   Hawkins incident 156
   shoots Groveland defendants 23, 116
McCarty, Dan (Florida governor) 67, 159
McClain, Charles 90
McClendon, James J. 25
McCloud, Azalie 205
McDaniel, Vernon 18
McGill, Samuel D. 8, 15, 17, 94
McGriff, Rutherford 187
McKissick, J. H. 175, 178, 230
McLin, Mrs. O. B. 207
McMillan, Paula 218
Meacham, Christina 5, 10, 25, 124
Meacham, Robert 2
Meharry Medical College 37
Meredith, James 87, 174
Miami 151, 154
   bus desegregation 83
   hearings by Johns Committee 168
Miami branch 144, 149, 154, 157, 161, 175
Miami Jewish Choir 219
Miami Times 149
Middleton, George S. 37
Middleton High School. *See* George S. Middleton High School
Mike, Marnie 21
Milner, M. P. 80
Mims, Elmo 66
Mims (Fla.) 61
   Moore bombing by KKK 111
   NAACP Youth Council 61
Minnis, Fred 48, 54, 123
miscegenation law 222
Miss NAACP pageant 67, 69
Mississippi
   legislation to outlaw NAACP 76
Mitchell, Clarence 70, 91, 141, 150, 209

295

Mizell, Von 218, 221
Moffett, Sandy 139
Montgomery (Ala.) Bus Boycott 75-76, 125, 131, 221
Moore, Evangeline 118-20
Moore, Harriett 111, 115, 119
   killed by KKK bombing of home 24, 118
   teaches Helen Strickland Saunders 61
   memorial service 121
Moore, Harry Tyson ix, 17, 19-21, 59-61, 65, 68, 71, 110-21, 131, 162, 178, 210, 222
   advocates suspension of McCall 116
   and Groveland case 115-17, 120
   and Helen Strickland Saunders 61
   and Progressive Voters' League 19
   and voter registration 115
   as Brevard County teacher 111
   as Florida NAACP executive secretary 115
   as Florida NAACP president 112
   criticized at 1951 state conference 23
   dismissed as NAACP executive secretary 116
   fired from teaching job 21, 115
   first elected Florida NAACP state conference president 19
   impact of his death 192, 204, 216, 227
   killed in KKK bombing of home 24, 111, 118, 222
      effect on membership 185
   leadership for state conference 185
   letter to Gov. Fuller Warren 117, 118
   memorial service 121
   NAACP salary past due 115
   organizes first NAACP state conference in Florida 18
Moore, Peaches 119, 120
Moore, Richard V. 63
Morrison's Cafeteria 128
Morsell, John 218
Motley, Constance Baker 80, 91, 196
Moultrie, Georgia 52
Mt. Herman A.M.E. Church (Ft. Lauderdale) 219

Murphy, Bettye 154, 155

N

NAACP (National Association for the Advancement of Colored People. *See also* individual headings in this index
   early history 3-24
   first Florida branch (Key West) 3, 9
   first state conference (Florida) 18, 219
   North Pinellas branch 194, 208
   Tampa branch organized by Johnson 9-10
   West Tampa local 3, 8-9,
NAACP Legal Defense Fund 22, 80, 142, 162-63, 167 212
NAACP Youth Council 58, 224-25, 192, 240
Nabrit, James 99
NASA (space agency) 223
National Colored Peoples Spiritualist Association 68
National Guard 22
National Negro Conference 7
National States Rights Party 236
National Youth Administration 44, 50, 52
Neal, Claude 16
Negro Chamber of Commerce (Orlando) 204
Negro Fort 4
Nerney, May Childs 8
New York City 35, 123, 234
New York Evening Post 7
New York Times 16
Newcross, Cole 126
Newman, DeQuincey 87
Niagara Movement 6
Nichols, D. Ward 35, 81
Nixon, E. D. 125, 131
North Boulevard 30
North Carolina Agricultural and Technical College 84
North Pinellas branch 194, 208
Nottage, Joseph A. 12
Nuccio, Nick (Tampa mayor) 134

O

Oates, G. J. 128
Ocala (Fla.) 13, 69
Ocoee Riot 12
Odom, Gordon G., Jr. 214
Office of Economic Opportunity 107
Office of Economic Opportunity (OEO) 88, 107
Okaloosa County branch 196-97
Orange County 203, 206
Orchid Club 208
Orlando (Fla.) 203-205
    fundraising concert by B. B. King 181
    mass meetings over Moore bombing 118
Orr, John B., Jr. 77
outhouses 32

P

Palatka (Fla.) 12
Palmer, Marie 205, 206
Panama City (Fla.) 198-200
Parks, Rosa 75
Patton, W. C. 87, 90, 129, 225
Payne, Jesse 113
Peak, Bill 230-32
Pearl Harbor 52
Pearson, Lloyd 144, 191
Pearson, Mary Ann 191
Pearson, Rutledge H. 144, 183-86, 193, 230
    1960 sit-in with youth council 188
    elected Jacksonville branch president 188, 191
    elected president of NAACP Florida State Conference 131, 191
    organization of Jacksonville youth council 188
    support for Berrier Ice Cream protests 191
    warnings of KKK attack 18
Peck, S. M. 62, 128
Pensacola (Fla.) 13, 195, 197, 200
Perkins, Daniel W. 10-11, 204
    as Jacksonville attorney 124
    as NAACP organizer 13, 124
Perkins, Paul 22, 60, 69, 203-204
Perry, July 12
Perry, Ruth 149
    called before Johns Committee 161, 168-69
Peterson, Preston 43
Pickett, Emma 21
Pinellas County 207
Pinellas County golf course 209
Pinellas County High School
    principal Curtis questioned by Johns Committee 164
Pinkston, Frank 224, 233-35, 239-40
    conference address 265-271
Plant City Strawberry Festival
    Black band in parade 38
Pohlhaus, J. Francis 91
police
    abuses of power 66
    discrimination against Blacks 42, 55, 131
    discrimination within force 211
    harassment of Blacks 41, 42
        detain Fordham 77
    kickbacks in Jacksonville 187
    protection of Tampa demonstrators 139
    provoking violence 180
    threats against President in Jacksonville 187
police brutality 113, 132, 227-28, 236
    in Amos President's death 188
    in Jacksonville 187
    in St. Augustine 241
    in Tallahassee 179, 181
    in Tampa 125
        beating of Black woman 126
        beating of Newcross 126
        killing of Ingram 126
policemen
    Black 39
Polk County 199
poll tax 4
    outlawed by 24th amendment 87
Ponce de Leon Hotel 229-30, 232
Ponder, Fannye Ayre 210
Porter, Gilbert L. 158
Porters Club 187

Potter, Marcellus D. ix, 5, 33-34, 36, 125, 128
Potter, Mrs. Mary E. 33, 36
Powell, Adam Clayton 66
Powell, Richard 121, 154, 157
   called before Johns Committee 161–162
Poynter, Nelson 209
President, Amos 187-88
Pressley, Leonard 125
Price, Joseph L., Jr. 22
Prichett, Altamese 207
Pride, Cheryle 139
Pride, Richard 127
Progress Village (Tampa) 137
Progressive Voters' League 19, 21,113, 162
protest marches 139, 181, 233
   in support of jailed Tallahassee students 179
protests
   for civil rights in Tampa 126
   in St. Augustine 226, 232
   in Tampa over police killing of Ingram 126
   NAACP defense of demonstrators 180
   Orange County 206
   St. Augustine 229, 241
   Wilkins for anti-lynching law 16
Publix grocery stores 206
Pughsley, Stubb C. 41
Purcell, Isaac L. 8
Puryear, Royal W. 229, 230

R

race riots 12, 142, 173
   Groveland 212
   St. Petersburg 207
   University of Mississippi 174
racial discrimination 54, 223
   highway signs 107
   in Cincinnati 56
   in Detroit 58
   in police 211
   in St. Augustine 235
   in St. Petersburg 207
   in Tampa 123, 124
   housing 126
racism 211
   avowed by Bryant 174, 233
Ragsdale, A. R. 139
Raiford (Florida state prison) 117
Railroad Voters League 187
Randolph, A. Philip
   ix, 49, 81, 125, 130-31, 187
Range, Althea 80
Ransom, Leon A. 15
Red Summer 12
Reddick, A. Joseph 81-82, 131
   elected state NAACP president in Tampa 77
Reddick, Harold N. 125, 129-30
Redding, Theodore 185
Reed, Horace 216, 218
Reeder, Dora 127
Reedy, George 232
Reeves, Frank D. 169, 221
Republican party
   Black loyalty to Lincoln's party 112
Reynolds, Herbert C. 18
Richardson, Dewey 69, 125
Riley, Z. L. 204
Ritter, Lou 193
Roberts & Sons Cigar Factory 26, 45
Roberts City (Tampa) 26-27, 30-31, 35, 45
   discrimination in 41
   ethnic mixture 30
Roberts City Garage 44, 47
Roberts, J. W. 27
Robinson, Jackie
   55, 81, 88, 211, 224, 251
Robinson, John C. 128
Robinson, Titus A. 211
Rodriguez and Fordham
   Tampa's first Black law partnership 127
Rodriguez, Francisco A. 77, 79, 100, 127, 141, 151, 154, 170, 213
   and Jesse Woods case 155
   Fruitland Park case 214
   lawyer in Mims case 66, 142
   Melvin Hawkins case 156
   on WHBO radio for NAACP 67
   Tampa NAACP president 127
Roger (musical show) 53
Rogers, Christina 31

Rogers Dining Room 39
Rogers, James W. 27
Rogers, Marie 35
Rogers, Marion E. Mathews 8, 27, 32, 34, 38, 124
   active in Tampa NAACP chapter 10
Rolfe, Everett 37, 52
Rollin, Metz 158
Rome Avenue 32
Roosevelt, Eleanor 25
   and Mary McLeod Bethune 50, 63
Roosevelt, Franklin D. 16, 49
   signs anti-discrimination order (Executive Order 8802) 18
Roosevelt, James 81
Rose, Eugene 209
Rosewood (Fla.) ix, 13, 94
Roxborough, Mildred 91
Royal American Shows 79
Rudd, John 84-85, 179
Rutledge, Talmadge 211

S

Satterwhite, Hunter 186
Saunders, Bobby. *See* Robert W. Saunders, Jr.
Saunders, Christina Rogers 29, 31-32, 35-36, 47
Saunders, Helen 79, 80, 90, 99, 208
Saunders, Helen Strickland 62, 78-80, 90, 99, 208
   acquaintance with Harry T. Moores 61, 111
   marries Robert Saunders 61-62
Saunders, John A. 29, 35
Saunders, Robert W., Jr, "Bobby" 143
   integrates Hillsborough County schools 85
Saunders, Robert W., Sr. 62, 90
   Army service 53-63
   early life 27-48
   education 36, 37, 38
      applies to Fisk University 55
      Bethune-Cookman College 50, 215
      college scholarship 44
      Detroit Institute of Technology 56
      high school graduation 44, 49
      University of Cincinnati 56
      University of Detroit Law School 57
      Wayne State University 56
   employment
      as NAACP Florida field secretary 59-64
      Cincinnati *Call and Post* 55, 123
      Detroit department store 58
      Florida Sentinel 67
      Ford Motor Company 56-57
      Office of Economic Opportunity (OEO) 88
   marriage 56
   Tampa Bulletin 36
   Florida civil rights activities 65 *et seq.*
   See individual headings in this index
Saunders, Willard 29, 31
school desegregation 20, 75
   first lawsuit for school system 196
   in Dade County 76
   in Hillsborough County
      by Bobby Saunders 85
   in Pinellas County 212
schools
   poor quality for Blacks 112, 114, 131
   source for Black community leaders 127
Scott, Shafter 128, 139
"Scrub" (Tampa) 126
Seaberry, Chester 37, 43
Seaboard White Citizens Council 168
Sears, Roebuck & Co. 192
   Jacksonville protests 189
segregation 30, 42, 72
   Florida's loss of Democratic convention due to 151
   in Tampa 123
      housing 137
      schools 126
   intra-state challenge 197
   Johns Committee support for 159
   of beaches 220
   of buses 218, 221
   of hotels and motels 137, 219
   of public facilities 124

of restaurants 140
of restaurants and dining rooms 141, 223
of schools and playgrounds ii
trains and train station 35
segregationists
   73, 141, 149, 174, 197, 201
   Connie Lynch 236
   Farris Bryant 174
   Liberty County 149, 150, 151
Selma to Montgomery March 87
Seventh Day Adventist Church 125
Shaw, Leander 227-28, 234, 241
Shepherd, Samuel 116-17, 120
Shinholster, Earl 121
Shoemaker, Joseph 30
Sholtz, David (Florida governor) 16
Shuler, Robert 212, 214
Sikes, Bob (congressman) 91, 141, 197
Silas, Elmer 222
sit-in movement 85-86, 179, 217
sit-ins 85, 128, 132, 139, 234
   Florida A&M students 175
   in Greensboro, N.C. 84
   in Jacksonville 189, 192
   in Tallahassee 175
   in Tampa 84, 122, 132, 138, 142-43
Sloan, Raynell 139
slums 133
Smathers, George 81, 230
Smith, Allie 205
Smith, Jimmy 55
Smith v. *Allwright* 19, 58
Snead, Taylor 205, 206
Snowden, Charles (judge) 76
Souls of Black Folk 6
Southern Christian Leadership Conference (SCLC) 76, 86, 233, 238, 240
   demonstrations in Albany, Georgia 174
   King's support for Meredith in Mississippi 174
Speed, Dan 201, 225
Speed, Leonard 225
Spence Field, (Ga.) 48, 52
Spencer, Rufus 38
Spingarn, Arthur 199

Spingarn Prize
   to Mary McLeod Bethune 50
Spotwood, Steven Gill 191
St. Augustine 9, 13, 74, 226-41, 233, 239
   KKK assaults 237
      arrests of Jacksonville Klansmen 238
   NAACP presence 86
   protests
      financial support for 218, 235
      Slave Mart 235
   quadricentennial 229
   racial strife 174, 234
St. Augustine branch 227-31
St. Augustine Market 226
St. Paul A.M.E. Church (Tampa) 5, 32-33, 46, 74, 79-80, 128, 139, 144, 152, 208
St. Petersburg
   race relations 209, 211
St. Petersburg branch 207
St. Petersburg Times 209
Stanford, Charles 128
Stanley, W. A. (judge) 190
Starke, George H. 18
Starke, Mavis 206-207
State of Florida v. *Shepherd* 212
Stebbins, Charles 18
Steele, Charles Kenzie 75-76, 81, 175, 182
   address to state conference 257-264
   founder of SCLC 86
   organizer of March on Tallahassee 176-77
   considers inviting King 178
   national reputation from 178
   plaintiff in Leon County 201
   shooting of home 81
Stevens, Dr. 201
Stevens, Patricia 175
Stewart, Garland V. 37, 127
Stone, Melvin 80
Stone, Rudy 223, 224
Straughn, Elder 125
street car
   racial seating in 43
Strickland, Henry J. 61
Strickland, Lucy A. 61

Student Nonviolent Coordinating Committee 86
Sturgis, Charles S. 8, 11
Sumter County 152
  kidnapping of Jesse Woods 152
Sunderlin, James B. 212
SuperTest Oil Company
  segregation protest 128
Supreme Court (U.S.) 99, 120, 159, 166, 171
  landmark cases 14, 71
    "all deliberate speed" ruling 73
    Brown v. The Board of Education of Topeka, Kans. 71, 127, 128
    James Meredith 174
    Johns Committee contempt citation overturned 175
    ruling with NAACP against Johns Committee 170
    Smith v. Allwright 19
    throws out Montgomery bus case 77
    orders Mississippi to admit Meredith 174
    overturns Groveland case decision 116
Sutton, C. S. 14
Swain, Jimmy L. 211
Swain, Robert 209
Sweatt v. Painter 20
swim-ins 84

T

Taft-Hartley Labor Relations Act 131
Taliaferro, Harry 209
Tallahassee 13, 140, 155, 200, 224-25
  Boy Scout jamboree 34
  NAACP branch activities 175
  protests and marches 172-74, 179, 181
    Saunders's pride in Black community 181
    Saunders's testimony before Johns Committee 161
Tallahassee Bus Boycott 75-77, 172-73, 175, 183, 225
Tallahassee Bus Protest 182-83

Tampa
  Florida's next-to-largest city 29
  fundraising concert by B. B. King 181
  labor union officials 125
  NAACP chapter 13, 124, 127, 132-33
    housing committee 134
    housing initiatives 136, 138
    sit-ins 122, 138, 142-43
    urban renewal 133, 135-36
  "Negro Housing Project" 125
  racial problems 142
  "Scrub" area 126
Tampa Bay Hotel 27
Tampa branch 123-145,
Tampa Bulletin 5, 33, 36, 54, 125, 128
Tampa Daily Times 42, 67
Tampa Freedom Fund 88
Tampa Housing Authority 138
Tampa NAACP youth council 50, 142-43
Tampa Tribune 213
Tampa Urban League 125
Tarpon Springs branch 194
Taston, Reverend 193
teacher salaries
  inequality for Blacks 113, 207
teachers 201
  discrimination against 200
  reprisals against 222
Thomas, Bob 139
Thomas, W. Carey 38
Thompson, Frankie 37
Tillman, Eugene C. 178, 217, 224
Tim, Gwendolyn 139
To Secure These Rights 21
Tolbert, Abraham 196, 197
Tolbert v. Escambia County Board of Public Instruction 196-97
Toomer, Reverend 206
Trailways bus company 197
Trammell, Park 8
Truman, Harry S 21, 59
Turner, Elsie 37
Turner, Henry McNeal local (West Tampa NAACP chapter) 9
Turner, Levy 128

301

Turney, Hilda 18, 37
Tuskegee Army Air Field (Ala.) 48, 53, 63

U

Union Station (Tampa) 152
unions 56, 131
University of Cincinnati 56
University of Detroit Law School 57
University of Florida
    desegregation of undergraduate programs and housing 173
    integration 86, 162
        Hawkins lawsuit 162-65
        Moore involved in 1947 suit 111
University of Georgia 219
University of Mississippi 87, 174
University of South Florida
    investigated by Johns Committee 170
University of Tampa
    desegregation lawsuit 128
University of Texas
    Law School admissions suit 20
Urban League 13, 33-34, 79
    in Tampa
        cooperation with NAACP 125
        Maryland Avenue Project 136
urban renewal 133-35
    commissions 136
    objections from Tampa NAACP 135-36
    objections to Tampa plan 136
Urban Renewal Administration 136

V

Van, Terasea 139-40
Vanderhorst, Charles ("Charlie Moon") 40, 132
    gunned down 40
    helps feed needy 40
    McAden convicted for murder of 41
Vaught, Charles 185
    rebuilding Jacksonville NAACP membership 186
Veteran's Administration 223

Villard, Oswald Garrison 7
Vinson, Eddie "Clean Head" 55
violence
    against Blacks in Tampa 29
    with KKK baseball bats 192
Virginia Union College 233
Volusia County 180, 215-17
voter registration 12, 19, 57, 89, 100, 112-13, 115, 125, 129, 138, 183, 224
    Liberty County 149-51
voting rights 8, 19, 115, 150-51
    Democratic White primary overturned 19, 195
    for women 12
Voting Rights Act of 1965 85, 87

W

Wall, Charlie 40
Ware, Dan 204-205
Warren, Fuller (Florida governor) 22, 59-60, 116-18
    letter from Harry T. Moore 117-18
    response to Moore bombing 118
Warren, Willie 125
Warthen, Hollie 63
Washington, Booker T.
    death of 9
    influence of 5-6
    opposition to Du Bois 7
    visit to Florida 5
Washington, Glen 186, 188
Washington High School. *See* Booker T. Washington High School
Washington Junior College 165
Watson, LeRoy 62
Wayne State University 56
Weatherly, Chief 123
Weaver, Robert C. 136
Weirsdale (Fla.)
    and Groveland defendants 117
Wells, Mr. 227
Wells, W. O., Jr. 223-24
West Palm Beach 199, 208
West Tampa 26-27, 47, 123
    impact of urban renewal 137
West Tampa Elementary School 32

WHBO radio 67
Wheeler, Berneice 205-206
White, Alton 180
White Citizens Council 179
White House (Washington, D.C.) 145
White, J. A. ix, 10, 25, 33-34, 124
White, Moses 39, 132
white supremacists 160, 179
White, Walter
    16, 21, 25, 59, 63, 65, 69, 70, 132
  and Harry T. Moore 21
  appointed to civil rights commission 59
  as NAACP executive secretary 14
  attends state conference meeting in St. Petersburg 18
  death in 1955 73
  helps amend draft law 49
  keynote speaker at 1952 Florida NAACP 66, 219
  outrage over bombing of Harry T. Moore home 118
Wiggins, Garrett T.
  questioned by Johns Committee 165
Wildwood (Fla.) 152
  suspected lynching of Woods 153-54
  Wilkins on train 152
Wilkins, Roy 25, 70, 91, 107, 132, 152, 176, 179, 229, 231, 236
  Johns Committee 160
  picketing in Neal case 16
  praise for FAM students in March on Tallahassee 178
  Woods incident 152
Williams, Albert 190
Williams, "Big Jim" 43
Williams, Doris 42
Williams, Dorothy 42
Williams, Earl 211
Williams, Eli 211
Williams, F. Henry 186-87
  failure to meet with executive committee 187
Williams, Frank 91
Williams, Franklin 22
Williams, Helen 208
Williams, J. L. 18
Williams, Jesse 79
Williams, Robert L. 197

Williams, Nick, 155
Williams, Ray 79
Williams, Wilma 62
Williamson, Jack 14
Wilson, Charles
  Tolbert lawsuit 196
  Williams lawsuit 197
Wilson, Clarence O. 139, 238
Wilson, Helen 37
Wimbish and Alsup, et al. v. The Pinellas County Commission 209
Wimbish, Ralph 209-10
Winn-Dixie grocery stores 206
Wood, Jack E., Jr. 135, 138, 223
  denunciation of Tampa's urban renewal plan 135
Woodley, Georgia N. 206-207
Woods, Jesse 152-57
  beating of 153
  search for 154-56
Woodward, Walter 14
Woolfork, Norris 207
Woolworth department store 139, 142-43, 192, 206
  DeLand sit-ins 217
  Jacksonville protests 189
Work Projects Administration (WPA) 36
  band 38
  music program in Tampa 38
World War II 49
Wright, E. J. 14
Wright, Herbert
  praised by Hughes 87
Wright, Thomas W. 227, 230
Wyland, Ben F. 209

Y

Yates, James 213, 214, 215
Ybor City (Tampa)
  impact of urban renewal 133
Young Adults for Progressive Action 140
Young, Andrew 241
Young, Daisy 175
Young, Nathan B. 13
Youngblood, Timothy 198

Youth Council
  Brevard County 223
  Clearwater 212
  Daytona 217
  Fort Lauderdale 220
  Jacksonville
    members arrested 190
    national model for action 191
    organized by Pearson 188
  Orlando 206
  St. Augustine 233
  St. Petersburg 210, 211
  Tallahassee 148
  Tampa 180
Youth for Freedom Encampments 74

Robert W. Saunders, Sr.

About the Author

Robert W. Saunders, Sr., was born on June 9, 1921, in the area of West Tampa known as Roberts City. He attended Bethune-Cookman College in Daytona Beach and after military service completed a BA degree at the Detroit Institute of Technology before entering the University of Detroit Law School. In January of 1952 he suspended his legal studies to accept a position as Florida field director for the NAACP after the state's first field director, Harry T. Moore, was killed in a Ku Klux Klan bombing of his home.

Assuming a difficult and dangerous leadership role, Saunders guided the state through challenging years of change, including landmark legal decisions on voting rights, school desegregation, the integration of public beaches, facilities, and housing, equal pay for Black teachers, and many other milestones, many of which are described in this book.

In 1966 he left his position with the NAACP to work with his friend Roy Wilkins at the U.S. Office of Equal Opportunity, serving for a decade as the chief of civil rights for the southeast region. He returned to Tampa in 1976 and directed the Office of Equal Opportunity for the Hillsborough County Board of County Commissioners until his retirement in 1988. Since that time he has remained an active and outspoken community leader.

The *St. Petersburg Times* featured him in its "Millennium Magazine" among the most inspiring Floridians over the past century as one of "Twenty-five Who Mattered." In that profile, *Times* columnist Bill Maxwell concluded by quoting Saunders on the reasons for his continuing activism.

"I need to go back to a meeting we had with Thurgood Marshall in 1955 regarding the *Brown* v. *Board of Education of Topeka* decision," Saunders said. "Thurgood made this comment: 'There are going to be ups and downs. There are going to be enemies fighting us. But you can't give up. Remember, when you're driving a car up a hill and you take your foot off the accelerator, the car slows down. You've got to continue to apply the gas. . . . We're at the point now where the fight for justice is just beginning."